A History and Genealogy of the Davenport Family,

In England and America, from A. D. 1086 to 1850

A. Benedict Davenport

Alpha Editions

This edition published in 2020

ISBN : 9789354023378

Design and Setting By
Alpha Editions
email - alphaedis@gmail.com

TO THE

DESCENDANTS OF

REV. JOHN DAVENPORT,

THE FOUNDER AND PATRIARCH

OF

NEW HAVEN, CT.,

WHO CHERISH THE PRINCIPLES, EMULATE THE VIRTUES,

AND ILLUSTRATE THE EXAMPLE

OF THEIR DISTINGUISHED ANCESTOR,

THIS VOLUME IS RESPECTFULLY INSCRIBED BY

THE AUTHOR.

INTRODUCTION.

"Not to know what took place before one was born," says Cicero, "is to remain forever a child." History is the herald of the past. To search into that past, to learn the lessons which it teaches, to profit by its experiences, avoiding its errors and cherishing its virtues, is alike the duty of the scholar, the patriot, and the Christian.

The history of nations is chiefly that of individuals. It is the individual character that gives shape and color to any age, that effects great moral and political revolutions, that evolves and illustrates great principles or heroic achievements. Such was that of the Puritan fathers of New England. *They were constructors of society.* They laid the foundations of that mighty edifice which they were about to build, upon a broad and imperishable basis.

The vine which God brought out of Egypt has spread its shadows over our land, till millions are now enjoying the rich legacy of their toils, their labors, and their prayers.

In the following pages, the author lays no claim to originality. That the long winter of age might not bury the leaves and fruit of our pious ancestors in America, the pleasing task was undertaken, to collect and preserve, in this simple form, some memorials of their principles and their virtues, for future generations.

In commencing the preparation of this work, the writer had no idea of extending it to its present limits, or of going further back than to the original settler of New Haven. But in his researches, he was led backwards by a series of successes, by which he is enabled to present a line of ancestry for nearly eight hundred years, authenticated by the clearest proofs and evidences.

Most of the information in regard to the family in this country has been obtained from probate and town records, sepulchral monuments, and local or general histories. To those who have aided him in making these collections, the author would here tender his grateful acknowledgments.

After much labor bestowed, in collecting and preparing materials, the work is sent forth as a vade mecum to the Family, with the hope that it may stimulate the present and future generations, to emulate the piety, the love of civil and religious liberty, and that devotion to "the common welfare of all," which characterized the Puritan fathers of New England.

A. B. Davenport

BROOKLYN, N. Y.,
January 1, 1851.

FAMILY OF DAVENPORT.

Arms of Davenport.—Argent, a chevron sable between three cross crossletts fitchée of the second.

Crest.—On a wreath a felon's head, couped at the neck proper, haltered Or.

Office indicated, Magisterial Sergeancy.

(See page 15.)

FAMILY OF DAVENPORT.

HISTORICAL.

The family name of Davenport is of local origin. The township of Davenport is situated in a sequestered part of the Hundred of Northwich, County of Chester, England; and is about twenty-five miles from the ancient city of Chester. It stands on high ground above a range of rich meadows, through which the river Dane flows rapidly, with a winding and irregular course. The banks on each side are remarkably lofty; those on the Davenport side are a series of verdant slopes, bearing evident marks of having been covered with timber at some former period; the opposite ones have been broken by the force of the current, and are more precipitous.

These features of the circumjacent landscape constitute some of the most pleasing scenery of the hundred; and they are backed by what must have had no ordinary charms for the ancient chiefs of Davenport, the adjoining hills of Macclesfield—the scene of their favorite sports and their feudal power.*

The manorial history of this township involves a subject of rare occurrence even in England—the descent of a family in one uninterrupted male line from the Norman Conquerors of the palatinate, possessing at the present day the feudal powers with which the local sovereigns of that palatinate invested it, and preserving in its archives, in a series of original documents, the proofs of its ancient history, and its unbroken descent.

Davenport occurs in that part of the description of the Venables estates, in which the founder of the barony is termed "venator." Isdem Gislebertus (Venator) tenet Deneport. Godvinus tenuit; ibi dimidia hida geldabilis: terra est una cacura; ibi est cum uno Radman; et III bovariis, et III bordariis; et una acra silvae. Valebat III solidos; wasta invenitur.

Shortly after this vill was given, either by the Norman grantee or by his grandson (who appears to have succeeded him), to Orme, the ancestor of the Davenports, who assumed the local name, as is proved by his attestation to a charter at that period.

* History of Cheshire, by George F. Ormerod, A.M., F.R.S., F.A.S.

Orme de Davenport appears to have been born in the 20th year of William the Conqueror, 1086, and must have been fifty years old at the birth of his son Richard, who married Amabilia, daughter of the second Gilbert Venables, the Norman grantee of Davenport, &c., before 1086.

Hugh Kevelioc, Earl of Chester, granted by charter to Richard de Davenport, the master forestership of the forests of Leek and Macclesfield, about 1166, which was an hereditary office, and is nominally held at the present time.

This Richard de Davenport had also in marriage with Amabilia, a moiety of the township of Marton, by grant from her brother William de Venables, and the same has continued by hereditary descent in the Davenport family to the present day.

This township is noticed in the Domesday survey, and was held, together with other estates, by the Saxon thane Goderic. From various coincidences in the Domesday account, it appears that *Wulfric*, who lived in the time of Edward the Confessor, 1040, and who was grandfather to Margaret Venables, the mother of Amabilia, was heir (probably brother) to Goderic, and that the Norman conquerors who had dispossessed this family in the first instance, re-admitted them to Marton, Cranage, &c.

Of the Manor, Hall, and Chapel, of Marton, which has passed through successive generations to the late Davies Davenport, Esq., member of Parliament for the county of Chester, we shall speak hereafter.

Thomas de Davenport, son of Richard, lived in the time of Henry II., or before 1189.

Vivian de Davenport, son of Richard, and grandson of Thomas, and the fourth in descent from Orme de Davenport, had a grant of the magisterial sergeancy of the hundred of Macclesfield, from Randle Blundeville, earl of Chester, by charter made during the justiceship of Philip de Orreby, between 1209 and 1226. It appears that the grant was made to Vivian Davenport, *against his will*, as a compensation for the park and vivaries of Macclesfield, of which the earl had deprived him, but which Vivian did not consider an adequate compensation.

The powers of this office were the highest which the earl could bestow, as it placed, in several cases, at the disposal of the sergeant and his itinerant subservients, the lives of his subjects, without delay, and without appeal.

At this period, the illusive crest of the Davenports is said to have first been adopted, and to have been borne upon the helmets of the master sergeants in their perambulations through the peak hills, and the forests of Leek and Macclesfield, to the terror of the numerous gangs of banditti which then infested those wild districts.

There is now in the possession of the family at Capesthorne, a long roll (without date, but very ancient), containing the names of the master robbers who were taken and beheaded in the times of Vivian, his son Roger, and grandson Thomas de Davenport, and also of the fees paid to them in right of this sergeancy. From this, it appears that the fee paid for a master robber was 2s. and one salmon, and for their companions 12 pence each. There is also an account of the master robbers, and their companions slain by the sergeants, and the fees thereon.*

* On the roll is a note by the first Davies Davenport, of Woodford, Esq., to wit: "The numbers are great, and though the roll is very ancient and much defaced, yet several of the names appear."—*Communicated to Ormerod by the Rev. Walter Davenport, in* 1819.

The same gentleman, now the Rev. Walter Davenport Bromley, adds, in a letter to the writer, dated September

Many particulars connected with this sergeancy are found interwoven with the subsequent history of the family in England. At times, it has been sought to wrest the powers of this office from those who have held them, but such efforts have been unsuccessful.

This charter, as subsequently interpreted, seems to have given to the master sergeant, within the fee of the hundred of Macclesfield, all goods and chattels of felons and fugitives condemned, and to be condemned, and whatever properly belonged to them.*

28, 1850: "Though the office of grand sergeancy since the time of Queen Elizabeth has been comparatively obsolete, yet Waifs, Estrays and Mortuaries were claimed as late as when my father succeeded to the estates; and I remember the old steward. The roll of names of persons beheaded still exists, and I think the names are visible."

* The original inquisition, under the seals of the jurors, is preserved among the deeds of the grand sergeancy at Capesthorne, at the present day.

Davies Davenport, Esq., member of Parliament from 1806 to 1830, held the grand sergeancy, and had in his possession many original papers, and much other matter pertaining to the family. The same passed to his son, the late Edward Davies Davenport, Esq., who succeeded to his father's estates in 1838, and who died in 1847.

A few general remarks may here be introduced in regard to the origin and use of arms.

Arms in heraldry are ensigns armorial or marks of honor, borne upon shields, banners or coats of mail, in order to distinction. These may belong to individuals, to families, or to countries.

Badges, and emblems on shields and helmets, occurred in the earliest times. Allusion is made to this in Numbers, (chapter 1: 52,) where the children of Israel are required to pitch their tents, "every man by his own camp, and every man by his own standard," with the ensigns of his father's house.

Reference is also made by the Greek and Roman poets, to the use of such devices; and Xenophon relates that the kings of Media bore a golden eagle on their shields.

But notwithstanding these traces of armorial bearings in the ancient world, modern heraldry is no older than the tournaments, and seems to have first prevailed in the eleventh or twelfth centuries.

The Crusades, which were expeditions to the Holy Land against the Infidels, during the twelfth century, tended to bring this science to its present degree of perfection. From these originated several new figures before unknown in arms, besides a great number of crosses variously formed, which are to be seen in the arms all over Europe.

In process of time, these tokens, now called arms, became remunerations for services, and were bestowed by emperors, kings, generals, and chief-commanders in the field, upon martial men, as a reward for heroic acts, the remembrance of which would thus be preserved to posterity.

At first, arms were allowed to be taken up at any gentleman's pleasure, but according to the present laws of the college of arms, in England and most other countries of Europe, no person is allowed the bearing of them but such as belong to the family, except by special grant or purchase.

The crest is considered the highest part of the ornament of a coat of arms, and is placed on a wreath. Anciently, they were worn on the heads of commanders in the field, to distinguish different families, armies or nations.

The Davenport crest, denoting the office of magisterial sergeancy, may be reckoned among the most ancient in England, and the same family coat of arms, with filial distinction, appertains to all the different branches through which the line of descent will here be given.

Sir Thomas Davenport, of Davenport, knight, son of Roger, and grandson of Vivian de Davenport, married for his first wife, Agnes, daughter of Thomas de Macclesfield, in 1287. She was the mother of his issue. His second wife was Roesia, daughter of Ralph de Vernon, and widow of Sir William de Brereton.

In 1309, he grants a lease of the office of sergeancy for two years to his son Thomas, and his pledges for two years, at an annual rent of sixteen marks of silver.

This Thomas, second son of Sir Thomas, was male ancestor of the Davenports of Whetrough, Bromhall, Henbury, Coventry, and Woodford (now of Capesthorne).*

Sir John Davenport, knight, eldest son and heir of Sir Thomas, married his father's step-daughter, Margery, daughter of Sir William Brereton, by Roesia Vernon; to his second wife he had Agnes de Bradford.

* From this time, the name, which had been previously written Dauneporte and Davenporte, was usually spelled as at this day. The name was sometimes vulgarly called Damport.

The first of these marriages took place in 1301, when "Thomas, son of Roger de Davenport," grants to Sir William Brereton, knight, the marriage of his eldest son John, (to marry him to Margery, daughter of the said William,) for 60 marks. Witnesses, Hugh Massey, Ralph Vernon, Hugh de Venables, knights, &c.; dated at Brereton. Harl. MSS. 2074 : 148. Four years after this, a sentence was procured from the Court of Chester, declaring the marriage null, having been celebrated without the consent of the parties, both being under age. The pedigrees, however, make Margery Brereton the mother of Sir John's children, which must of course suppose them to have been reunited; which fact seems further proved by a settlement, in 12th year of Edward II., (1319,) when Thomas de Davenport obtained from Richard, Chaplain, of Prestbury, the manors of Davenport and Marton, remainder to *John his son and Margery his wife;* remainder to the heirs of Thomas.

The issue of Sir John were as follows: 1st, Thomas; 2d, John, who became rector of the Church in Swettenham, (a village on the side of the Dane, opposite to Davenport,) in 1335, of which Church his father and several of the succeeding Johns were patrons;* 3d, Ralph, the continuer of the direct male line; 4th, Richard; 5th, Roger; 6th, Urian, who was distinguished for his great stature and military achievements; 7th, Arthur, ancestor of the Davenports of Calveley, who was slain on the part of the Percies in the battle of Shrewsbury, in 1403.†

Sir John Davenport, in the reign of Edward III., (1343,) founded a chantry in the Chapel of Marton, which was dissolved at the Reformation, or after 1500. After the dissolution, the site of the Chapel was granted by the Crown, to the Davenports of Davenport, in

* The Church is a neat building of brick, with a tower and side aisles, the former of which forms an interesting object in several romantic views along the banks of the Dane.

The Harl. MSS. 2151: 68. have notes of this Church. On the windows are many figures, arms, &c. On one is this inscription: "Of yr charitie pray for Rondell Mainwaring and Margaret and Ellen his wyves, which made this window A'no D'mi M°CCC°XL.°

In the same window, the arms of Davenport, and Davenport impaling Savage.

† Sir John's daughters were *Margaret*, who married Sir John Hyde, son of Robert Hyde, Lord of Norbury, and *Isabella*, who married Robert Eaton, baron of Stockport, and re-married to John de Stafford.

which family it has continued to the present day.

The present Chapel, consisting of a belfry, with a small spile, porch, nave and chancel, with side aisles, is built exclusively of timber, except the chancel, which has been rebuilt of brick. The side aisles are separated from the body by rudely hewn timber beams, resting on pillars of the same materials, and in some of the windows are fragments of ancient painted glass.

The only monuments here, worthy of notice, are two mutilated figures placed in the Church-yard, to the south of the Chapel, representing knights armed, as far as can be traced, in plate armor, with conical helmets, and boots pointed at the toes and much curved.

The hands are clasped in prayer; the feet of each figure are pressed against an animal, and under the head of each is the Davenport crest, a felon's head couped; the rope is only visible round one of the heads, the other is placed on something which has more the appearance of a chapeau, or cap of maintenance, than the wreath and helmet with which it has usually been borne. These figures are supposed to be those of Sir John Davenport, and his son Urian.*

About a quarter of a mile from the Chapel,

* The church notes of this Chapel, Harl. MSS. 2151, p. 54, contain a drawing of the monuments in the Church-yard, with this note, "It is said by auncient people that the were Sir Jo. Davenp't and Vivian [Urian] his sone, who founded the Chappell of Merton, and they lie buried there." In the painted glass was a kneeling armed figure, with surcoat, quarterly, 1 and 4, a chevron between three martlets; 2 and 3, Davenport. In the windows also arms of Davenport, Siddington and . . . . . barry of 4 sable and argent, the second and third indented.

(The Siddingtons, as far as can be judged from their coat of arms, were originally Davenports, their coat differing from the latter family, only in the addition of three cross crosslets fitchée in the base.

The Davenports had estates in Siddington as early as the time of Edward I., 1272–1307.)

Among the Davenport deeds is a grant from Sir John de Davenport, knight, to Robert de Bradshaw, &c., of 4 messuages, and 60 acres of land, with the appurtenances in the woods and wastes and all other profits in the ville of Merton, &c., of the one part, and Yeaton on the other, to maintain a fit priest celebrating mass in the Chapel of Merton, for the souls of himself, his parents, and successors, and all faithful people deceased forever; and he also grants to them common of pasture in all pastures in Merton, till they should be appropriated; and if any heir of Davenport should contradict his will and grant, they should incur God's indignation. Witnessed, 1390.

is the present Hall of Marton, a plain building, built with timber and plaster. The center and wings of the front project and terminate in gables. The porch in the center opens to a hall in which some long pikes yet remain suspended; on the left is a wainscoted parlor, over the mantle-piece of which, amongst old carvings in oak, apparently older than the building, are the arms and crest of Davenport, inlaid with various colored wood.

Behind the hall, to the west, is a mere which gave name to the township, and near which is the site of a more ancient mansion.

Sir Ralph Davenport, knight, succeeded his father, Sir John, and was engaged in the service of king Richard II., binding himself by indenture in 1380, to serve the king with three archers, well mounted and armed, to make war for a year beyond the sea where God pleased.

This Ralph Davenport, chevalier, held, *inter alia*, lands in Swettenham, from St. John of Jerusalem, also the manors of Davenport, Withington, Marton, &c. He died in 1383.*

* Among the notes of the tenures by which Sir Rafe Davenport held his grand sergeancy, is a bill from John Davenport of Davenport, Esq., to King Richard II., (1383,) showing that Randle, Earl of Chester, granted to Vivian

John Davenport, son of Ralph, and grandson of Sir Ralph, was a minor in 1416, and was married to Joan, daughter of Randle Mainwaring, of Peover, on whom were estated the manor of Swettenham, and the advowson of the Church and all the lands which Thomas de Swettenham, lord of Swettenham, had in Cheshire, by deed, dated Monday, in the 4th week in Lent, 21 Henry VI. (1443).

About the latter end of the same reign, (1460,) before the last struggle of this king with the house of York, Prince Edward, earl of Chester, issued his writ to John Davenport, Esq., his sergeant, for keeping the peace within the hundred of Macclesfield, also to take 120 persons who had been outlawed in the seven

de Davenporte the office of Master-Sergeant, worth not above the yearly sum of £12 6s. 8d., in exchange for the park, &c., of Macclesfield, worth about £40 a year, and though the petitioner and supplicant, and his ancestors, had, time out of mind, had and received £12 6s. 8d. yearly, as puture or kelk of the inhabitans and towns within the hundred, yet that Sir John Stanley, and others, would not suffer their tenants to pay the same, and therefore, he prays the king's letters under the privy seal to the bishop of Exeter, president of the council, with the king's daughter, the princess, and other his commissioners in the marches of Wales, to call the persons before them, and cause payment to be made of the money.

preceding years, and who are mentioned by name.* He died about 1475.

It may here be added that twelve pitched battles were fought between the houses of York and Lancaster, which desolated the kingdom for the space of nearly thirty years, cost the lives of eighty princes of the blood, and almost annihilated the ancient nobility of England.

After a series of successes and defeats by each party, the contest was decided by the battle of Bosworth, 1485, which was won by the Lancastrians, and Richard III. slain. Henry VII., of the second branch of the house of Lancaster, then ascended the throne.

John Davenport, of Davenport, Esq., son of John, held the office of sergeant on the death of his father in 1475. He married Elizabeth, daughter of Sir John Savage, of Clifton, knight. Died in 1482.

John Davenport, Esq., son of Ralph and grandson of John, was born 1480. Married 1st, Matilda, daughter of Sir Andrew Brereton, knight, of Brereton ; 2d wife, Jane, daughter of Ralph Arderne, Esq. ; and 3d, Blanch, daughter of Robert Latham,

* Communicated by Rev. Walter Davenport to Ormerod.

of Tabley, Esq. He died about 1553, aged 74 years. His children were, 1st, John; 2d, William; 3d, Thomas; 4th, Roger; 5th, Ralph; 6th, Randle; 7th, Parnell; 8th, Alice; 9th, Mary; 10th, Katharine; 11th, Margaret; 12th, Margery; 13th, Ellen.*

John Davenport, of Davenport, Esq., son of the preceding John, was born in 1505. Married 1st, to Elleanor, daughter of Thurston Holland, Esq., of Denton County, Lanc.; 2d wife, Jane, daughter and coheiress of Richard Massey; 3d wife, Anne, daughter of Randle Mainwaring, of Carincham, Esq. By his first

* Thomas Davenport, a younger brother of the above John, (son of Ralph,) married Elizabeth, sole daughter and heiress of Robert Handford, of Chorley, Cheshire, who thus became possessed of Chorley Hall, in whose descendants it remained vested for four generations, as follows: Robert, son of Thomas; William; Henry; William Davenport, who married Jane Bromley, and who sold Chorley, and whose grandson Henry was high sheriff of Shropshire, in 1683, and was the lineal ancestor of the Rev. Edward Sharington Davenport, of Davenport House, county of Salop, who died February 27, 1842. His son, William Sharington Davenport, of Davenport House, was born July 30, 1808, and was married December 22, 1835, to Catharine Louisa, only daughter of Samuel Warindin, Esq., of Chestleton, County of Salop, and has issue: William Bromley, born October 14, 1836; Edward Henry, born August 9, 1839, and Louisa Warindin.

wife, he had eight children, by his second, seven, and by his third, fifteen, making *thirty* in all, as follows: 1st, John; 2d, Anne; 3d, Alice; 4th, Ellen; 5th, Bridget; 6th, Urian; 7th and 8th, two who died before baptism; 9th, Richard; 10th, William; 11th, Hugh; 12th, Ralph; 13th, Parnell; 14th, Jane; 15th, Anne; 16th, Elizabeth; 17th, Mary; 18th, Katharine; 19th, Bridget; 20th, Anne; 21st, Jasper; 22d, John 2d (died young); 23d, Henry; 24th, Francis; 25th, George; (these three last all died young;) 26th, Arthur; 27th, Thomas; 28th, Peter; 29th, William 2d; 30th, Edward.*

Sir John Davenport, of Davenport, knight, son of John, and grandson of the above John (the father of so numerous offspring), was born in 1549. He married Elizabeth, daughter of Thomas Wilbraham, of Nantwich, Esq.

Webb, in his King's Vale Royal, gives an interesting incident concerning the knighting of this John D.

John Davenport, in 1617, was high sheriff of the county, and performing his service and

* These thirty children of John Davenport, added to the thirteen of his father, and the fourteen of his eldest son, make the three persons the fathers of fifty-seven children!

duty to his excellent majesty James I., while making his tour through this county, so pleased his royal highness, that upon his taking leave of him in the confines of the county, his majesty not only gave him thanks for his attention, but calling him to come to him, bestowed upon him the degree of knighthood, and graced him with this pleasant, princely farewell: "*You shall carry me this token to your wife*:" for which honor, Sir John had to thank his majesty as far as himself was concerned; but to inform him that his gentlewoman had already attained to a better ladyship, having gone to her Lord and Saviour in heaven.

Sir John Davenport died in 1625, aged seventy-six years.

John Davenport, of Davenport, Esq., son of John, grandson of John, and great grandson of Sir John, and the twentieth in lineal male descent from Orme de Davenport, married Anne, daughter of Sir Peter Richaut, knight, of London. She died at Manchester, county of Lancaster, September 27, 1665; and was buried at Swettenham, October 6, 1665. Their children were John Davenport, only son and heir apparent, born in London, October

6, 1653; died in 1658, and was buried at Swettenham, aged five years; second, Elizabeth, eldest daughter and co-heiress, baptized at Swettenham in 1655, and married Robert Davies, gent, of Moldsworth, son and heir of John Davies, of Manley, county of Chester, March 23, 1676, and on her was settled the manor and mansion of Davenport; third, Anne Davenport, second and youngest daughter, co-heiress with her sister, baptized at Swettenham, 1658, and married to John Davenport, Esq., of Woodford, March 6th, 1676, at Prestbury.

Between the husbands of these co-heiresses, the real and personal estate of the above mentioned John Davenport was divided, by an agreement signed March 23, 1689.

Mr. Davies had the manor and mansion of Davenport, and a moiety of Marton, from whom it descended to Salisbury, daughter and sole heiress of Thomas Davenport Davies, of Manley, Esq., wife of Sir William Deane, of Dromore, who sold Davenport to Richard Davenport, of Calveley, Esq., who was the representative of the eldest known existing male line of its ancient possessors.

Under the will of Mr. Davenport, this

manor passed to Phœbe (daughter of his own daughter Phœbe, wife of Davies Davenport 2d, of Woodford and Capesthorne, Esq.), which Phœbe was wife of Eusebius Horton, of Catton, Esq., and the same became vested in Anne, wife of Robert Wilmot, Esq., M.P., son of Sir Robert Wilmot, baronet.

John Davenport, of Woodford, Esq., had the *other moiety of Marton* (which has never been out of the family since the marriage of Richard de Dauneporte with Amabilia Venables, nearly seven hundred years ago), and also the *grand sergeancy* of Macclesfield hundred, and the *forestership* of Macclesfield. After his death, without issue, the same passed to his nephew Davies Davenport 2d, of Woodford and Capesthorne, Esq., and thence to his son Davies Davenport 3d, Esq., member of Parliament from 1806 to 1830, and the same passed at his death in 1838, to his eldest son Edward Davies Davenport, of Woodford and Capesthorne, Esq., its late proprietor, who was of *the twenty-fifth generation*, and who died in 1847, leaving eldest son and heir Arthur Henry, born June 9th, 1832.

The office of *hereditary master forester*, held in fee by the Davenports of Davenport, appears, after the demise of the local earldom, to have been rather an honorary office, and to have been superseded, as far as its active powers were concerned, by that of *stewards*, who were appointed and removed at pleasure, until the reign of Edward IV., when the stewardship of the forest and hundred of Macclesfield was granted to Thomas, Lord Stanley, in which family it has since remained.

The magisterial duties of the office of *grand sergeant*, still held by the Davenports, have become less frequent of later years, and partaken of that tendency to disuse, to which all feudal tenures have been subject, but its privileges remain in full force in the hundred. The office is noticed in the successive wills and inquisitions, and was included in a recovery, 18 George II. (1745.)

In possession of the family at Woodford and Capesthorne is still retained a collection of very numerous documents, clearly proving its general exercise; consisting of reports of coroners, letters describing the goods of felons, and announcing sudden deaths, and in some instances treasure trove; and the rights of the grand sergeancy have been exercised by late sergeants with respect to forfeited goods and chattels of felons, felos de se, and fugitives, estrays and deodands, within the limits above specified.

The present hall of Davenport is a low building of various materials, still used as the residence of a gentleman's family, and doubtless retaining in its walls many relics of the ancient mansion which occupied its site.

Capesthorne, a vill about six miles from Davenport, passed from the ancient family of the Capesthornes to the family of the Wards, and through Mary (eldest daughter, and finally sole heiress of John Ward, who died in 1748,) to her husband, the first Davies Davenport, of Woodford, Esq.

This place is now the residence of this branch of the Davenport family, and is situated in one of the most pleasing parts of the hundred.

The hall is a spacious building, in the style of architecture used in the early part of the last century, and stands upon extensive grounds to the left of the road leading to the city of Manchester, which is about twenty miles to the north.

This sketch will now be continued, and present somewhat of the history and lineage of the other most distinguished collateral branches, after which the full genealogical line of descent will be given in its regular succession.

WHELTROUGH HALL.

The township of Lower Withington (which lies adjoining Capesthorne), with its appurtenances and liberties, was given by Randle Blundeville, Earl of Chester and Lincoln, with twenty shillings rent out of the mills of Macclesfield, besides various lands held by his father and grandfather, to Robert, son of Salmon, to be held by a pair of gilt spurs, for which Robert remitted and quit-claimed to the earl and his heirs all the lands which his father held in Normandy.

These deeds were executed during the justiceship of Philip de Orreby, between 1209 and 1226.

Harl. MSS. 2074, 183. Robert de Salmon gives to Roger, son of Vivian de Davenport, in frank marriage with Mary his daughter, one half of Withington, with homages, relief and wardships; half of Tunsted, Lundris and Wardshaw; half of Hewood and Weltrok, subject to foreign service and suite in the court of Weverham.

In this township is a singular hill called *Tunsted*, which precisely resembles in form an enormous tumulus, which is the commencement of the natural undulations of surface which distinguish Macclesfield hundred, and gradually increase in size and number towards the eastward, until they form the bold barrier of hills ranging along the Staffordshire frontier.

On the northern side of this hill is *Wheltrough Hall*, an ancient timber mansion, embosomed in trees, in which a branch of the Davenports (as above stated) seated themselves during the reign of Edward the First, or between 1250 and 1300, and from which descended the collateral lines of *Bramhall*, *Henbury*, *Coventry*, and *Woodford*.

The moiety of the manor settled on the Davenports of Davenport, by inquisitions postmortem, is shown to have been held by Sir Ralph Davenport of Davenport, his son Ralph, and Ralph of the thirteenth generation; also John Davenport of Davenport, of the fourteenth generation, his son John, and also by his grandson John Davenport of Davenport.

Harl. MSS. 2119, p. 225, &c. Arms and

crest as Davenport of Davenport, with filial distinction.

Thomas Davenport of Wheltrough was the second son of Sir Thomas Davenport of Davenport, by Agnes de Macclesfield.

In 1309, his father grants him a lease of the office of sergeancy for two years, at an annual rent of sixteen marks of silver. He had lands from his father, in Withington, Tunstede and Marton. Married Elizabeth, daughter of ——, who survived her husband 12 Edw. III. (1355).

Their children were, 1st, Thomas, the continuer of the direct line in Wheltrough; 2d, John, ancestor of the Davenports of Bromhall, fifth in the Henbury entail, 1366; 3d, Sir John (called also Jenkin, to distinguish him from his brother of Bromhall), kt. justice of Lancastershire, 1384, and purchaser of Henbury; 4th, Alice, wife of Sir John de Hide of Urmetson.

From Thomas, the oldest son and heir, the line of descent in Wheltrough is as follows: Richard; Richard (1452); Richard; Ralph (1499); Richard (1542); Richard (1566); Richard; Richard (1618); Richard (1647); Richard, son and heir, will dated 1677;

shortly after which, the family appear to have left Wheltrough.

Sir John (alias Sir Jenkin) Davenport, third son of Thomas of Wheltrough, and grandson of Sir Thomas Davenport of Davenport, married Elizabeth, daughter and co-heiress of Peter Legh of Betchton. Their children were, 1st, Thomas, ancestor of the Davenports of Henbury; 2d, John, living 1366; 3d, Nicholas, ancestor of the Davenports of Woodford and Capesthorne, living 1371; 4th, Griffin Davenport.

Thomas Davenport of Henbury, eldest son of Sir Jenkin, married Margaret, daughter of Hugh Venables, living in 1371. From him the Henbury line of descent was as follows: Hugh, son and heir; Thomas; Thomas; Thomas; John (Inq. post-mortem 1556); Randle (Inq. p. m. 1614); William (fifteen years old in 1580); John; William, whose only child and heiress was Isabella, who became the wife of Sir Fulk Lucy, kt. member of Parliament for the county of Chester in 1664, and who thus came into possession of the Henbury estate.*

* The township of Henbury lies about twelve or fifteen miles from Davenport, and two miles from Macclesfield.

Several more names of this branch of the family will

BRAMALL, OR BRAMHALL, CHESHIRE.

This township lies about twenty miles from Davenport, two from Stockport, and about eight miles south of the city of Manchester. From the Domesday survey, it appears that two manors existed in this township in the Saxon period, the proprietors of which were ejected, to make way for the baron of Durham Massey.

A charter from the third baron of Durham, in the time of Henry II. (1154—1189), confirms to Mathew de Bromeale, the manors of Bramall, Duckenfield, and two parts of Baggiley, which had been previously held by his father, whose name is not mentioned, but who was probably younger son or near kinsman of Hamo de Masci, the Norman grantee.

In 1278, Richard de Bromhall obtained a conditional release for himself and his tenants, in Bromhall, Duckenfield, &c., from Hamon de Massey, from being impleaded in the court of Dunham. He is called Sir Richard in the

be found in the genealogical line of descent. Of all these branches, the writer has in his possession hundreds of names belonging to the various pedigrees, which are not here used, his object being simply to give an outline of the descent of the different branches.

pedigrees of this family, "son of William, son of John, son of Edward," and is allowed for his armorial coat, sable, a lion rampant Or, which might have had reference to the lion rampant on the early seals of the lords of Durham.

Sir Richard de Bromhall had issue, Sir Geoffry de Bromhall, whose daughter and heiress, according to Dugdale, and other pedigrees, married John Davenport, second son of Thomas Davenport of Wheltrough, in the twenty-second year of Edward III. (1349), and who thus became proprietor of the manor, and the same has continued in the Davenport family to the present day.

The children of John Davenport, by Alice his wife, are given as Robert, oldest son and heir living in 1399; Thomas, who married Ellen, sister of Sir Ralph de Moburley; and Margaret, wife of William Hyde of Hyde.

Sir John Hyde of Norbury and Hyde, kt., father of William, and son of Robert Hyde, lord of Norbury, married for his first wife Margaret, daughter of Sir John Davenport of Davenport, and was the ancestor of the distinguished Edward Hyde, earl of Clarendon, Lord High Chancellor of England, whose daughter, Anne Hyde, was the wife of James II., and the mother of Queen Mary (the wife of William Prince of Orange), and also of Queen Anne, successive sovereigns on the throne of England.

John Davenport, son of Robert, and grandson of Robert, married for his first wife, Cicely, daughter of Lawrence Warren, of Poymton, by whom he had William, eldest son and heir; second wife, a daughter of John Pagot, of Staffordshire, by whom he had John Davenport, of the County of Somerset. He died in 1497.

Sir William Davenport, of Bromhall, knight, was the son of William, and the grandson of the above William. He married for his first wife, Margarie, daughter of George Booth, of Durham; second wife, Anne, daughter of Sir Richard Brereton, of Patton, knight. His first marriage took place in 1566. He died Sept. 13th, 1577.

Sir William Davenport, of Bromhall, knight, son of William, and grandson of Sir William, married *Dorothy*, daughter of [Edward] Warren, of Poynton.

Of the product of the handicraft of this dame Dorothy Davenport, we shall speak in giving an account of the interior of the present hall attached to this manor. Sir William died in 1641.

The following account of Sir Humphrey Davenport, knight, lord chief baron, younger brother of Sir William Davenport, (last mentioned,) is drawn from Wood's Athenæ Oxonienses.

Humphrey Davenport, younger son of William Davenport, of Bromhall, in Cheshire, by Margaret, his wife, daughter of Richard Ashton, of Middleton, in Lanc., knight, was born of an ancient and genteel family at Bromhall, and became a commoner of Baliol College, Oxford, in the beginning of 1581, being then in the fifteenth year of his age, and matriculated, or made a member of the University, as a Cheshire man born, or an esquire's son. He was brought into trouble by the members of the Long Parliament, which hastened the end of this good man, esteemed by all who knew him, as *an able lawyer*, *a loyal subject*, *hospitable*, *charitable*, *and above all*, *religious*. He died in 1645.*

* The trouble into which he was brought by the Long Parliament, was that of several impeachments drawn up against him; 1st, for being one of the judges that advised the king in the matter of ship money; 2d, for ordering the

His wife was Mary, daughter and coheiress of Francis Sutton, of Sutton. They left one son, James Davenport, of Sutton, who was born about 1610, and who married Anne, daughter of Sir Henry Robinson, county of Northampton.

William Davenport, of Bromhall, Esq., son of Sir William, was baptized at Stockport, March 25, 1584, and buried April 24, 1655. His oldest son William, and most of his other children, having died in the lifetime of their father, he was succeeded by his youngest son, Peter Davenport, Esq., who was baptized at Stockport, July 31, 1622, and buried April 8, 1658.

Rev. Warren Davenport, of Bromhall (heir to his brother William), was the son of William, and grandson of William, the son of Peter Davenport, Esq., baptized at Stockport, September 30, 1698. He married Achsah, daughter of Caleb Storrs, of Stockport, in

seizing of the goods of Samuel Vassal, a merchant, because he refused to pay the imposition due for them; 3d, for acting injuriously in the case of Peter Smart, Prebendary of Durham, for preaching a factious sermon.

He was ably defended in 1641, in a speech before the joint houses of Parliament, by the Earl of Clarendon, Lord High Chancellor.

1744, and was succeeded by the late proprietor of Bromhall, William Davenport, Esq., only son and heir, who was born November 18, 1749, and who married Martha, youngest daughter of Rev. John le Tourcey, April 27, 1767. The following sketch is subjoined of the present seat of this ancient branch of the family—compiled from Ormerod.

The first appearance of the Hall, pertaining to this domain, is unusually striking, exhibiting a long and lofty line of irregular buildings of timber and plaster, standing in a considerable elevation at the intersection of two deep valleys, near the bank of a rivulet. The building was originally quadrangular, but the western side of the quadrangle was removed by a former proprietor, who also took down a long gallery which extended along the top of the eastern side, and added much to the imposing effect of the building.

A porch admits from the court on the east side into the great hall, whence a spiral staircase, composed of solid blocks of oak, leads to the drawing-room, a noble apartment about twelve yards square, wainscoted nearly to the top. Over the wainscot are ornaments in stucco, and the arms of the successive alliances of the Davenports. The ceiling is enriched with pendants. On the mantle-piece, which ascends to the top of the room, are the arms of Queen Elizabeth, and the date 1592 occurs in the ornamental castings of the door posts. Round the apartment is hung a fine series of family portraits, commencing with Sir William Davenport, aged 65, and Dorothy his wife, aged 66, 1627. Among other portraits, are originals of Edward Warren, of Poynton, 1594, aged 32; Sir Urian Legh, of Adlington, aged 39, 1632; and Henry, earl of Derby, 1583, aged 51, being then lord-lieutenant of Lancastershire and Cheshire.

Beyond this are the plaster-room, (so called from the materials of the floor,) hung round with buff coats, imperfect suits of armor, and military weapons, and a bed chamber, called "*The Paradise room*," from a bed in which the entire history of the Fall was worked in worsted by the hands of dame Dorothy Davenport, who appears to have labored upon it from 1610 to 1614. The entire arrangement of this little room is probably unequaled as a specimen of the furniture and decorations of the time. A wainscoted apartment in the south-east angle leads hence to the banqueting room, which occupies nearly all that remains of the first story on the south side of the quadrangle. This singularly curious room is about forty-two feet by twenty-one; the floor is plaster, and the sides are timber and plaster, painted with figures and foliage in imitation of tapestry. The roof is divided lengthways into six compartments, supported by massive arched timbers, the alternate ones being supported by uprights, resting on obtuse arches of oak, sprung from pilasters: the sides of these arches are ornamented with foliage, rosettes, &c., and finished at the top with embattled mouldings. There have been originally three windows in each side, divided by upright mullions only, with highly carved gothic heads. The center window on the north side projects out into the quadrangle, resting on a bracket below, on which, among some bold carvings in oak, is the shield of the ancient Bromhall family. In these windows are armorial bearings in stained glass with damasked grounds.

The domestic Chapel, which is in the south-east angle under the wainscoted room before mentioned, has a flat roof supported by brackets, is fitted up with oaken benches, and retains much ancient painted glass in its windows.

At the end of one of these benches is a curious carving in oak, the aera of which, from the devices, consisting of the rose and fetterlock, the feathers of the principality, the ragged staff and the rampant bear of the heiress of the earls of Warwick, may be referred indubitably within the reign of Richard the Third.

In this Chapel is the family vault, over which is an inscription commemorating

MARTHA, WIFE OF WILLIAM DAVENPORT, ESQ.,
WHO DIED
DECEMBER 25TH, 1810,
AGED 63 YEARS.

Mr. Davenport died in 1838, and was succeeded by Sir Salisbury Davenport, of the cross of the Bath, and knight of the cross of the Hanoverian Order, Rear Admiral of the White, whose patronymic was Humphreys, (son of Rev. Evan Humphreys,) and who married for his second wife, in 1816, *Maria*, daughter and heiress of William Davenport, Esq., of Bromhall Hall, by whom he has issue. He assumed his present surname, by royal license, on succeeding, through his wife, to the Davenport estate of Bromhall. He is acting magistrate for the counties of Chester, Derby, Lancaster, and Gloucester, and the borough of Stockport.

Arms and crest, those of the old family of Davenport.

WOODFORD, CHESHIRE.

The township of Woodford, with those of Withington and Capesthorne, lies in the parish of Prestbury, not far from the original seat of the Davenports of Davenport. It is unnoticed in the Domesday survey, but in the reign of King John, between 1199 and 1216, it occurs among the estates of Sir John Arderne of Alfdord.

In 1356, the manor and appurtenances of Wydeford, (Woodford) were granted by John Stafford and Isabella his wife to John Davenport, third son of Thomas Davenport de Wheltrough, for the life of Isabella, wife of said John Stafford. (This Isabella was the daughter of Sir John Davenport of Davenport, by Margaret, daughter of Sir William Brereton, and was first married to Robert de Eaton, baron of Stockport.) John Davenport was knighted, and chief justice of Lancastershire, and is styled indifferently of his father's estates of Wheltrough and his own manors of Henbury and Woodford. He enfeoffed his brother Robert, chaplain, with the manor of Woodford, for the use of his son Nicholas, by deed, dated 1371, at Woodford, who resettled the same on John and his wife Margaret, for life, remainder to this Nicholas and his male heirs.

Christopher Davenport of Widford, eldest son of Nicholas, married Alica, daughter of Hugh Arderne; marriage articles dated 1415. Their children were John, eldest son, who died in 1415; Randulph, parson of Wilmslow; Charles; and Nicholas, who married Agnes, daughter of Robert Davenport of Bromhall.

Nicholas Davenport, son of John, and grandson of Christopher, married Margaret, daughter of Sir Christopher Savage, knight, son of Sir John Savage of Clifton, knight, feoffment for her jointure Feb. 3, 1490. He died Feb. 9, 1522, and his wife 1542, and was buried with her ancestors at Macclesfield. Their children were John, who married Margaret, daughter of William Davenport, Esq., of Bromhall, who died in 1575, surviving William, his eldest son and heir; Nicholas; Lawrence; and Christopher Davenport, ancestor of the Davenports of Locrosse, who married Emma, daughter of John Blunt, upon Trent, County of Stafford—Harl. MSS. 2094.

William Davenport of Woodford, son of John, was married to Ellen, daughter of John Davenport of Davenport, Esq., by dispensation from Thomas Wolsey, Cardinal Archbishop of York, they being of the third and fourth degree of kindred, dated at Westminster, July 3, 1529. He was buried at Prestbury, January 6, 1570.

William Davenport, son of Christopher, and grandson of William, married for his first wife Dorothy, daughter of Robert Hyde of Norbury, Esq., by Jane his wife, sister of Sir William Davenport of Bromhall; marriage articles signed January 26, 1569. His second wife was Elizabeth, daughter of William Dimocke of Chester, who was a widow to Hugh Bromley of Hampton Post, County Chester. His third wife was Anne, daughter of John Warren of Pointon, Esq. He died at Woodford, and was buried at Prestbury, April 2, 1632.

William Davenport, son of John (by Mary, daughter of Hugh Bromley, Esq.), and grandson of William, married Elizabeth, daughter of William Rawlinson, Esq., county of Derb. He died at Woodford, and was buried at Prestbury, November 6, 1656.

John Davenport, son of John, and grandson of William, married Anne, daughter and co-heiress of John Davenport of Davenport and Marton; marriage articles signed March 23, 1676. He was major of the Cheshire forces raised at Nantwich in 1689, and died February 4, 1733, and was buried at Marton.

Monk Davenport, brother of the above John, and heir by survivorship, married Elizabeth, daughter of John Davies, Esq., of Manley and Moldsworth, county of Chester, and died February 24, 1735.

Davies Davenport, Esq., of Woodford, Marton, and of the Inner Temple, London, heir to his father Monk, and uncle John Davenport, Esq., was baptized at Prestbury, March 14, 1696. He married Mary, daughter and sole heiress of John Ward, of Capesthorne, Esq., and of the Inner Temple, October 19, 1721. Their children were, 1st, Davies Davenport, Esq., of Woodford, Marton and Capesthorne, and of the Inner Temple, born in Red Lion Square, London, October 2, 1723, and who married Phœbe, daughter and co-heiress of Richard Davenport of Calveley and Davenport, and died at Capesthorne in 1758; 2d,

William Davenport, born in London, October 8, 1725, buried at Liverpool; 3d, Philip Davenport, born 1726, died in 1727; 4th, Richard Davenport, born August 20, 1729, and died in 1799; 5th, Christopher Davenport, born November 4, 1730, and was buried at Liverpool; 6th, Thomazine Davenport, born in Red Lion Square, March 28, 1732, and died at Capesthorne, unmarried, in 1766; 7th, Sir Thomas Davenport of Hendon, knight, born 1733; and baptized at St. George's (London), died on the York Circuit, and was buried in the Minster. His wife was Jane, daughter of John Seel, Esq.; 8th, Charles Davenport, born in Bloomsbury Square, London, April 7, 1735, was rector of Brereton, county of Chester, and was buried at Capesthorne, March 16, 1767.

Davies Davenport of Woodford, Marton, Calveley and Capesthorne, Esq., only son and heir of the above Davies Davenport, was born August 29, 1757. He married Charlotte, daughter of Ralph Sneyd, Esq., of Keel, county of Stafford. He was first chosen a member of Parliament for the county of Chester in 1806, and continued to represent that county in successive parliaments till 1830, when he resigned. He died February 6, 1837.

Edward Davies Davenport, Esq., eldest son of the above Davies Davenport, M.P., was born at Catton Hall, county Derby, April 27, 1778, and succeeded to his father's estates in Woodford, Marton, Calveley, Capesthorne, &c., in 1837. He was married November 8, 1830, to Catharine Anne, daughter of Richard Hunt, Esq., of Wirksworth, and had a son and heir, Arthur Henry, born June 9, 1832. Mr. D. died in 1847, in the seventieth year of his age. His widow is now living at Capesthorne.

Rev. Walter Davenport Bromley, youngest son of the above Davies Davenport, Esq., M.P., was born in Upper Seymour Street, London, Feb. 5, 1787, and baptized in the parish of St. Mary-le-bone. For some time he was vicar of Ellaston, county of Stafford. He was first married July, 1818, to Caroline Barbara, daughter of John Gooch of Praxlingham, county of Norfolk, Archdeacon of Sudbury. For his second wife he married, February 22, 1829, Lady Louisa Dawson, sister of the earl of Portarlington. He assumed the surname of Bromley by royal license, and for some years owned and resided at Baginton Hall, about four miles from the city of Coventry.* His present country residence is at Wootton Hall, county of Stafford, about five miles from Ashbourne.

Harriet Catharine Davenport, daughter of the above Davies Davenport, Esq., M.P., was born in Harley Street, London, April 4, 1791, and married Sir John Williams, knight, Judge on the Bench of Queen Victoria.

DAVENPORT OF CALVELEY, CHESHIRE.

Arms and Crest as Davenport of Davenport, &c.

Calveley lies about fourteen miles from the city of Chester, on the left of the road leading

* Baginton Hall was long the seat of the Bromley family. The estate was purchased by the family in the reign of James I., and the original Hall was built by Secretary Bromley. This gentleman was Speaker of the House of Commons during the reign of Queen Anne. In proof of the high estimation in which he was held, the following circumstance may be cited: In 1706, the family seat at Baginton was reduced to the ground by fire. Intelligence of this calamity was conveyed to the owner while attending his duty in the House of Commons, and a considerable sum was immediately voted by Parliament towards a restoration of the edifice.—*Dugdale's England and Wales Delineated.*

from thence to London. The township was granted by Richard de Vernon, in the beginning of the thirteenth century, to Hugh de Calvelegh, and from the tenure of the Davenports under the Vernons of Shipbrook and their successors the Savages, as specified in the inquisitions post mortem. The son of the grantee was Richard de Calvelegh, who received a confirmation of this title from Elena, daughter of Matthew de Vernon. This Richard de Calvelegh had issue by Leuca his wife, as follows: Hugh de Calvelegh, his successor, William (living in 1339), and Robert. From Hugh de Calvelegh, the estate passed to his son Kenric de Calveley, who by his wife had issue Robert de Calveley, son and heir, as also David de Calveley, the father of the celebrated Sir Hugh Calveley of Lea, knight, the founder of Buxbury College.

Robert de Calveley married Eliza, one of the daughters and co-heiresses of Ralph, son of David de Haselwall, who was a widow in 1350, when the Black Prince presented in her stead to the church of Haselwall, in consequence of an alienation without her license. By his wife, Robert de Calveley had a son, who dying without issue (inquisition post mortem, 1362), was succeeded in the joint estate of Calveley and Haselwall by Catharine, the sister and heir of this son of Robert de Calveley, in whom the male line thus terminated.

Catharine de Calveley, who thus became heiress, brought the manor of Calveley and a moiety of Haselwall in marriage to her husband, Arthur Davenport, who presented in her right to the church of Haselwall, in 1369 and 1394, and after whose death Catharine presented as a widow in 1405. The said Arthur and Catharine Davenport had a release for their lands in Wirral forest, from William, son of William, son of John Stanley (Harl. MSS. 2079: 147), and the marriage is further proved by an inquisition post mortem, 17 Richard II. (1394), in which Hugh Calveley of Lea is stated to hold lands in Calveley, from Arthur Davenport and Catharine his wife, in right of said Catharine.

This Arthur Davenport, as appears by a very elaborate pedigree drawn up from original deeds (Harl. MSS. 2119: 224), was sixth son of Sir John Davenport of Davenport, knight, by Margery, daughter of Sir William Brereton. He was one of the Cheshire men who were zealously attached to King Richard the Second, and was slain on the part of the Percies at the battle of Shrewsbury in 1403. According to Holinshed, two hundred Cheshire esquires and gentlemen fell on that bloody day.

Henry Davenport, son of Arthur, had issue by Isabella, his wife, Arthur Davenport, who died before his father, leaving issue, Hugh, grandson and heir of Henry, who married a daughter and heiress of William Handford, of Handford. Inquisition post mortem 1472.

Ralph Davenport, of Calveley, Esq., son of Hugh, married Isabella Spurstow, of Spurstow, in the 9th year of Edward IV., 1470. He died on Whitsunday, 14th year of Henry VIII., (1523.)

John Davenport, of Calveley, Esq., son of Hugh, and grandson of the above Ralph, married Eleanor, daughter of Sir George Calveley, of Lea, knight, 1522. He died October 20th, 1567. His children were, Katharine, Elizabeth, Dorothy, Jane, Hugh, John, Arthur, Randle and Anthony.

Hugh Davenport, Esq., son of the above John, held the manor of Calveley, and lands and tenements therein, from Sir John Savage, knight, by military service, by the services of the sixth part of a knight's fee, and the sixth part of the twenty-ninth part of a knight's fee, also a moiety of the advowson and lands of Haselwall, Wythington, Somerford, Macclesfield, &c. By his first wife, he had John, eldest son, who died young (August 21, 1570), Jane, Catharine, Arthur, who married Eleanor, daughter of John Davenport, of Davenport, and Randell; by his second wife, he had George, William, and Dorothy.

Arthur Davenport, oldest surviving son, dying without male issue in 1625, the estate passed to his younger brother, by the second marriage, George Davenport, Esq., who died in 1638.

Samuel Davenport of Calveley, Esq., son of George, and grandson of the above George, was baptized at Bunbury, June 28, 1652, and married Mary, daughter of the Right Hon. Richard Verney, Lord Willoughby de Broke.

Richard Davenport, of Calveley, Esq., son of George, and grandson of the above Samuel, purchased from Sir Matthew Done, bart. (who in the right of his wife Salisbury, daughter and sole heiress of Robert Davies, of Manley, was the representative of the Davenports of Davenport, in the female line), the original seat of his ancestors, and died without male issue in 1771, leaving two daughters and coheiresses, Bridget, who married John Bromley, Esq., of Baginton, (near Coventry,) County of Warwick, and Phebe, who became the wife of Davies Davenport, of Capesthorne, Esq., the representative of the Davenports of Woodford, in the hundred of Macclesfield. On the death of John Bromley, Esq., without issue, who possessed the Manor and Hall of Calveley, in right of his wife, the same passed to Davies Davenport, Esq., only son of the coheiress, who was knight of the shire for the County of Chester, in several successive parliaments, and who died in 1838.

Nearly the whole township is now in the possession of the family at Capesthorne. The ancient hall of Calveley was pulled down during the latter part of the last century. The enclosure contained about two acres. The present house is an old timber building cased with brick. There are no family paintings found here. The park and paddock adjacent to the house contain about sixty-three acres, in which have been kept a large number of deer.

DAVENPORT OF COVENTRY, WARWICKSHIRE.

Arms and Crest as Davenport of Davenport, Wheltrough, Henbury, &c.

The city of Coventry was founded at a very early period, probably while the Romans inhabited Britain. It was anciently spelled Coventrie, the final syllable being evidently the British Tre, a town; and its prefix as given by the Saxons, is supposed to express the circumstance of a covent, or convent, having stood upon the spot. In 1016, when Edric invaded Mercia, a house of nuns in Coventry is said to have fallen a prey to their ferocity. After the Norman conquest, the lordship of Coventry became vested in the Earl of Chester, by the marriage of Leucia, granddaughter of Leofric, (by Countess Godiva), the fifth Earl of Chester, who was descended from Leofric, Earl of Chester, in the time of Ethelbald, 857–860.

The city and certain villages in its vicinity, as a mark of special favor, were constituted by Henry VI. in 1451, an entire county by themselves, so that the citizens of Coventry had no political connection with Warwickshire, and the mayor and aldermen of Coventry have been justices of the peace for the county, and held quarter sessions in the same manner, and with the same powers as counties at large. The freeholders, as such, are not even entitled to vote for the return of any member to parliament, and the public offices are required to be filled from the tradesmen and artisans, rather than from the landed proprietors.

The city of Coventry, having been peculiarly favored in escaping any extensive conflagration, till recently has preserved the aspect of a city of the sixteenth century. The streets were narrow, and the upper parts of the houses projected, so as almost to form an arch, and were evidently constructed with little intention of affording a free circulation of air. Many houses replete with traces of the fifteenth century, till recently were standing, and though age had impaired their freshness, it had not served much to weaken their timbers of massive and impregnable oak. A specimen of these buildings yet remains in that of the Bablake School, to which reference will be made hereafter.

In this city, a younger son of the Henbury branch of the Davenport family in the County of Chester, settled soon after the year 1500, and became the ancestor of the Davenports of that city. Here they were not, as in Cheshire, landed proprietors; but as merchants, artisans, &c., were men of wealth, piety, and influence; four of whom were mayors of that city—an office, as before remarked, held by the latter class of citizens, rather than the former.

In this connection, we find John Davenport, the father of those distinguished brothers—REV. JOHN DAVENPORT, the PURITAN, and REV. CHRISTOPHER DAVENPORT, alias FRANCISCUS A SANCTA CLARA, who, like two mighty forces, diverging from a common center, arose, the one to plant in this western world, a system of Church polity, which should give the purest freedom to all the members of Christ's house; the other, endowed with like genius, and energy of will, to lend his influence to promote that system of Ecclesiastical despotism, which a Wickliffe, a Luther, and a Melancthon, had labored to overthrow. Of these two brothers, and other members of this branch, we shall further speak in the genealogical line of descent to be now given.

PLAN OF THE GENEALOGY.

The Arabian figures mark the number in the line of descent. The Roman letters number the children of a family.

To trace backwards the line of descent, take the Arabian number prefixed to any name, and refer to the number of the person whose issue is there given, and repeat the same with each preceding generation, thus: (42) III. shows John Davenport to be the third son of Sir John Davenport, No. 38. Turning to No. 38, Sir John Davenport of the ninth generation is shown to be the third son of Thomas Davenport, No. 21, of the eighth generation, &c.

GENEALOGY OF THE DAVENPORT FAMILY.

FIRST GENERATION.

(1.) Ormus de Dauneporte, born in 1086, and assumed the local name in the County of Chester, England. He witnessed a charter of enfranchisement of Gilbert Venables, in the time of William II., or Henry I.

SECOND GENERATION.

Issue of Ormus de Dauneporte, (*No.* 1.)

(2.) I. Richard de Dauneporte, born in 1136, to whom Hugh Kevelioc, earl of Chester, granted by charter the *chief forestership* of the forests of Leek and Macclesfield, about 1166, and who had a moiety of the township of Marton by marriage, about 1176. His wife was Amabilia, the daughter of Gilbert Venables, baron of Kinderton, whose father, Gilbert Venables, was the Norman grantee of Kinderton, Davenport, &c., before 1086.

THIRD GENERATION.

Issue of Richard de Dauneporte, (No. 2.)

(3.) I. Thomas de Davenporte, living in the time of Henry II., or before 1189.

FOURTH GENERATION.

Issue of Thomas de Davenporte, (No. 3.)

(4.) I. Richard de Davenporte, to whom Randle Blundeville, earl of Chester, granted by charter acquittance from suit in the Shire and Hundred Court, for himself and heirs, between 1209 and 1226.

FIFTH GENERATION.

Issue of Richard de Davenporte, (No. 4.)

(5.) I. Amicia Davenporte, who became the wife of Randle de Cheldleton, and had lands in the Abbacy of Dierlacres.

(6.) II. Vivian de Davenporte, to whom Randle Blundeville, earl of Chester, granted by charter, the grand sergeancy of the forests of Leek and Macclesfield, between 1209 and 1226, and also acquittance of juris of County and Hundred. Married Beatrix, daughter of Bertrand de Hulme. Harl. MSS. 2094.

(7.) III. Walter Davenporte, second son, had lands in Somerford Booths.

(8.) IV. Peter Davenporte, living in 1263. Harl. MSS. 2119.

SIXTH GENERATION.

Issue of Vivian de Davenporte, (No. 6.)

(9.) I. Roger Davenport of Davenport, who married Mary, daughter of Robert Salemon of Wythington, with whom her husband had a moiety of Wythington, also a part of Tunstede and Wultroke (Wheltrough).

By an inquisition taken before Reginald de Gray, 16 year of Edward I. (1288), it is found that Roger de Davenport held his sergeancy in the Hundred of Macclesfield in the Bach &c., and that he shall find eight sergeants (one a horseman) to keep the peace, who shall come at the king's summons, at their own cost in the county, and at the king's cost when they shall have passed the Dee, or gone out of the county. The same Roger, in 1248, witnessed a deed of Alexander Wythington. He seems to have died in 1291.

(10.) II. Edward de Davenport de Newton, living in 1272. He assumed the name of Newton, and became the ancestor of the Newtons of Newton.

(11.) III. Richard de Davenport, who was the father of Roger de Tornock, and who had lands in Somerford Booths.

(12.) IV. Robert de Davenport, living in 1272; he assumed the name of Lawton, and was ancestor of the Lawtons of Lawton.

(13.) V. Beatrix Davenport, in some pedigrees called the wife of Bertrand de Hulme.

(14.) VI. Thomas de Davenport.

SEVENTH GENERATION.

Issue of Roger de Davenport, (*No.* 9.)

(15.) I. Peter de Davenport, son and heir, died without issue.

(16.) II. Sir Thomas Davenport of Davenport, knight, married, 1st, Agnes, daughter of Thomas de Macclesfield, who was born in 1287. She was the mother of his issue. His second wife was Roesia, daughter of Ralph de Vernon, and widow of Sir William de Brereton. Sir Thomas died in 1320, and his widow survived him in 1322.

(17.) III. John de Davenport, who married Matilda, daughter of William de Rode, by whom he had issue, Richard.

(18.) IV. Ellen Davenport, who was married to William de Burklegh, eldest son and heir of Robert Burkley, Esq., and ancestors of the lords Burkley.

(19.) V. Henry Davenport of Marton, who also had lands in Macclesfield in 1292. He had one son, Roger, who married, 1st, Mary, widow of William Mainwaring de Peover; and 2d, Margaret, widow of Thomas de Swettenham.

EIGHTH GENERATION.

Issue of Sir Thomas Davenport, (No. 16.)

(20.) I. Sir John Davenport of Davenport, knight, married for his first wife in 1301, Margery, daughter of Sir William de Brereton, by Roesia his wife, daughter of Sir Ralph Vernon. She was the mother of his issue. His second wife was Agnes de Bradford. Sir John founded a chantry in the Chapel of Marton, in 1343, which was dissolved after the Reformation. His second wife survived him, and was remarried to Robert Massey, senior, of Sale, in 1358.

(21.) II. Thomas Davenport de Wheltrough, to whom his father gave lands in Withington, Wheltrough, Marton, &c., &c., who became the ancestor of the Davenports of Wheltrough,

Henbury, Coventry, Bromhall, and Woodford, (now also of Capesthorne.) He married Elizabeth .... who survived her husband in 1339.

(22.) III. Roger Davenport, senior.

(23.) IV. Peter Davenport, who assumed the name of Denton in 1329.

(24.) V. Roger Davenport, who had lands in Whittington, by gift of his father and brother Roger.

(25.) VI. Mallicent Davenport.

(26.) VII. Roesia Davenport.

NINTH GENERATION.

Issue of Sir John Davenport, (No. 20.)

(27.) I. Thomas Davenport of Davenport, who married for his first wife Matilda ...... in 1343, and was afterwards married to Eve ... He died in 1380 without issue.

(28.) II. John Davenport, who became rector of the Church in Swettenham, (a village on the side of the Dane opposite to Davenport,) in 1335. He married, 1st, Johanna, daughter of Sir Henry Delves, of Dodington, knight. His second wife was Margaret, daughter of Henry Done, who remarried Sir William Brereton, knight.

(29.) III. Sir Ralph Davenport, knight, the continuer of the direct male line of the Davenports of Davenport, who married Joice . . . . . . In 1380, Sir Ralph bound himself by indenture to serve King Richard, with three archers well mounted, to make war for a year beyond the sea where God pleased. He died in 1383. His wife held the grand sergeancy, by letters patent from Richard II., during the nonage of Ralph, son and heir, dated December 11, 1384.

(30.) IV. Richard Davenport, living in 1350.

(31.) V. Roger Davenport, living in 1350.

(32.) VI. Urian Davenport, distinguished for his great stature, was buried at Marton.

(33.) VII. Arthur Davenport, of Calveley, who married Katharine de Calveley, and became the ancestor of the Davenports of Calveley. He was slain on the part of the Percies, in the battle of Shrewsbury, in 1403.

(34.) VIII. Margaret Davenport, who married Sir John Hyde, lord of Norbury, from whom descended the distinguished Edward Hyde, earl of Clarendon.

(35.) IX. Isabella Davenport married Robert de Eaton, baron of Stockport; remarried to John de Stafford.

NINTH GENERATION—Continued.

Issue of Thomas Davenport of Wheltrough, (No. 21.)

(36.) I. Thomas Davenport, with whose son and heir Richard, the direct line of Wheltrough continued.

(37.) II. John Davenport, who married Alice, daughter and heiress of Godfrey de Bromhall, and who became the ancestor of the Davenports of Bromhall, 1366.

(38.) III. Sir John Davenport, (called also Jenkin, to distinguish him from his elder brother of that name,) knight, justice of Lancastershire, 1384, and who became the purchaser of Henbury. He married Elizabeth, daughter and coheiress of Peter Legh of Betcherton.

(39.) IV. Alice Davenport, married Sir John de Hyde, knight, ancestor of the Hydes of Urmetson.

TENTH GENERATION.

Issue of Sir John Davenport, (No. 38.)

(40.) I. Margaret Davenport, married Thomas de Leghes, Jr.

(41.) II. Thomas Davenport, ancestor of the Davenports of Henbury, named 1st, in the Henbury entail, 1366, and 3d, in the Woodford entail, 1371. He married Margaret, daughter of Hugh Venables, who was afterwards married to Sir William Newport.

(42.) III. John Davenport, living in 1366.

(43.) IV. Nicholas Davenport de Widford, ancestor of the Davenports of Woodford, &c., living in 1371, and had lands as by indenture in 1413 in Bredbury, Romiley, &c. He married Ellena, widow of Edward Massey, of Timberley, in 1371. She died a widow in 1423.

(44.) V. Griffin Davenport, living in 1371.

ELEVENTH GENERATION.

Issue of Thomas Davenport, (No. 41.)

(45.) I. Hugh Davenport of Henbury, who married for his first wife, Ellen, daughter of William Massey, Esq. She was the mother of his issue. His second wife was Jane, daughter of Sir Thomas Whootton of Chester, knight, Inq. post mortem, 1418.

(46.) II. Thomas Davenport of Butley.

TWELFTH GENERATION.

Issue of Hugh Davenport, (No. 45.)

(47.) I. Thomas Davenport, of Henbury, who married Margery, daughter of Randle Mainwaring of Carincham.

(48.) II. Margery Davenport, who married Ralph Davenport of Davenport.

(49.) III. Margaret Davenport, married Randle Mainwaring of Carincham.

(50.) IV. Parnell Davenport, married William Somerford of Somerford.

(51.) V. William Davenport.

(52.) VI. John Davenport.

THIRTEENTH GENERATION.

Issue of Thomas Davenport, (No. 47.)

(53.) I. Thomas Davenport of Henbury, married Katharine, daughter of Sir John Ratcliffe, knight.

(54.) II. Parnell Davenport, married Robert Downes, of Worth.

(55.) III. Agnes Davenport, married William Ward of Capesthorne.

(56.) IV. William Davenport.

(57.) V. John Davenport.

(58.) VI. Richard Davenport, who appears from the pedigrees to have first removed to the County of Northampton, adjoining Warwickshire, and then to have settled at Coventry, in the latter County, about the year 1510. His wife was a daughter of ..... Venables.

(59.) VII. Ralph Davenport, of Boughton, living in 1542.*

FOURTEENTH GENERATION.

Issue of Richard Davenport, (*No.* 58.)

(60.) I. Edward Davenport of Coventry, who married a daughter of John Harford, Alderman of Coventry. In 1534, he was chosen to the city office of Chamberlain, and in 1540 to that of Sheriff. In 1550, he was chosen Mayor of Coventry, and during the time of his Mayoralty overruled all this county.†

* Boughton lies in the immediate suburbs of Chester, a part of it forming a continuation of the streets of that city. The principal manor of this place became the property of Ralph Davenport, youngest son of Thomas Davenport, Esq., of Henbury, from whom it descended as follows: Hugh Davenport, son of Ralph, living in 1589; William, who died in 1621; Hugh, who died without issue in 1634, when Jane Davenport, aunt of Hugh, brought the manor of Boughton, by marriage, to Thomas Hand, merchant, of Chester, from whom it descended to his son Thomas Hand, of Chester and Boughton, gent., whose daughter Mary married Hugh Folkes, from whom the estate passed to Robert Folkes, and then to their daughter Mary, who married William Currie of Chester, M.D., who died in 1813.

† The writer is indebted to Mrs. M. A. [Davenport] Bruen, of New York, for information pertaining to the Coven-

FIFTEENTH GENERATION.

Issue of Edward Davenport, (No. 60.)

(61.) I. Henry Davenport, of Coventry, who married, 1st, Winifred, daughter of Richard Barnabit. She was the mother of his issue. His second wife was Elizabeth, daughter of Thomas ——— of Gloucestershire. He was chosen Sheriff of Coventry, in 1602, and seems to have succeeded his younger brother as Mayor, in 1613.

(62.) II. Christopher Davenport, who married a daughter of William Hopkins, Alderman of Coventry. He was chosen Sheriff, in 1593; and Mayor, in 1602. [On Thursday, about 2 o'clock, March 24, 1603, deceased Queen Elizabeth, at Richmond, when Hon. Mayor Davenport proclaimed James I. King of England. Harl. MSS.]* Christopher Davenport

try branch, collected by her while in London, from the Harl. MSS., and also to the Rev. W. Davenport Bromley, England, for pedigrees furnished through Panizzi, the chief of the Literary Department in the British Museum.

* Rickson's MS. History says that he "was proclaimed during the Mayoralty of Christopher Davenport, at Cross Cheaping, Coventry, by Alderman Rogerson, in the presence of Lord Berkley and divers others of good account."—Communicated by George Eld, Esq., of Coventry, to whom the writer is obliged for information gathered from the Leet Books and Annals of that city.

founded what is now known as the Bablake School. This is one of the most celebrated of the free schools of Coventry, and for nearly two centuries and a half has furnished a thorough system of instruction to a large number of youth. Its funds are also used for the maintenance of a certain number of superannuated teachers.* It derives its name from a small sheet of water near which the school is located, called Bablake, from the circumstance of a babe having there been drowned. The master of this school is still appointed by the General Charity Trustees of Coventry. A portrait of Christopher Davenport is to be seen in St. Mary's Hall, which stands a little south of St. Michael's Church, with those of other benefactors of the city. In these rooms are also to be found many ancient paintings, figures, arms, &c.: also half-length portraits of Queen Elizabeth, James I., Charles I.: whole lengths of Charles II., James II., &c.: William and Mary (copies) in their coronation robes: originals of Anne, George I., George II., and Caroline, in their coronation robes, &c.

* Communicated by Mr. J. Oliver, of Brooklyn, N. Y., formerly a teacher in Coventry.

SIXTEENTH GENERATION.

Issue of Henry Davenport, (No. 61.)

(63.) I. Barnabas Davenport of Coventry, who married Mary, daughter of Simon Glover, by whom he had issue, Christopher, Anne, and Elizabeth.

(64.) II. Edward Davenport, who married Sarah, daughter of John White, Alderman of Coventry, by whom he had issue, Christopher, Winifred, Elizabeth, and Phillipa.

(65.) III. Christopher Davenport, who married Frances, daughter of John Higginson, by whom he had one daughter, Elizabeth.*

* A Christopher Davenport was Sheriff of Coventry, in 1632, and Mayor in 1641, when Charles I. made his tour through the country, and sent to the Mayor and Sheriffs of Coventry, demanding an entrance into the city, which was refused by the inhabitants. Whether this was the third son of Henry, or one of the sons of that name by his elder brothers, I am not able to ascertain.

The following monumental inscription, found in Whatcote Church, Warwickshire, was communicated by Rev. Walter Davenport Bromley. The inscription is in Latin. "Here lies John Davenport, for 70 years and 6 months Rector of this church, who died the 20th day of July, 1688, aged 101 years. Together with the husband lies his most loving wife, who died in 1656, aged 88 years." What connection this John Davenport may have had with the Coventry family, if any, is not known.

(66.) IV. Henry Davenport.

(67.) V. John Davenport, who married Elizabeth Wolley.

SEVENTEENTH GENERATION.

Issue of John Davenport, (No. 67.)

[The following account of these two brothers is principally drawn from Wood's Athenæ Oxonienses, and Biographia Britannica. The numbers are given in inverted order.]

(69.) II. Christopher Davenport, second son of John, by Elizabeth Wolley his wife, was born in the city of Coventry, Warwickshire, in the year 1598, and in grammatical learning there educated. At about fifteen years of age, he and his brother John were sent to Merton College, in the University of Oxford, in the beginning of the year 1613, and became the pupils of Samuel Lane, fellow of that house. Here they were battlers, and took of the cook's commons, but the warden, Sir Henry Savil, having received notice of them and their condition, dismissed them unless they would become commoners or students of the second rank, to which their relatives would not consent. John therefore immediately withdrew, and entered Magdalen Hall, while Christopher remained for a time longer, as Sir Henry was recalled to Eaton; but upon his return, he also withdrew, and by the invitation of a Romish priest, under whose influence he had fallen, went to Doway, and thence going to Ypres, he entered into the order of the Franciscans, among the Dutch there, in 1617. Thence he returned to Doway, where he read, first, philosophy, and afterwards became chief reader of Divinity in the College of St. Bonaventure, and in fine was made Doctor of Divinity of his order, but not of any University. Afterwards, he went into England under the name of *Franciscus a Sancta Clara.* He was well versed in school divinity, in the fathers and councils, in philosophy, and in ecclesiastical and profane histories. At length, he was made one of the chaplains to Henrietta Maria, the royal consort of Charles I., and became highly honored by all of his profession, and of many scholars, (whether Protestant or Papist,) for his great learning. For more than fifty years, he labored incessantly to promote the papal cause, by gaining many disciples, raising money among the English Catholics to carry on public matters beyond the seas, in traveling from one country to another, in printing books for the advancement of his religion and order, and by his perpetual and unwearied motion, day and night, to administer among his brethren, and by tending his services to consult and help warping protestants.

During the civil wars of Cromwell's time, he disappeared from public life, and spent most of those years beyond the seas, sometimes in London, at times in the country, and then at Oxford. After the restoration of Charles II., when a marriage was celebrated between that sovereign and Catharine of Portugal, he became her theologist or chief chaplain. He was four times chosen provincial Minister of his order for the province of England, and was accounted its greatest pillar, and the person most to be consulted in their affairs.

Among his published works were, 1st, Paraphrastica Expositio Articulorum Confessionis Anglicæ. For some reason, this book was much censured by Jesuits, who would fain have burnt it, but being soon after licensed at Rome, all further rumor about it stopped. 2d, *Deus, Natura, Gratia*, sive Tractatus de Predestinatione de Meritis, &c. This book was dedicated to Charles I., and Prynne contends that the whole scope of it, as well as the paraphrastical exposition of the articles reprinted in 1633, were designed to reconcile the king, the English Church, and the thirty-nine articles to the Church of Rome. [A copy of this work is to be found in the library of Brown University, Providence, R. I.] Christopher also published many other works, which have sunk into oblivion. He was so active in making converts, that one of the principal articles of impeachment against Archbishop Laud was his holding conferences with this Franciscan.*

He died at the palace of the Somerset

* "He was introduced to the Archbishop," as Bishop Heber, in his Life of Jeremy Taylor, tells us, "by his chaplain, Dr. Augustine Lindsell, as a person engaged in a work on the Operation of God's Grace, and a Defence of Episcopacy." Laud had some conversation with him about his work, (Deus, Natura, Gratia,) but denied in his trial that he had more than two or three conferences with Sancta Clara after this, and that he did not give him encouragement in his work, but remarked, "that the bishops of England were able to defend their own cause and calling, without calling in aid from Rome; and would in due time."—*Laud's Troubles and Trial, page* 385.

Bishop Heber suggests that the intimacy of Taylor with this Franciscan, "whose friendship," he says, "could have been no disgrace to Taylor," probably afforded in those suspicious times a foundation for the report that Taylor himself had a concealed attachment for the Romish communion.—*See Life of Taylor.*

House, in the Strand, London, on the 31st of May, 1680, and was buried, not according to his desire, in the vault under the Somerset House, which the Queen opposed, but in the church belonging to the Savoy Hospital.

(68.) I. John Davenport, eldest son of John, and grandson of Henry, was born in the city of Coventry, in the year 1597, and in grammatical learning there educated. He entered Merton College with his brother Christopher, in 1613. After passing two years at Merton, he removed to Magdalen Hall, in the same University, where, continuing under severe and puritanical discipline for some time, he left without taking the degree of A.M., retired to London, and became a minister of St. Stephen's Church in Coleman Street, and a Puritan of much note. In 1625, he returned to Magdalen Hall, and for some time performed his exercise for the degree of Bachelor of Divinity, accumulated and took that degree at the same time that he received his degree of Master of Arts, and in a short time after returned again to London, where he was esteemed a person of excellent gifts in preaching and other qualities belonging to a divine. Here he labored for some years, till becoming a decided non-conformist, he resigned his charge at St. Stephen's, in 1633, went into Holland, and after some time returned to England, and sailed for America.

REV. JOHN DAVENPORT IN AMERICA.

HISTORICAL SKETCH.

(68.) JOHN DAVENPORT, son of John, and grandson of Henry, was born in the ancient city of Coventry, Warwickshire, England, in the year 1597. His father was an eminent merchant of Coventry, of which city his grandfather was at one time Mayor. His mother was a woman of piety, but was early removed by death, leaving this son in his childhood, after having devoted him to the care and special service of God, with great fervor and faith, humbly relying on the divine promises to faithful parental dedication. And Heaven graciously accepted the offering of this believing parent, and gave to the dying mother's prayer an early answer.

His father possessed the disposition, not less than the ability, to give his son the best opportunities for education. The early application and vigorous genius of the son equaled the exertions and hopes of the father. He was placed at the grammar school in his native city, where he pursued his academical studies; and in 1613, at the age of sixteen, was admitted a member of Merton College, in the University of Oxford. A little previous to that event, he became a subject of the special influences of God's grace. Divine love now possessing his soul, seems to have had a governing influence in all the conduct of his future life.

While at the University, he was characterized by that close and diligent mental application which he maintained throughout his whole life. After passing two years at Merton College, he removed to Magdalen Hall, in the same University, where he received the degree of A.B., soon after which he commenced preaching. At about the age of twenty, we find him officiating, for a short time, as chaplain at Hilton Castle, in the neighborhood of Durham; thence he was invited to London, where he performed the services of assistant to a clergyman of that city, and soon after was made vicar of St. Stephen's Church, Coleman Street, where he labored constantly, and with great approbation.* His assiduity in his

* This church is mentioned by Disceto, in his survey, as

studies, and his diligence in the pursuits of science from early life, added to the gravity of his demeanor, and the warmth of his piety, gave him a popularity and influence unusual for his years.

early as 1182, and was named after the proto-martyr Stephen. The old building was destroyed by the great fire in 1666, and was rebuilt, in its present form, by Sir Christopher Wren, in 1676. The vestry room at the west end of the church contains a very curious painting of the "Stoning of Stephen."

I have not been able to ascertain the precise time when Mr. Davenport commenced his labors with this church. That it was as early as 1624 is proved by the following incident:

In the library of the American Antiquarian Society at Worcester, Mass., is a bound volume, consisting of miscellaneous tracts, pamphlets, &c., which belonged to the private library of Mr. Davenport. On a blank leaf, at the close of one of these pamphlets, containing the Thirty-nine Articles of the Church of England, is found the following declaration, evidently written with his own hand, and duly signed in the handwriting of the churchwardens. What adds additional interest to this incident is the fact that two of the names which appear as witnesses to this document are afterwards found among the members of the celebrated Westminster Assembly of Divines.

"Nov. 7, 1624.—John Davenport, clerk, vicar of St. Stephen's in Coleman Street, London, did, this day above written, being Sunday, publicly read this book of Articles herein contained, being in number 39, besides the ratifica-

About this time, the city of London was visited by a dreadful plague, which swept off thousands of the inhabitants. While many pastors deserted their flocks, and fled from the wasting pestilence, the youthful Davenport remained firmly at his post, and planting himself on those promises of divine protection and security, amid surrounding judgments, contained in the 91st Psalm, courageously passed this season of awful visitation, in proclaiming to the afflicted and the dying the consolations and hopes of the Gospel. His Christian fidelity

tion, and declared his full and unfeigned assent and consent thereunto, in the time of morning prayer, next after the second lesson, before the whole congregation; as also the said John did the same day administer the holy communion, in the said parish, in his surplice, according to the order prescribed by the Church of England, in the presence of those whose names are hereunto written.

Church Wardens,
HENRY WOOD,
WILLIAM SPURSTOWE,
SAMUEL ALDERSEY,
RICHARD SYMONDS,
THOMAS MASTON,
JOHN WELLS,
WILLIAM HILL,
ROBERT HOLMES."

Rev. Josiah Platt is now (1850,) vicar of St. Stephen's.

greatly endeared him to his flock, and raised him in the esteem of all.

To show that others besides his own congregation, were permitted to reap the harvest of his sowing, may be mentioned the circumstance, that about this time, he was the means of the conversion of William Kiffen, who became a distinguished minister of the Baptist denomination.

Having left the University without taking the degree of Master of Arts, Mr. D. retired to Oxford, and having gone through with the necessary exercises, received that degree, and at the same time was created Bachelor of Divinity, at Magdalen Hall, June 28, 1625, soon after which he returned to London.

"One of the members of his church in Coleman Street, was Theophilus Eaton, with whom, though six years older than himself, he had been intimate in childhood, the father of Eaton being one of the ministers of Coventry.*

* His father was Rev. Richard Eaton, who was descended from an ancient family in the County of Chester, near the original seat of the Davenports. He died in 1600, and left several children: Theophilus, a London merchant, who was for some time engaged in trade with Denmark and the ports of the Baltic; Samuel, who also became a

It had been the hope of Eaton's friends to see him in the ministry; but the Providence that controls all things had other designs concerning him; and therefore, the pious ambition of his friends was defeated. Being permitted to follow his own preferences, he became a merchant, and in that employment was eminent and successful. It may be presumed that Eaton's friendship for Davenport had something to do with bringing the young preacher to London, and fixing him there. Thenceforward the two lived in uninterrupted intimacy; they were rarely separated from each other; their history runs in one channel; their names are inseparably associated." *

During his ministry in London, Mr. Davenport enjoyed the acquaintance, and esteem, of the most distinguished persons belonging to the Puritan party in the Church of England. Among these may be mentioned Dr. John Preston, Master of Emanuel College, Cambridge. This man's popularity as a teacher

non-conformed minister, and came to America, and whose son, Nathaniel, was the first rector of what is now Harvard College, Cambridge, Mass.

* Historical Discourses, Rev. Dr. Bacon, New Haven, 1838.

was so great, that Fuller calls him the greatest pupil-monger ever known in England. "He was," says Mr. M'Clure, "a learned theologian, a most eloquent preacher, and also a deep politician. James I. made him chaplain to the Prince of Wales, and also to himself, and urged upon him the rich bishopric of Gloucester. On the death of King James, Dr. Preston rode up to London, in a close carriage, with the young king, and the Duke of Buckingham. He was again offered a bishopric, and the office of Lord Keeper of the Great Seal, which was the highest office in the State, and entitled the holder to preside in the house of peers. These tempting lures were offered, in the hopes of bringing over the Puritan party to the king's side, by means of Dr. Preston's vast influence. But the good man had a conscience, and could not be bought. He declined the proffered honors, and firmly adhered to his principles. Before he died, which was in 1628, this celebrated man showed his confidence in the young vicar of St. Stephen's, by leaving his writings to be published under Mr. Davenport's care, by whom accordingly they were edited." *

* Life of John Davenport, by Rev. J. W. M'Clure.

In 1627, an association was formed in London, the design of which was, by certain measures in connection with the Established Church, to promote throughout England, an able and evangelical ministry, and its measures seem to have gained much favor with the people, and to have promised usefulness. It was, in fact, a sort of Home Missionary Society. Funds, to a considerable amount, were raised by voluntary contributions to support able and faithful lecturers. The trustees who conducted the business of the association were called "feoffees in trust." These feoffees were twelve in number; four of them clergymen, of whom Mr. Davenport was one; four of them lawyers, of whom one was a king's sergeant; and four of them citizens, one of whom was the Lord Mayor of London.

As most, or all engaged in this association, were zealous Puritans, the opposing party soon took the alarm. Laud, then Bishop of London, and his adherents were warmly aroused, and took decisive measures to crush these developments of the principle of voluntary association, and of church reform. Through the influence of Laud with the king, the trustees were soon after arraigned before the Court of the Exchequer, where the association was condemned as dangerous and illegal; the whole of the funds collected, (about six thousand pounds,) were confiscated to the king's use; and the feoffees were referred for punishment to that infamous tribunal, the Star Chamber. The unpopularity of the proceedings, however, caused the matter to be dropt, and the fines and penalties with which these excellent men were threatened, in their pious and laudable undertaking, were never executed.

It was on this afflictive occasion, that Mr. Davenport wrote the following passages in his great Bible :—

"Feb. 11, 1632. The business of the feoffees being to be heard the third time at the Exchequer, I prayed earnestly that God would assist our counselors in opening the case, and be pleased to grant, that they may get no advantage against us to punish us, as *evil doers*; promising to observe what *answer* he gave. Which, seeing he hath graciously done, and delivered me from the thing I feared, I record to these ends :—

"1. To be more *industrious* in my family.

"2. To check my *unthankfulness*.

"3. To quicken myself to *thankfulness*.

"4. To awaken myself to more *watchfulness* for the time to come, in remembrance of his mercy.

"Which I beseech the Lord to grant; upon whose faithfulness in *his* covenant, I cast myself to be more faithful in *my* covenant.

John Davenporte."

But the troubles of this good man did not end here. The storm of religious intolerance yet continued to lower, and threatened to spend its fury against these first buddings of Puritanism. Soon after, Mr. Davenport was convened before the High Commission as a notorious delinquent, because he had united with some other worthy persons in promoting a private subscription in behalf of the poor distressed ministers of the Palatinate of the Rhine.

These ministers had been driven into exile by the religious persecution of Ferdinand II., the papist Emperor of Germany. The Queen of Bohemia (the wife of Frederic V.), who was sister to Charles I., desired that aid might be rendered them from England. The king was disposed to grant her request, and the brief was prepared authorizing the collections. Objections were at once raised against these proceedings by Laud, because these impoverished ministers, suffering as they were for the faith of Christ, were Calvinists or Presbyterians. Swayed by these and other arguments, the brief was altered and the public collections soon ceased. Upon this, Mr. Davenport united with Doctors Sibbs, Gouge, and other Puritan divines in promoting a private subscription, and thus sought to afford relief through their individual efforts to their afflicted brethren. This was the sum of his offence, and for so notorious an exhibition of the broad principle of charity, the arm of the devout bishop was raised against him. These very proceedings, however, as we shall see, were but working out the designs of an all-wise Providence for still greater good.

How blessed is the school of affliction to the true child of God ! It is here that God often fits his people for those most important services which they are to render to his church and the world. As gold refined in the fire is separated from the dross, so by trials is the true excellence of the Christian character brought out and the dross of human imperfection purged away.

Until now, Mr. Davenport had adhered to the Established Church, although there were many things in its communion which he could not approve, and which he sought to have reformed.

About this time his personal friend, Rev. John Cotton, of Boston, in Lincolnshire, had resigned his charge, having become a non-conformist. He was now on a visit to London. Mr. Davenport and some others, sought an interview with him for the purpose of convincing him that he ought not to leave his flock, but retain his connection with the English Church. The result of this interview was, that instead of bringing Mr. Cotton over to his views, Mr. Davenport, before somewhat "staggered in his conformity" became fully convinced by the strong reasonings of his pious and erudite friend, and was fully brought over to *his* side.

Before, however, he openly declared his intentions, he had several interviews with Laud. The bishop, whose most weighty argument in meeting all scruples of conscience in these matters, was in pointing to the Star Chamber, said, in reference to Mr. D., "*I thought I had settled his judgment;*" but found himself greatly mistaken when he discovered that he had openly "declared his judgment against conformity with the Church of England," that he had resigned his benefice, and even made his escape from the warrant which was out against him, by fleeing into Holland. And yet this was the man who afterwards, in a speech before the House of Lords, spoke of Mr. Davenport as "a most religious man, who fled to New England for the sake of a good conscience."*

* Answer to Lord Say's speech.

A brief extract from Prynne as given by Neal,[1] will throw light on some points of history to which allusion has now been made. In describing the subsequent trial of Archbishop Laud, he says: "The managers went on to charge the Archbishop with his severe persecution of those clergymen who had dared to preach against the dangerous increase of Arminianism and Popery, or the late innovations: They instanced Mr. Chauncey, Mr. Workman, Mr. Davenport, and others; some of whom were punished in the High Commission, for not railing in the communion table, and for preaching against images, and when Mr. Davenport fled to New England to avoid the storm, the Archbishop said *his arm should reach him there.* They ob-

[1] Neal's Puritans, vol. ii., p. 282.

Previous, however, to his embarkation for Holland, Mr. Davenport called together the principal people of his charge, desiring their opinion and advice, when he acknowledged

jected further, his suppressing afternoon sermons on the Lord's day, and the laudable design of buying in impropriations which was designed to encourage such lectures. Laud replied that the censures passed upon these men was the act of the High Commission and not his, and if he did say his arm should reach Mr. Davenport in New England, he sees no harm in it, for offences against good order should be dealt with by law.

He [Laud] confessed that he overthrew the design of buying up impropriations, and he thanked God that he had destroyed it, for he conceived it to be a plot against the Church, for if it had succeeded, more clergymen would have depended on the feoffees than on the king, and on all the peers and bishops besides, and he proceeded against them according to law, and if the sentence was not just, it must be the judges' fault and not his. The Commons replied that it was notorious to all men how cruel he had been toward all those who had dared to take a stand against his proceedings, and put him in mind of many who had been forced into Holland and America, to avoid the ruin of themselves and family. . . . . . . As to the impropriations, there was no design in the feoffees to render the clergy independent of the bishops, for none were presented but comformable men, nor did any preach but such as were licensed by the bishop; indeed the design being to encourage the preaching of the Word of God, the feoffees were careful to employ such persons as would not be idle; and their right to him as their pastor, and declared that "*No danger should drive him from any service which they should expect or demand at his hands.*" With a noble disinterestedness of soul, which reflected great honor upon them, and demonstrated their affection for their pastor and their respect for what he considered the rights of conscience, and yet thoroughly aware of their loss, they advised him for his own safety to resign his office.

Having sent in his resignation in 1633, and finding that no peace or quietness could be enjoyed while in the midst of those hungry pursuivants who were continually seeking to draw him into their power, he betook himself during the same year into Holland.

Soon after his arrival in Holland, a Presbyterian church of English Christians in the city of Amsterdam, under the pastoral charge of the Rev. John Paget, sent an invitation to Mr.

when they perceived the Archbishop was bent on their ruin, Mr. White went to his *grace* and promised to rectify anything that was amiss, if the thing itself might stand. But he was determined to destroy it, and by his mighty influence obtained a decree that the money should be paid into the Exchequer, by which an end was put to one of the most charitable designs for the good of the Church, that has been formed these many years."

Davenport to come among them as a colleague. Here, for a time, he labored, but a disagreement was soon found to exist between the two pastors on the subject of administering baptism to the children of irreligious parents—a practice which Mr. P. and the Dutch classes of presbytery insisted on, but to which Mr. D. would not conform—and therefore, in 1635, he gave up his pastoral relation to this church.

Having resigned his charge, he opened a catechetical exercise at his own lodgings every Lord's day evening, after the public services of the city were over. But the popularity of his talents soon collected great numbers of hearers, which increased the jealousy and opposition of the adverse party, and his meetings were finally broken up. A warm tractarian controversy ensued on the subject of promiscuous baptism. Several works were published on both sides, the last of which was Mr. Davenport's "Apologetical Reply to a book called 'an Answer to an Unjust Complaint of W. B.,' &c.," published at Rotterdam in 1636. That this disputation was conducted in a kind and Christian spirit by Mr. Davenport, at least, is evident from a review of his works yet extant. In proof of this may here be cited a few remarks introductory to the work above mentioned, and touching the spirit which should govern all religious controversies.

Addressing the Christian reader, he remarks: "Though the testimony of a good conscience is of itself a sufficient cause of rejoicing in all the tribulations of this pilgrimage, and of confidence in all our apologies against false accusers, in which respect, blessed Paul, according to the wisdom given unto him, did 'exercise himself to have always a conscience void of offence both towards God and man;' yet, next to a good conscience, a man is bound to provide for 'a good name,' it being in Solomon's judgment 'better than precious ointment.' But the regard to our good name must be exercised upon higher ground than self-respect, else it is but vain glory. God's name must be dearer to us than our own; and our care must be, not so much to shun our duty, as his dishonor; our esteem for his glory, therefore, ought in some proportion to answer to his dignity and eminency."

"Again, it is enjoined that our speech be well filled and well seasoned. It is well filled when it expresseth the sanctifying graces of the Spirit; as the fruits of the earth are then fully ripe, when they have attained to the perfection of their kind. The best rise of a good conscience is from a gracious heart, which is declared to be a 'good treasure,' which *sendeth forth good things, and to be full of goodness.* When good speeches flow from the *abundance* within, and are filled with the Spirit, then the words will express the delightful and amiable sweetness of those 'fruits of the Spirit, which are love, joy, peace, long-suffering, gentleness, goodness, faith,' which fruits are well pleasing to Christ, and delightful to good men, as the savor of that ointment which Mary poured on the head of Christ was to those that were in the house.

"Thus an answer is well filled when it expresseth Godly wisdom, and Christian prudence and discretion, which enable a man to observe a due proportion to the causes, persons, times, places, and whatever circumstances are considerable; as that harsh speech be forborne when a soft answer should be given; that a friend be not wounded as an enemy, nor be reviled as a brother, and that the answer which should serve to mend the garment, doth not make the rent worse." Such principles, for the government of a controversy, are well worthy of imitation in modern times.

Finding no door of usefulness now open before him in the land where so many of the Puritans, for a short time, had found refuge, Mr. D. soon after returned to his native country for the purpose of emigrating to America.

For some years, he had been familiar, chiefly through his personal friend, Rev. John Cotton, with the weighty affairs that were going on in New England. He had taken an early interest in the formation of the Massachusetts colony, and contributed £50 towards the procurement of its charter. He was present at the meeting of the company in London, March 23, 1629, and also at those of March 30, April 8, August 28, 29, and those of November and December following.*

He now resolved, with his friend Theophilus Eaton, to collect a band of colonists whom, under God, they might lead out of spiritual Egypt, the house of bondage and oppression, into the distant land of promise. Many of those who had formerly enjoyed the ministry of Mr. Davenport, in Coleman Street, were ready to join them.

* Prince's Annals, 257.

"He who divided the Red Sea before the Israelites, gave this little company as safe a passage across the ocean. They arrived at Boston in the Hector and another ship, on the 26th of June, 1637. Among other passengers who came with this expedition was Edward Hopkins, son-in-law of Governor Eaton, and himself for many years Governor of Connecticut colony. By his will, he became a distinguished benefactor of Harvard College and several other institutions of learning in New England. With these came also Lord Leigh, son and heir of the Earl of Marlborough, a youth of nineteen, humble and pious, who came merely to see the country, and returned to England a few weeks after, in company with Sir Henry Vane."*

Mr. Davenport was heartily welcomed by Mr. Cotton and his associates, and more particularly as his assistance was now required in helping to stay the prevalence of Antinomian error, which seemed at this time, through the fanaticism of Ann Hutchinson and others, to have threatened the peace and purity of the churches. His preaching, and also his counsels

* Lives of the Chief Fathers of New England, by Rev. A. W. M'Clure. Vol. ii. p. 270.

in the Synod of that year, evidently had a favorable influence in the suppression of those dangerous errors. At the request of the Synod, he closed the proceedings by a sermon on the text, Phil. iii. 16: "Nevertheless, whereto we have attained, let us walk by the same rule; let us mind the same thing." In this discourse, he declared the result of the assembly, and "with much wisdom and sound argument," urged to unity and harmony. These difficulties being in a good degree removed, it became an object with Mr. Davenport and his company to fix upon a place of settlement.

The wealth, intellectual endowments and moral worth of this newly arrived company of emigrants, made it very desirable with the already organized colonies of Plymouth and Massachusetts, to retain them among them: and to this end, very liberal offers were made them. But reasons existed in their own minds why these urgent invitations could not be complied with, "the refusal to accept which," says Mr. M'Clure, "was regarded as almost an unkindness by those who coveted this accession to their strength."

It was thought that Mr. Davenport's residence in Massachusetts might draw down upon that colony the speedier wrath of Laud, who loved them not before. When he heard Mr. Davenport had fled to New England, to avoid the storm of prelatical indignation, the persecuting archbishop had boldly said, "*My arm shall reach him there.*" It was supposed that the scattering of those who were obnoxious to Laud into different places might lessen the motives for stretching out his potent arm against them. Although he obtained a commission from the king to carry out these designs, yet the political excitements by which they were surrounded at home, obliged him and his monarch (Charles I.) to confine their activity to resisting a revolution which eventually resulted in the overthrow of their own power. As John Cotton expressed it, "God rocked three nations with shaking dispensations to procure some rest for these infant churches."

Another probable reason why Mr. Davenport and Eaton wished to form an independent colony, beyond the limits of any existing grant or patent, was, that they might carry out their peculiar views in regard to a civil state. They seemed to have desired the formation of a community in some respects different from any that existed elsewhere; one more thoroughly *scriptural*—more in accordance with the ancient Jewish system—one fashioned throughout in the strictest conformity to the rules of the Bible.

In the Fall of 1637, Mr. Eaton and others of the company, made a journey to Connecticut, to explore the lands and harbors on the coast. They came to a place lying at the head of a harbor, which sets up about four miles from Long Island Sound. Its Indian name was Quinnipiac. The explorers were much taken with the beauty and fertility of this tract of country, and most of them being Londoners, and accustomed to commercial pursuits, they deemed it a desirable site for the establishment of a commercial town. This place was, therefore, fixed upon for the location of their colony. On what is now the south corner of Church and Meadow Streets, they erected a hut, in which a few men remained for the winter to make preparations for the commencement of the settlement, while the rest returned to Massachusetts.*

* Seven men were left by Eaton, one of whom was John Beacher, (from whom the venerable Dr. Lyman Beecher descended)—another was Joseph Atwater. One of the party died during the winter. Mr. Atwater was a gentleman of distinction and opulence, and built himself a house

Early in the Spring the colonists prepared to remove to their new home in the wilderness. After taking an affectionate leave of their friends and gratefully acknowledging the many kindnesses they had there received, the company sailed from Boston for the place of their destination on the 13th of March, 1638.*

"This band of pilgrims reached Quinnipiac, the future New Haven, on the 14th of April, 1638. Mr. Davenport was then forty-one years of age. The next day is the Sabbath. A drum beats in the rude and hasty encampment. The armed men with their wives and children gather at this signal under a branching oak.†

on what is now Fleet Street, which has stood for more than two hundred years, and was occupied till lately by descendants of its original proprietor.

* See letter No. 1, Note A., Appendix.

† This tree stood near the present corner of George and College Streets, and was standing till after the revolutionary war, when it is said to have been cut down by Mr. David Beecher (the father of Rev. Dr. Beecher), and to have been burnt in his shop which stood in College Street, near George.

On the 25th of April, 1838, was celebrated the second Centennial Anniversary of the settlement of New Haven. A procession was formed at the State House, comprising the various classes of citizens and strangers, which proceeded to the intersection of College and George Streets, at

They meet to consecrate to God a new region reclaimed from heathen darkness. For the first time the aisles of that forest-temple re-

which place Mr. Davenport preached his first sermon, just two hundred years before. Here the procession halted for religious exercises. The number of persons assembled around this spot was variously estimated from four to five thousand. Many roofs of the houses were covered with people, and some had taken their station in the trees. After singing, an appropriate and impressive prayer was offered (on a stage which had been erected near the spot where the oak tree is supposed to have stood) by the venerable Rev. Frederick W. Hotchkiss (since deceased), of Saybrook, whose mother was a direct descendant of Gov. Jones, the son-in-law of Gov. Eaton.

After the religious exercises were closed the procession again formed, and moving through George and State Streets passed the place in Elm Street where the houses of Gov. Eaton and Mr. Davenport formerly stood, and then down Temple Street to the First Congregational Church, where the society whose first pastor was Mr. Davenport, worship, and near which the first house of worship was erected. Here after singing and reading a portion of Scripture, prayer was offered by the present pastor, Rev. Leonard Bacon, after which an historical discourse was delivered by Professor James L. Kingsley, of Yale College, and the services were closed by prayer, singing, and the benediction. See Appendix to Kingsley's Discourse 109–115.

At this time there was a medal struck representing on the one side Mr. Davenport preaching under the oak, and on the other New Haven as it then (1838) appeared.

sounded with the praises of the Host High. Here are men who were nurtured in the halls of Oxford and Cambridge; and women used to all the elegant refinements of the British metropolis. They are gathered under the oaken tree. Why are they here? Why this change in their condition? Why are they here, far from the haunts of civilization, confronting privation and suffering in every form? It is for conscience, to keep that sacred thing unspotted;—it is for posterity:—for eternity:—for God!

["What sought they thus afar?
Bright jewels of the mine?
The wealth of seas? the spoils of war?
They sought a faith's pure shrine!

There is also in the possession of Mr. James Brewster, of that city, a large oil painting by Rossiter, giving the landing of Davenport and his followers, and representing him under the oak preaching his first sermon.—Communicated by Mr. William A. Reynolds, of New Haven.

During the same year (1838), the eloquent pastor of the First Church (Rev. Dr. Bacon), delivered a series of Historical Discourses, which were published in a quarto volume of 400 pages, containing a mine of valuable information in regard to the "first settlers," and the history of New Haven generally. To that work and the admirable discourse of Professor Kingsley, the writer is greatly indebted for copious extracts made in preparing the present sketch of the Rev. John Davenport.

Ay, call it holy ground,
  The soil where first they trod!
They have left unstained what there they found,
  Freedom to worship GOD !"]

Surely angels rejoiced while Infinite Love smiled upon the scene. Mr. Davenport preached from the text, Matthew iv. 1 :—'Then was Jesus led up of the Spirit into the wilderness to be tempted of the devil' ;—and his subject was, 'the temptations of the wilderness.' Every place, however sequestered, has its trials. In every place we have need to watch and pray."* At the close of these services Mr. Davenport remarked that "*he had enjoyed a good day.*"

Soon after their arrival at Quinnipiac, at the close of a "day of fasting and prayer," these exiles formed and subscribed what they denominated a "plantation covenant." By this instrument they engaged "that as in matters that concern the gathering and ordering of a church, so also in all public offices, which concern civil order, as choice of magistrates, and officers, making and repealing laws, dividing allotments of inheritance, and all things of like nature, they would all of them be ordered by the rules which the Scripture held forth to

* Life of John Davenport by Rev. Mr. M'Clure, p. 276.

them." This may be considered the original civil constitution of the New Haven colony.

It may here be stated that the planters of this colony, like the immortal Penn, did not disregard the rights of the Indians. On this point Dr. Bacon says:

"The most ancient record in existence at New Haven is, as it ought to be, the record of two treaties with the aboriginal proprietors, by which the soil was purchased, and the relations thenceforward to subsist between the Indians and the English were distinctly defined." These treaties commenced thus: "Articles of Agreement between Theophilus Eaton and John Davenport, and others, English planters at Quinopiocke, on the one party, and Momaugin, the Indian Sachem of Quinopiocke, and Sugcogisin, Caroughood, Wesaucucke, and others of his council, on the other party, made and concluded the 24th day of November, 1638, Thomas Stanton being interpreter," &c. Here follow the treaties, which are duly signed by Eaton and Davenport, and by the Sachem, his council and sister, by their respective marks.*

* "Copies of these Indian marks may be seen in Barber's History and Antiquities of New Haven, p. 27. The first is a rude resemblance of a bow; the second of a fish hook.

These treaties were held in good faith, by both parties, and the colony lived in much peace and security from the hostile attacks of the surrounding tribes. By these treaties the Indians considered themselves under the protection of the English, while they retained the right to hunt in their forests, to fish in the streams, with the pledge not to disturb the corn-fields or pastures of the English, or to interrupt their trade. The colonists showed themselves the friends of the natives and enjoyed their unlimited confidence—a confidence which history forbids us to think in this case was ever violated.

More than a year, after their arrival, was spent in erecting their dwellings and in clearing their lands, while they were often together praying and consulting in reference to the fundamental principles which should form their system of civil polity. During this period, Mr. Davenport prepared his "Discourse about

The third is a horizontal line, neither straight nor of any curve known to mathematicians. The fourth is a small block. The fifth may be imagined to stand for a war club. And the squaw's mark is perhaps as much like a tobacco pipe as the cloud which Hamlet showed to Polonius, was 'like a whale.'"—*Bacon's Discourses*, p. 335.

Civil Government in a New Plantation, whose Design is Religion." This treatise was published many years after, in 1673. It was a vindication of the practice long maintained by our fathers of allowing the rights of voting and holding office to only such as were members of the Church.

Having given themselves time for mature deliberation and wise counsel, and practically recognizing the principle that "governments are instituted among men, deriving their just powers from the consent of the governed," "all the free planters"—by which was meant all who were engaged in planting the colony—on the fourth of June, 1639, convened in a large barn of Mr. Newman, and in a formal manner proceeded to the organization of a civil government. "No reference, direct or indirect," says Professor Kingsley, "was made by those concerned in this transaction to their native country; as at the time the colonists signed their plantation covenant, so now they seem to have supposed that since they were in fact beyond the actual control of any existing sovereignty, they had a perfect right to constitute a government for themselves." The business of the occasion, in conformity to the views of those assembled and the propriety of the case, was opened with prayer, and Mr. Davenport is said to have preached a sermon from Prov. ix. 1: "Wisdom hath builded her house, she hath hewn out her seven pillars."

Mr. Davenport then proposed several queries to the planters, and urged them "to consider seriously in the presence and fear of God, the weight of the business they met about, and not to be rash or slight in giving their votes to things they understood not; but to digest fully and thoroughly what should be propounded to them, and without respect to men, as they should be satisfied and persuaded in their own minds, to give their answers in such sort, as they should be willing should stand upon record for posterity. They then unanimously resolved "that the Scriptures do hold forth a perfect rule for the direction and government of all men in all duties, which they are to perform to God and men as well in families and commonwealth as in matters of the Church."

After this, they renewed their assent to their plantation covenant, and mutually bound themselves, not only in their ecclesiastical proceedings, but also "in the choice of magistrates, the making and repealing of laws, the dividing of inheritances, and in all civil matters, to submit themselves to the rules held forth in the Word of God."

"Then," as the record informs us, "Mr. Davenport declared to them by the Scripture, what kind of persons might best be trusted with matters of government; and by sundry arguments from Scripture, proved that such men as were described in Exod. xviii. 21; Deut. i. 13; with Deut. xvii. 15; and 1 Cor. vi. 1, 6, 7—[viz.: "Able men, such as fear God; men of truth, hating covetousness;" "men of wisdom and understanding, and known among your tribes;" "not strangers, but brethren, and those whom the Lord your God shall choose;" "not the unjust or the unbelieving, but the holy"]—ought to be intrusted by them, seeing they were free to cast themselves into that mould and form of commonwealth which appeared best for them in reference to the securing the peace and peaceable enjoyment of all Christ's ordinances in the Church."

After some further consideration, the company, among other fundamental regulations, adopted this: "that church-members only should be free burgesses, and that they only should choose magistrates and officers among themselves, to have the power of transacting all the public civil affairs of the plantation; of making and repealing laws; dividing inheritances; deciding differences that may arise; and doing all things and business of like nature."

Such was the civil polity established by the colonists of New Haven; and whatever may have been its imperfection, the history of mankind may be challenged to show a State community organized under more favorable auspices, or a settlement that for so many years has enjoyed a greater share of social happiness.

Having founded their civil commonwealth, they proceeded to the organization of their church. On the twenty-second of August, 1639, *seven persons* chosen out of their number, among whom Mr. Davenport was one, entered into a covenant with one another, and with Christ, and thus was constituted the first Church of New Haven. Being thus organized, they proceeded to admit others of the company to their fellowship.

Shortly after the church was instituted, Mr. Davenport was chosen pastor. He was ordained by the hands of two or three of the lay brethren, though Mr. Hooker, and Mr. Stone, the reverend pastors of the church in Hartford, were present, and one of them made the prayer. This ceremony was not used because the validity of his ordination in the Church of England was doubted, it being, in fact, but an *installation* or solemn recognition of his new relation to a particular church.

With an organization so simple and scriptural; with a minister, whose genius, wisdom and piety enabled him to bring forth from the word of God things new and old, it is not a matter of wonder that success should have crowned their enterprise. And such was emphatically the case. The ministry of their pastor was abundantly blessed. His church continued in great unity during the whole period of his pastoral relation of nearly thirty years, and often received additions of those who were "heirs of the grace of life." He was strict in his examination of those who were to be admitted to membership, yet his church was large, and they walked together in prayer and love. But few instances of public censure occurred in his flock, though seldom has one had a deeper sense of the importance of the discipline of Christ's house than he.

About two months after the organization of the church, on the 25th of October, 1639, the General Court, as it was termed—consisting at first of the "seven pillars" chosen to form the church, but afterwards of all the free burgesses—proceeded to constitute the body of freemen, and to elect their officers. Mr. Davenport expounded several passages of Scripture to them, describing the character of civil magistrates given in the Sacred Oracles. To this succeeded the election of officers. Theophilus Eaton, Esq., was chosen Governor; Robert Newman, Matthew Gilbert, Nathaniel Turner, and Thomas Fugill were chosen Magistrates. Mr. Fugill was also chosen Secretary, and Robert Seely, Marshal.

Mr. Davenport gave Governor Eaton a charge in open court, from Deut. i. 16, 17: "And I charged your judges at that time, saying, Hear the causes between your brethren, and judge righteously between every man and his brother, and the stranger that is with him. Ye shall not respect persons in judgment, but ye shall hear the small as well as the great; ye shall not be afraid of the face of man, for the judgment is God's; and the cause that is too hard for you, bring it unto me, and I will hear it."*

Governor Eaton was annually chosen to preside over the colony, as its chief magistrate, for nearly twenty years, till his death, which occurred in January, 1658. This good man was accustomed to say: "Some count it a great matter to die well; but I am sure it is a greater matter to live well. All our care should be, while we have our life, to use it well: and so when death puts an end to that, it will be an end of all our cares." "And God would have him die well," says the quaint historian Mather, "without any room or time then given to care at all; for he enjoyed a death sudden to every one but himself."

On the evening of the 7th of January, after family worship, as usual, "he took a turn or two abroad, for his meditations," and then came to bid his wife good-night, who was confined by sickness in another apartment. She said to him, "Methinks you look sad." He replied, "The differences in the church of Hartford make me sad." She then, discontented as she long had been, said, "Let us go back to our native country." To which he answered,

* Records of the Colony of New Haven.

"You may, but I shall die here." This was the last word she ever heard him speak. He retired to his chamber; and about midnight, he was heard to groan: and to some one, who instantly came in to inquire how he did, he answered only, "Very ill," and immediately fell asleep in Jesus. His grave is just behind the pulpit window of the First Church.*

So intimately is the history of Governor Eaton connected with that of Mr. Davenport, that one or two brief extracts in reference to him may not be deemed wholly out of place.

Mather, in writing the life of Eaton, whom he calls the Moses of New Haven, says—"He carried in his very countenance, a majesty which cannot be described; and in his dispensations of justice he was a mirror for the most inimitable impartiality, but ungainsayable authority of his proceedings, being awfully sensible of the obligations which the oath of a judge lays upon him. Hence he who would most patiently bear hard things offered to his person in private cases, would never pass by any public affronts or neglects, when he appeared under the character of a magistrate. But he still was the guide of the blind, the staff of the

* Bacon, His. Dis. p. 110.

lame, the helper of the widow and the orphan, and all the distressed. None that had a good cause was afraid of coming before him. On the one side, in his days did the righteous flourish; on the other side, he was the terror of evil doers."

Hubbard, who was partly his cotemporary, says: "This man [Gov. Eaton] had in him great gifts and as many excellencies as are usually found in any one man; he had an excellent princely face and port, commanding respect from all others; he was a good scholar, a traveler, a great reader, of an exceeding steady and even spirit, not easily moved to passion, and standing unshaken in his principles when once fixed upon, of a profound judgment, full of majesty and authority in his judicatures, so that it was a vain thing to offer to brave him out, and yet in his ordinary conversation, and among friends, of such pleasantness of behavior, and such felicity and fecundity of harmless wit as can hardly be paralleled; but above all, he was seasoned with religion, close in closet duties, solemn and substantial in family worship, a diligent and constant attender upon all public ordinances, taking notes of the sermons he heard exactly, and improving them accordingly; in short, approving himself in the whole course of his life in faithfulness, wisdom, and inoffensiveness before God and man." *

When the day arrived for the election of a

* Governor Eaton, by will, disposed of his estates, both in this country, and "in the parish of Great Budworth, in the county of Chester, England:" and among other small legacies, gives "to my wife's son, Thomas Yale, five pounds; to my dear son-in-law, Mr. Hopkins, and to my reverend pastor, Mr. John Davenport, to each of them ten pounds, as a small token of my love and respect."

Mrs. Eaton, soon after her husband's death, returned to England, taking her children, and also her grandchild, Elihu Yale, then about ten years old, from whom Yale College was afterwards named.

The Rev. Samuel Eaton came to America with his brother, Theophilus, and for a year or two was Mr. Davenport's assistant. He returned to England in 1640, with a view of collecting a company of emigrants to settle Branford—that tract of country having been granted him for such friends as he should bring over from England. But the temporary peace which he found enjoyed by those who had before suffered from the persecuting spirit of the times, induced him to settle as a teacher over a Congregational church in Duckenfield, in Cheshire, his native county, whence he removed, probably with some of his congregation, to the neighboring borough of Stockport. He was one of the two thousand ministers who, in 1662, were silenced in one day, by the act of uniformity. He died on the 9th of June, 1665, at Denton, Lancastershire, and was buried in the chapel there.

new Governor, Mr. Davenport preached an election sermon, as was usual on such occasions, taking for his text the first words in the book of Joshua: "Now, after the death of Moses, the servant of the Lord, it came to pass that the Lord spake to Joshua, the son of Nun, Moses' minister, saying, Moses, my servant is dead; now, therefore arise, go over this Jordan, thou and all this people." The unanimous choice of the electors fell upon Francis Newman, who had been one of the bench of magistrates, and for many years Secretary of the colony.*

Deeply did Mr. Davenport feel the loss of his beloved Eaton, who for more than twenty years had been his copartner in the work of rearing a republic, and from childhood his most intimate friend and companion. The following eloquent passage is from Dr. Bacon's invaluable Historical Discourses:

"Davenport, and his friend Eaton, built their dwellings over against each other, on the same street,† and the intimacy begun when

* Historical Discourses, page 114.

† These houses were large and commodious. Governor Eaton's stood upon the north corner of Elm and Orange Streets. It was built in the form of a capital E, had many

they were children, and strengthened in their earlier manhood, is prolonged without interruption, till in a good old age death separates them for a little season, to meet again in heaven. They were never out of each other's thoughts; and rarely could a day pass by in which they did not see each other, and take counsel together. The voice of prayer, or the evening psalm, in one of their dwellings, might be heard in the other. Whatever changes came upon one family, the other was sure to partake immediately in the sorrow or the joy. In such neighborhood and intimacy, these two friends passed their days here, till the full strength of manhood in which they came had gradually turned to venerable age. They saw trials, many and various; trials such as weigh heaviest upon the spirit, and cause the heart to faint; but in all their trials, they had one hope, one consolation; and how refreshing to such men, in such vicissitudes, is the sympathy

apartments in it, and nineteen fire-places. Mr. Davenport's house, on the opposite side of Elm Street, near State Street, was built in the form of a cross, with the chimney in the centre. "That Mr. Davenport's house had also many apartments, and thirteen fire-places," says President Stiles, in his History of the Judges, "I very well remember, having frequently, when a boy, been all over the house."

of kindred souls, well-tried and true. Strong in themselves, with the gifts of nature, the endowments of education and experience, and the unction of Almighty grace; strong in their individual reliance upon God, their help and Saviour; they were the stronger for their friendship, the stronger for their mutual counsels, the stronger for the sympathy by which each drew the other towards the great fountain of strength, and love, and life.

"Such are the friendships of good men. Their intimacies make them better, holier, happier, more patient for endurance, wiser for counsel, stronger for every Godlike action."

The fathers of New England were not professedly separatists, but non-conformists. They did not design so much to withdraw themselves from the Church of England, as to promote a reformation from what they considered to be the errors that had crept into their communion. But the reformation which they sought, and effected, laid the foundation for a system of church polity which, both in its simplicity and practical operations, was most nearly allied to that of the apostles of Christ. They still felt themselves in communion with the truly good and pious, whether in the Church of England, or in any other Christian denomination; and especially in the former, there were many to whom their hearts still clung with the warmest Christian attachment.

A work written by Mr. Davenport, in 1639, and published in London, in 1641, entitled "An Answer of the Elders of the Several Churches in New England, unto nine Positions sent over to them by divers reverend and Godly ministers in England," exhibits most clearly his views, and those of the first ministers of New England, in regard to this work of reformation.

In the preface to this epistle, he says, "In our native country, where we were first called to the ministry, many of us took some things to be indifferent, and lawful, which in time we saw to be sinful, and could not continue in the practice of them there. Afterwards, some things that we bare as burdens—that is, as things inexpedient, though not utterly unlawful, we had no cause to retain and prescribe the same things here, which would have been not only inexpedient, but unlawful—such things as a man may tolerate when he cannot remove them; besides some things we practiced there, which, (we speak it to our shame and grief,) we never took it into serious consideration whether they were lawful and expedient, or no, but took them for granted, and generally received not only by the most reformed churches, but by the most judicious servants of God amongst them, which, nevertheless, when we came to weigh them in the balance of the sanctuary, we could not find sufficient warrant in the word to receive them as established there."

In closing this opening address of the work, he says: "If anything [in this answer] appears to be unsound, and dissonant to the word, (which we, for our part, cannot discern,) we shall willingly attend to what further light God may send unto us by you. In the mean time, we entreat you in the Lord, not to suffer such apprehensions to lodge in your minds, which you intimate in your letters, as if we justified the ways of rigid separation which, sometimes amongst you, we formerly bore witness against, and so build again the things which we destroyed, as those who separate from your congregations as no churches, from the ordinances as dispensed by you *as mere antichristian*, and from yourselves as no

Christians. But we profess unfeignedly, we separate from the *corruptions* which we conceive to be left in your churches, and from such ordinances administered therein, as we fear are not of God, but of men; and for ourselves, we are so far from separating, as from no visible Christians, as that you are under God in our hearts (if the Lord would suffer it) to live and die together, and we look at sundry of you as men of that eminent growth in Christianity, that if there be any visible Christians under heaven, amongst you are the men who for these many years have had written in your foreheads, 'holiness to the Lord,' which we speak, not to prejudice any truth which ourselves are here taught and called to profess, but we still believe, though personal Christians may be eminent in their growth of Christianity, yet churches have still need to grow from apparent defects to purity, and from reformation to reformation, from age to age, till the Lord have utterly abolished Antichrist with the breath of his mouth, and the brightness of his coming to the full and clear revelation of all his holy truth, especially touching the ordering of his house, and public worship. As a pledge of this, our estimation of you, we have sent you these answers to your demands, and shall be ready, by the help of Christ, to receive back from you, wise and just and holy advertisements in the Lord. Now, the Lord God, and Father of our Lord Jesus Christ, lead you and us into all truth, and purge all leaven out of his churches, and keep us blameless and harmless in his holy faith and fear to his heavenly kingdom, through Him that hath loved us, in whom we rest."

During the year 1642, letters were received, signed by Oliver Cromwell and several members of both houses of parliament, and also from some ministers in England, inviting Mr. Davenport, with Mr. Hooker of Hartford, and Mr. Cotton of Boston, to return to their native country, to assist in settling the affairs of the great revolution, which was then in progress there, and more particularly with reference to securing the independency of the churches. "The condition," say they, "wherein the state of things in this kingdom doth now stand, we suppose you have from the relation of others; whereby you cannot but understand how great need there is of the help of prayer, and improvement of all good means, from all parts, for the settling and composing the affairs of the Church. We, therefore, present to you our earnest desires of you all. To show wherein, or how many ways, you may be useful, would easily be done by us and found by you, were you present with us. In all likelihood you will find opportunity to draw forth all that helpfulness which God shall afford by you. And we doubt not, these advantages will be such as will fully answer all inconveniences yourselves, churches or plantations, may sustain in this your short voyage and absence from them. Only the sooner you come the better."

Upon the receipt of this invitation the subject was duly weighed by the several ministers and other leading men of the colonies, and while many deemed it "a call of God," yet it appears that Mr. Hooker was averse to the proposal, "nor thought it any sufficient call for them to go a thousand leagues to confer with a few persons that differed from the rest in matter of church government." Mr. Davenport, on the contrary, was strongly inclined to go, but his church considering the case, came to the conclusion, "that in regard they had but one officer, they could not see the way clear to spare him for so long a time as such a journey required." Mr. Cotton was in favor of accepting the invitation, and would have gone if the others had not declined.*

In the cause of popular education, Mr. Davenport has been justly styled a leader. "It has been a matter of some curiosity," says Professor Kingsley, in his Historical Discourse, "to ascertain, to what man, or class of men, the honor of having originated our system of schools belongs. A distinguished citizen of Connecticut remarked more than forty years ago: 'Did I know the name of the legislator, who first conceived and suggested the idea [of Common Schools], I should pay to his memory the highest tribute of reverence and regard. I should feel for him a much higher veneration and respect than I do for Lycurgus and Solon, the celebrated legislators of Sparta and Athens. I should revere him as the greatest benefactor of the human race; because he has been the author of a provision which if it should be adopted in every

* It is said that letters were also received during the same year—probably not official, but private—inviting the above ministers to come over, that they might have seats in the famous Assembly of Divines at Westminster.—*His. Discourses*, 103, 104.

country, would produce a happier and more important influence on the human character than any institution which the wisdom of man has devised.'*

"Perhaps the honor of devising the scheme of popular education, which has prevailed in New England, belongs exclusively to no individual. It originated rather in the general wish to bring all directly to the Scriptures for religious knowledge and in a regard for popular rights, both of which were distinguishing traits of Puritanism, than in the sagacity and benevolent efforts of any one man. But if the inquiry should be to whom is to be ascribed the honor of establishing the school system of the New Haven Colony, the question is easily answered. It is the just due of Theophilus Eaton and John Davenport; or if a distinction must be made here, abundant evidence exists in the colony records that the pre-eminence belongs to the latter. In John Davenport was that deep conviction of the value of general intelligence, especially, in his view of the subject, as the means of diffusing sound religious instruction, that energy, and that reso-

* "I. Swift's System, 159."

lution, which are essential to the successful introduction into a community, of a practical Common School System; and it is to men like him, that the credit should be given of having by their influence carried this system forward to its full execution."

In 1654, Mr. Davenport brought forward the plan of establishing a College in New Haven, for which the town made a donation of land. Through the correspondence of Davenport and Eaton, a donation of £500 sterling was also made by Governor Hopkins, who soon after died in England. With these funds the General Court erected the college school into a College for teaching the three learned languages, Latin, Greek, and Hebrew, and for the education of youth in good literature to fit them for the public service in church and commonwealth, and settled £40 a year out of the colony treasury, upon the preceptor or rector, besides the salary from New Haven School, with £100 for a library.*

* Stiles' History of the Judges.

It was in 1660, that Mr. Davenport appeared before the General Court reinforced with the legacy of Gov. Hopkins, and entreated them "not to suffer this gift to be lost from the Colony, but as it becometh fathers of the Common-

Mr. Davenport took the care of the colony school for several years, but in 1660, the Rev. Jeremiah Peck was appointed to that post. The convulsions of the time in 1664, the small number of inhabitants in the colony, and the subsequent removal of Mr. Davenport to Boston, prevented the carrying out of their designs for a College, and left the institution to terminate in a Grammar School, which continued to hold the Hopkins' fund.*

wealth, to use all good endeavors to get it into their hands and to assert their right in it for the common good; that posterity might reap the good fruit of their labors and wisdom and faithfulness; and that Jesus Christ might have the service and honor of such provision made for his people."

The letter of Mr. Davenport resigning the Hopkins' fund into the hands of the General Court of New Haven, may be found in Trumbull's History of Connecticut, vol. 1, p. 532.

* This was not the origin of Yale College. In the year 1700, several individuals met in New Haven and formed themselves into a Society, to consist of eleven ministers including a rector, and agreed to found a College in the Colony of Connecticut. At a subsequent meeting, the same year, at Branford, each of the trustees brought a number of books, and presented them to the Association, using words to this effect, as he laid them on the table, "*I give these books for founding a College in Connecticut.*" About forty

The following extract from the record of "a town meeting, held in New Haven, Feb. 7,

folio volumes were contributed on this occasion. This act of depositing the books has ever been considered the origin of Yale College.—*Quarterly Register*, Vol. 8, p. 14.

The College for some time was located at Saybrook, till in the year 1717, it was removed to New Haven, "where," says President Woolsey, "from being almost an airy nothing, it received a local habitation and was also in the course of the year 1718, destined to have that name given to it, by which, since the charter of 1745, the whole institution has been designated."

The following extract from a manuscript written at this time by one of the College officers, the Rev. Samuel Johnson, D.D., afterwards first President of King's [Columbia] College, New York, will not be uninteresting:—

"The building went forward apace, so that the hall and library were finished by Commencement. A few days before Commencement, came the news of the good success of some gentlemen's endeavors to procure some donations from Great Britain. For at Boston, arrived a large box of books, the picture and arms of King George, and two hundred pounds sterling worth of English goods, all to the value of eight hundred pounds in our money, from Governor Yale of London, which greatly revived our hearts and disheartened our opposers. [We were] favored and honored with the presence of his Honor Governor Saltonstall and his lady, and the Hon. Col. Taylor, of Boston, and the Lieutenant-Governor, and the whole Superior Court at our Commencement, Sept. 10, 1718, where the trustees present—those gentlemen being present, in the hall of our New College,

1668," affords a specimen of the early proceedings, in reference to this subject :—

"Mr. John Davenport, senior, came into the meeting, and desired to speak something concerning the school, and first propounded to the town, whether they would send their children to the school, to be taught for the fitting them for

first most solemnly named our College, by the name of Yale College, to perpetuate the memory of the Hon. Gov. Elihu Yale, Esq., of London, who had granted so liberal and bountiful a donation for the perfecting and adorning of it. Upon which the Hon. Col. Taylor represented Gov. Yale in a speech expressing his great satisfaction, which ended, we passed to the church, and there the Commencement was carried on. In which affair in the first place, after prayer, an oration was had by the saluting orator, James Pierpont, and then the disputations as usual, which concluded, the Rev. Mr. Davenport [one of the Trustees and Minister of Stamford] offered an excellent oration in Latin, expressing their thanks to Almighty God and Mr. Yale under him for so public a favor, and so great regard to our languishing School. After which, were graduated ten young men; whereupon the Hon. Gov. Saltonstall, in a Latin speech, congratulated the Trustees on their success, and in the comfortable appearance of things with relation to their School. All which ended, the gentlemen returned to the College Hall, where they were entertained with a splendid dinner, and the ladies at the same time were also entertained in the Library, after which they sung the four first verses in the 65th Psalm, and so the day ended."

the service of God in church and commonwealth. If they would, then, he said that the grant of that part of Mr. Hopkins his estate formerly made to this town stands good, but if not, then it is void; because it attains not the end of the donor. Therefore, he desired that they would express themselves. Upon which Roger Alling declared his purpose of bringing up one of his sons to learning; also Henry Glover, one of Mr. William Russell's, John Winston, Mr. Hodshon, Thomas Trowbridge, David Atwater, Thomas Meeks [Mix]; and Mr. Augur said that he intended to send for a kinsman from England. Mr. Samuel Street declared that there were eight at present in Latin, and three more would come in summer, and two more before next winter. Upon which Mr. Davenport seemed to be satisfied; but yet declared that he must always reserve a negative voice, that nothing be done contrary to the true intent of the donor, and it [the donation] be improved only for that use, and, therefore, while it can be so improved here, it shall be settled here. But, if New Haven will neglect their own good herein, he must improve it otherwise, unto that end it may answer the will of the dead. His desire was, that a farm may be purchased, that the revenues of it may ease the town; and therefore propounded, that if any knew of any farm to be purchased, they would acquaint the committee with it.; and then desired to know whether the town would grant this to be recorded, with this condition. The town fell into some debate about it, and so nothing was done further at this time."

A goodly number of pupils were fitted for College at this Hopkins' Grammar School.*

* This School is still kept on the corner of Temple and Crown Streets.

Mr. Ezekiel Cheever (or Cheevers), who came to New Haven with Mr. Davenport, taught a Grammar School there for many years. He was the father of New England school teachers. He was born in London, in 1615, and was one of those who signed the Plantation Covenant in Mr. Newman's barn in 1639. Of this man, Mather wrote: "He was a pious and learned divine, as well as preceptor. He wore his beard to the day of his death. He much formed and established the New England pronunciation of Latin and Greek. He printed an English Accidence still in use. The hair of his head and beard were white as snow. 'He died, leaning like old Jacob upon a staff; the sacrifice and the righteousness of a glorious Christ, he let us know, was the staff which he leaned upon.' 'He wore a long white beard terminating in a point, and when he stroked his beard to the point, it was a sign to the boys to

Says Professor Kingsley, "Of the graduates of Harvard College, from its foundation [1638] to the year 1700, as many as one in thirty, at least, were from the town of New Haven. When it is considered that so late as the year 1700, the number of inhabitants in New Haven could have very little if at all exceeded five hundred, this fact deserves notice. The explanation is found in the exertions of Mr. Davenport, which continued to produce their effect long after his death. Indeed, his influence in favor of liberal education has never ceased; but commencing in the infancy of the colony, has with the progress of time, and the increase of population, been more and more strengthened and more widely diffused." "How aptly," adds Dr. Bacon, "might that beautiful apostrophe of one of our poets have been addressed to him:

stand clear.' He died in Boston, August 21, 1708, in the ninety-fourth year of his age; after he had been a skillful, painful, faithful schoolmaster for seventy years; and had the singular favor of Heaven, that though he had usefully spent his life among *children*, yet he had not become *twice a child*, but held his abilities, with his usefulness, in an unusual degree to the very last."

'The good begun by thee shall onward flow
In many a branching stream, and wider grow;
The seed that in these few and fleeting hours
Thy hands, unsparing and unwearied, sow,
Shall deck thy grave with Amaranthine flowers,
And yield thee fruit divine in Heaven's immortal bowers!' "

The name of Mr. Davenport, more than that of almost any other man, has been associated with the history of those individuals, commonly known as "*the regicides.*" These were men who had conspired against the tyrannical rule of Charles I., the result of which was, the overthrow of that monarch who was condemned to the scaffold.

On the restoration of Charles II., in 1660, some who had been active in the times of the Commonwealth, under Cromwell, were put to death, and others fled for their lives. The surviving members of the Court that condemned the king to the scaffold, were pursued with special fury. Of these regicide judges, four at least escaped to this country, two of whom, Edward Whalley and William Goffe, came to New Haven. These two were among the most prominent of those who signed the death-warrant of the king. They arrived in Boston, on the 27th of July, 1660, in the same ship that brought the first news of the king's restoration.

"Whalley was closely connected with Cromwell by kindred, as well as by the tie of a common political interest. He was the colonel of that regiment of cavalry in the Parliament's army, in which Richard Baxter was chaplain, and between him and the author of the Saint's Rest, there was an intimate friendship, not only while Baxter continued in the army, but afterwards, when Whalley had become, under the Protectorate of his cousin Cromwell, one of the chief officers of the empire. To him, in token of their continued friendship, Baxter dedicated one of his works in an epistle, which is among the most beautiful examples of that kind of composition.

"Goffe was the son-in-law of Whalley, and like him, having distinguished himself in the army, in which he rose to the rank of Major-General, he became a member of Cromwell's House of Lords, and was one of the principal supporters of the Cromwell dynasty. So eminent was he, that it was thought by some, that he might, in time, become the head of the empire.

"When these men arrived in Boston, with the news of the king's restoration, they were at first received with undisguised attention by the Governor of that Colony and the principal inhabitants. For some time, they resided openly at Cambridge, where they attended public worship, and were active in private religious meetings, and were received to occasional communion in the church, by virtue of letters which they brought from the churches in England, with which they had been previously connected. As they became personally known, they were greatly respected for their piety, as well as for their talents and intelligence. It was hoped that in so distant a part of the world as this, they would escape the notice of their enemies; and the first rumors that followed them from England, gave some confirmation to the hope. But in November, the act of indemnity arrived, which secured all, with certain exceptions, against being called in question for anything they had done against the government since the beginning of the civil wars; and it appeared that these two men, with many others, were excepted from the general pardon; still, however, compassion and friendship prevented the government of Massachusetts from taking any measures to arrest them.

"On the 22d of February, 1661, the Governor called his council together, to consult about seizing them, but the council not having yet received any special order on that subject, refused to do anything. Four days after this, the two regicide judges, foreseeing that a warrant or order for their arrest must soon arrive from England, and that Governor Endicott, and their other friends there, would, in that case, be unable to protect them, left Cambridge, and passing through Hartford, where they were hospitably received by Governor Winthrop, arrived at New Haven on the 7th of March."*

Here, the minds of the people were well prepared to receive them. Mr. Davenport at once espoused their cause with great courage and boldness. There seems to be no evidence that Mr. Davenport ever preached a special discourse, as he is usually represented to have done, with reference to the cause of the regicides. That he alluded to them in terms which were not likely to be misunderstood, in a series of sermons which were preached just before their coming to New Haven, and which were afterwards published in his "Saint's Anchor Hold," is quite evident. In speaking of the general state of the church, both in this and

* His. Discourses, 123, 124.

other lands, and of the persecutions and trials to which God's people have been subject in all ages, he uses the following language:

"Brethren, it is a weighty matter to read letters, and receive intelligence in them concerning the state of the churches. You had need to lift up your hearts to God, when you are about to read your letters from our native country, to give you wisdom, and hearts duly affected, that you may receive such intelligences as you ought; for God looks upon every man in such cases, with a jealous eye, observing with what workings of bowels they read or speak of the concernments of his church. You see, in Amos vi. 6, how his wrath was incensed against those who solaced themselves with their private prosperity, but were not sick; their hearts asked not for the afflictions of Joseph.

"Again; let such know that if they withdraw from being helpful to the church, God will do good to his church, without them; but he will be avenged upon them that desert or neglect his cause and people. This argument, Mordecai used to Esther (Esther iv. 13, 14); and it prevailed mightily with her, to run the utmost hazard of her own person when there might be hope of some good to the church thereby (verse 16). For the contrary, Meroz was cursed by the angel of the Lord, because they 'came not up to the help of the Lord against the mighty.' (Judges v. 23.)

"Though men cannot help the Lord essentially or personally, yet they may be said to help him relatively in his cause and people; when they own his cause and people, and appear on that side, when Satan and his instruments raise persecutions and reproaches against them. Though the Lord needs not men's help in such cases—'for when he saw that there was no man, no intercessor, his own arm brought salvation unto him' (Isa. li. 16)—yet it is our duty to show on whose side we stand. For Christ will look upon us as his enemies, that disown his cause and people at such times; as he saith: 'He that is not with me, is against me.' (Matt. xii. 30.) 'Are the people and ways of God under reproach? Christ is reproached *in* them, and *with* them.' (Rom. xv. 3.)

"But it is objected, we are called fools and fanatics! This is the reproachful title put by profane men upon the people of God, in all ages. But if he is a fool who will be laughed out of his coat, much more is he a fool who will be laughed out of heaven; that will hazard the loss of his soul, and salvation, to free himself from the mocks and scoffs of a profane and sinful world.

"If Christ had not, for our sakes, endured the cross, despising the shame, we could never have been redeemed and saved. 'Let us go forth, therefore, unto him without the camp, bearing his reproach.' (Heb. xiii. 13.) In the same epistle, the Christian Hebrews are exhorted to 'call to remembrance the former days in which, after they were illuminated, they endured a great fight of afflictions, partly whilst they were made a gazingstock, both by reproaches and afflictions, and partly whilst they became companions of them that were so used.' (Heb. x. 32, 33.) Let us do likewise, and own the reproached and persecuted people, and cause of Christ, in suffering times.

"Withhold not countenance, entertainment and protection, from such, if they come to us from France, Germany, [England,] or any other place. 'Be not forgetful to entertain strangers, for thereby some have entertained angels unawares.' 'Remember them that are in bonds, as bound with them, and them who suffer adversity, as being yourselves also in the body.' (Heb. xiii. 2, 3.) The Lord required this of Moab, saying: '*Make thy shadow as the night in the midst of the noon-day*'—*i. e.*, provide safe and comfortable shelter, and refreshment, for my people, in the heat of persecution and opposition raised against them—'*Hide the outcasts; bewray not him that wandereth. Let mine outcasts dwell with thee, Moab; be thou a covert to them from the face of the spoiler.*' (Isa. xvi. 3.)

"But, again, it may be objected, so I shall expose myself to be spoiled or troubled? He therefore, to remove this objection, addeth, 'for the danger is at an end, the spoiler ceaseth, the treaders down are consumed out of the land.' While we are attending to our duty in owning and harboring Christ's witnesses, God will be providing for their and our safety by destroying those that would destroy his people.

"Two helps I shall propound to arm you against those fears of reproach, or danger, whereby men are apt to be drawn to flinch from the cause and witnesses of Christ in suffering times.

"First, strengthen your faith. A sight of the

invisible God and an eye to the recompense of reward so quickened and strengthened the faith of Moses, that he chose rather to suffer affliction with the people of God, than to enjoy the pleasures of sin for a season, esteeming the reproach of 'Christ greater riches than the treasures in Egypt.' (Heb. xi. 25, 26.)

"Secondly, exalt God as the highest object of your fear. Fear God as he ought to be feared, fear him above all. The greater fear will expel the lesser. Therefore, the Lord prescribes this fearing him aright, as the best remedy against all carnal fears, whereby men are wont to be hindered from obeying God in those duties that will expose men to hurt from the creature. (Isa viii. 12, 13.) *The balking of any duty which God commandeth is the ready way to bring upon you, by the wrath of God, that very evil which you fear that the doing of your duty will expose you to by the wrath of men.*"

With such a state of feeling in the public mind at New Haven, the two Colonels, as they were called, met with that kind reception which was considered due at least to uncondemned criminals. Soon after they had left Massachusetts, the king's proclamation denouncing them as traitors was received at Boston.

Before the news of this reached New Haven, they had showed themselves openly there as at Boston. Now they were obliged to secrete themselves. For more than a month they were hid in Mr. Davenport's house, when they removed across the street to Governor Eaton's, then occupied by Mr. Jones.

Near the last of April, the royal mandate arrived requiring the Governor of Massachusetts to cause the two Colonels to be arrested.*

* The following is a copy of this mandate found in Mass. His. Col. 3d Series, Vol. vii., p. 123.

"GOVERNOR OF NEW-ENGLAND TO APPREHEND WHALLEY AND GOFFE.

" *To our trusty and well-beloved, the present Governor, or other Magistrate or Magistrates, of our Plantation of New-England.*

CHARLES R.

Trusty and well-beloved,—Wee greete you well. Wee being given to understand that Colonell Whalley and Colonell Goffe, who stand here convicted for the execrable murder of our Royall Father of glorious memory, are lately arrived at New England, where they hope to shroud themselves securely from the justice of our laws;—Our will and pleasure is, and wee do hereby expressly require and command you forthwith, upon the receipt of these our letters, to cause both the said persons to be apprehended, and with the first opportunity sent over hither, under a strict care to receive according to their demerits. Wee are confident of your readiness and diligence to perform your duty; and so bid you farewell.

" Given at our Court at Whitehall, the fifth day of March, 1661.

" By his Majesty's command,

"EDW. NICHOLAS.

" JNO. ENDECOTT, Governor."

The whole community was now alarmed, and the Governor and Council of Massachusetts seem to have set about in earnest to apprehend and deliver up the victims. They deputized two zealous royalists, Thomas Kellond and Thomas Kirk, just from England, to go through the Colonies in pursuit of them. They came into the jurisdiction of the New Haven Colony and called upon Governor Leete, at Guilford, then acting magistrate. He assured them that he had not seen the men in several weeks, and that they had probably gone out of the jurisdiction. They came to New Haven two days after, with a letter from the Governor to the magistrate of the town, advising the town court to be called together, and search to be made. Various hindrances for some days prevented any further progress in the matter. Governor Leete, who had now arrived at New Haven, objected to giving them a special warrant authorizing their search, because the king's mandate which they brought with them was addressed to the Governor of New England, and he would not recognize any such officer. When they asked the magistrates if they would honor and obey the king in this affair, the Governor replied, "We honor his Majesty, but we have tender consciences." When further asked, whether they would own his Majesty or not, they replied, "That they would first know whether his Majesty would own them."

The pursuers insisted that the regicides were hid somewhere in the town, and pointed to the houses of Mr. Davenport and Mr. Jones. They had proof that they had been seen at Mr. Davenport's, and threatened him with severe penalties for concealing and comforting traitors. They also offered great rewards to any who should aid in their arrests. After various delays the court gave them authority to proceed. A diligent search was made throughout the colony, but the fugitives were not to be found.

During all this time the Colonels were in the immediate vicinity of New Haven. On the day in which their pursuers arrived at Guilford, they had left their concealment at New Haven, and escaped to a mill at West Rock, where they spent the Sabbath. For two days, they were secreted by some friends at Woodbridge, and on the 15th of May took up their residence in a cave at West Rock, a mountainous and almost inaccessible wild in the vicinity of New Haven. Here they were concealed till the 11th of June, while the whole colony was searched. "Once, when they ventured out of the cave for provisions, they hid themselves under a bridge, while their pursuers passed over it. At another time, they met the sheriff, who had the warrant for their execution, in his pocket, but they fought for their lives, and before they could procure assistance, escaped into the woods."*

While at the cave, they were informed of all that was going on, and stood ready to surrender themselves, rather than that any one should suffer through their concealment. At last, finding that Mr. Davenport was in danger of suffering on their account, they came into the town for the purpose of surrendering themselves. Here they remained for two days, and were seen so publicly, as to clear Mr. Davenport from the charge of still concealing them.

On the second day, while the Governor and Magistrates were consulting in reference to their case, the two Colonels suddenly disappeared, and when the search for them was renewed, they could not be found. They had betaken themselves to the cave, which contin-

* Stiles' History of the Judges.

ued to afford them a safe asylum, and where they were supplied with things needful for their comfort. As their hiding-place continued undisclosed, the zeal of their pursuers gradually died away, the fugitives retired to Hadley, Mass., where they lived for some years in devout seclusion, and at last died in peace.*

In reference to the matter of the regicides, it may be remarked, that while the magistrates wished to show their loyalty to the king, and as we have seen, made some efforts to aid the pursuers in their arrest, still, but few knew, or desired to know their hiding-places, and

* James Dixwell, another of the regicide Judges, resided for some years at New Haven, where he was known by the name of James Davis, Esq. He died in 1689, and was buried in the rear of the First (Centre) Church, close to the graves of Governor Eaton and Governor Jones. An ancient stone, in the old burying ground, marked the spot, with this charged inscription: "J. D., ESQ., DECEASED, MARCH Y^e^ 18TH, IN Y^e^ 82D YEAR OF HIS AGE, 1688–9."

It is said that the bodies of Whalley and Goffe were secretly conveyed to New Haven, and also buried near this spot; and the tradition is strongly confirmed by the two stones there standing, on one of which are the initials "E. W., 1678," and on the other "M. G., 80," the M of which, with a line drawn under (evidently intentional), may be taken for an inverted W., and the number, as fixing the date of his death, 1680.

these could not be tempted, either by the fear of punishment, or the hope of reward, to betray them. The overruling providence of God preserved them in the midst of their threatened danger, and as Davenport afterwards wrote: "The same Providence could have done the same, in the same circumstances, if they had been in London, or in the Tower."

President Stiles, in his "History of the Judges," attributes thus much to Mr. Davenport: "While these matters were going on, everything depended upon Mr. Davenport's firmness. If he gave out, all was gone;" and adds, "Mr. Davenport was a man of intrepid resolution and firmness, of greater discernment in public affairs, and in every way superior in abilities to the Governor and all concerned. He saw they all gave up. He, like Mount Atlas, stood firm and alone, and took the whole upon himself. Better than any of the counsellors, he knew that all that had been done before the arrival of the royal mandate, could be vindicated by the laws of hospitality to unconvicted criminals, and could not, in a court of law, be construed into even a suspicion of treason. It might subject him to some inconveniences, perhaps prosecutions, but could not be fatal — a thing which, perhaps, the others doubted. Supported by his good sense, and deep discernment, he therefore felt himself secure. What staggered Governor Endicott, a man of heroic fortitude, and other hearts of oak at Boston, never staggered Mr. Davenport. Great minds display themselves on trying and great occasions. He was a man for *this* trying occasion. Davenport's enlightened greatness, fidelity and intrepidity, saved the Judges."

Dr. Bacon, in narrating the history of the Judges, also says: "These details show in a striking light the character of Mr. Davenport," and adds, "I know not what incident in history exhibits a more admirable combination of courage and adroitness, of fidelity to friendship, of magnanimity in distress, and of the fearless, yet discreet assertion of great principles of liberty, than can be found in this simple story of the protection of the regicides by the men of New Haven. And what gives to all the rest a higher dignity, is the fact, that the courage which feared not the wrath of the king, was not fool-hardiness or passion, but faith in God, who bade them hide the outcasts, and be a covert to them from the face of the spoiler.

The rude munition of rocks that sheltered the fugitives when they were chased into dens and caves of the earth, is a monument more eloquent than arch or obelisk. Till the mountains shall melt, let it bear the inscription, 'Opposition to tyrants is obedience to God.'" *

In 1662, after his restoration, Charles II. granted through the agency of Governor Winthrop to the people of Connecticut a charter with the amplest privileges, which was also designed to include the colony of New Haven.†

* This inscription is placed by a modern hand on the Judges' Cave at West Rock.

† Governor John Winthrop, of Connecticut, was the son of Governor John Winthrop, "the father of Massachusetts." He was a man of eminent abilities and commanding influence, learned and pious. He so far ingratiated himself into the favor of Charles II. and Lord Clarendon, that while in England in 1662, he obtained from the king a charter embracing in its limits all that tract of country which lies between the Narragansett River and the Pacific Ocean, and conferring upon the colonists unqualified powers to govern themselves. Mr. Winthrop, it is said, had "an extraordinary ring," given to his grandfather by Charles I., which he presented to the king. This exceedingly pleased his majesty, and perhaps had some influence in procuring the grant. This was the charter which King James II. in 1686 sent Sir Edmund Andross to take away from the people of Connecticut, but by the adroitness of Capt. Wadsworth, it

Great efforts were made at this time to unite the two colonies. This was warmly opposed by a majority of the people of the New Haven colony. They were attached to their peculiar polity and feared such a union might have an unfavorable bearing on the purity of their churches, and on their general prosperity. Mr. Davenport took an active part in this resistance. The people of the Connecticut colony, however, endeavored by unfair means to bring them under their jurisdiction without their consent.

In October, after the arrival of the charter, the court of magistrates at New Haven, according to usage, appointed the 23d of that month, as a day of public thanksgiving, and at the same time ordered "that the 29th of this

was hid in a large hollow oak still standing in Hartford, and known by the name of Charter Oak.

Gov. Winthrop's principal residence in Connecticut was at Pequot, now New London. Great efforts were made by Mr. Davenport to induce his removal to New Haven and the town voted to give him a house. He declined their generous donation but resided there about two years. One reason why the people of New Haven were so anxious to have Mr. Winthrop make his residence there was his medical knowledge and skill. A number of letters from Mr. Davenport to Governor Winthrop, will be found in the Appendix.

month be kept as a day of extraordinary seeking of God by fasting and prayer for his guidance of the colony in this weighty business about joining with Connecticut colony, and for the afflicted state of the Church and people of God in our own native country, and in other parts of the world."

"Two days after that day of fasting," says Dr. Bacon, "the records of the town show us a meeting of the freemen at which a copy of the charter was exhibited, together with a writing from some gentlemen of Connecticut, signifying that they looked upon New Haven as being within their bounds. Mr. Davenport, and his colleague Mr. Street, were both present. Mr. Davenport appears to have addressed the meeting at great length. He stated some important facts, illustrating the haste, unkindness, and arrogance, with which their brethren of the other colony had proceeded in the matter. He showed what pledges he had received from Mr. Winthrop that so unrighteous an act should not be attempted. He went into an argument to prove, first, that New Haven was not of course included under the charter, and secondly, that New Haven ought not voluntarily to enter into such a union; and he concluded by giving directions as to the answer that should be returned to the men of Connecticut, 'that they may see their evil in what they have done, and restore us to our former state, that so we and they may live together in unity and amity for the future.' Mr. Street followed in the debate; he declared that he looked upon Mr. Davenport's arguments as unanswerable, he thought 'that both Church and town had cause to bless God for the wisdom held forth in them,' he exhorted the freemen 'to keep the ends and rules of Christ in their eye, and then God would stand by them;' and he concluded by seconding Mr. Davenport's directions respecting an answer, 'with one scripture out of Isaiah xiv. 32 [What shall one then answer the messengers of the nation?—that the Lord hath founded Zion, and the poor of his people shall trust in it]; and from thence did advise that the answer should be of faith, and not of fear.' The decision of the meeting, after a full debate, was in accordance with the advice thus given.

"Four days afterwards, the freemen of the whole colony were convened at New Haven, not by delegation but in full assembly. To that convention, Governor Leete submitted the communication which had been received from Connecticut, and the brief reply which had been made by the committee appointed by the last General Court. These writings having been read, together with the copy of the charter, the Governor called the attention of the meeting to the two distinct points which the communication from Connecticut presented for their consideration, namely, the claim that the charter necessarily included them, and that they were therefore bound to submit, and the invitation to a voluntary and peaceful union. After this, that the people might have time for consideration, the assembly was dismissed for an hour and a half, 'then to meet again at the beat of the drum.' When the meeting was again opened, Mr. Davenport was called upon by the Governor to express his views.

"Mr. Davenport said 'that according to this occasion he should discharge the duty of his place,' and proposed to 'read to them his own thoughts, which he had set down in writing, and which he desired might remain his own till they [the freemen of the colony] should be fully satisfied in them, for he would leave others to walk according to the light which God should give them in this business.'

Accordingly he read some reasons why the people of Connecticut ought not to construe their charter as including New Haven colony, and why New Haven might not voluntarily join with Connecticut—and then retired, leaving his written thoughts for the consideration of the assembly. The Governor carefully abstained from giving any opinion; but urged the freemen to speak their minds, that the substance of the answer might proceed from them. After the matter had been 'largely debated' the substance of the answer was agreed upon, and it was determined that the points of the reply should be, first, a 'due witness-bearing against the sin' of Connecticut in invading their independence; next, a demand that till Mr. Winthrop should return, or till they should otherwise obtain satisfaction, the whole matter should be deferred, and the jurisdiction of New Haven be permitted to proceed without interruption; and thirdly, a resolution to do nothing without taking advice from the other confederate colonies. A committee including all the magistrates and elders was appointed to prepare such an answer and to forward it to the authorities of Connecticut. The 'answer of the freemen drawn up into form by the committee,'* bears strong marks of the workmanship of Mr. Davenport.

"The correspondence thus begun between the two colonies was continued through several years, while Connecticut was gaining strength by steady encroachment, and New Haven, at first the weaker party, was gradually weakened by defections, and by the increasing burdens which the controversy occasioned. The great body of the people here loved their independence and their own peculiar polity. 'The ends for which,' said they, 'we left our dear native country, and were willing to undergo the difficulties which we have since met with in this wilderness, yet fresh in our remembrance,' were 'to advance the kingdom of our Lord Jesus Christ and to enjoy the liberties of the Gospel in purity with peace;' and these are 'the only ends we still pursue, having hitherto found by experience so much of the presence of God with us, and of his goodness and compassion towards us in so doing, for these many years.' To these ends their peculiar insti-

* Found in Trumbull's History of Connecticut, vol. i., 515.

tutions seemed in their judgment best adapted. To them their little republic seemed as near a perfect model of a Christian commonwealth, as could be in this world of imperfection. Cato in his 'little senate' at Utica, standing against the power of Cesar, for the ancient constitution of his country, was actuated by no sentiment higher or more admirable than that which actuated them. In all the negotiations of that crisis, the influence of Mr. Davenport was conspicuous. The numerous letters and remonstrances in which the claims of New Haven were argued, bear the stamp of his mind. Their clearness in the statement of the case, their cogency in the argument, their dignity of manner, with slight occasional manifestations of sarcastic humor, and the simple piety that breathes so naturally through them all, indicate him as the author." *

It was not till the beginning of 1665, that this controversy was ended. At that time an invasion of the rights of all the New England colonies was threatened by grants of large territories made to the Duke of York, the brother of the king, and a

* Historical Discourses, pp. 135–138.

general commission for him to settle the peace of the colonies and superintend their affairs. Fearful not only that their own interests but the common interests of all the other colonies, as well as the cause of truth and liberty, might now suffer, the New Haven colony came to a unanimous decision to submit to the claims of Connecticut, and Mr. Davenport, yielding with many regrets to the necessity of the measure, was chosen one of the committee for consummating the union.

In 1651, the second church in Boston, then just formed, had extended a call to Mr. Davenport, to settle among them, which however, he felt it his duty to decline. Sixteen years had now passed away. Mr. Davenport had become an old man. His beloved Eaton and many more of his fellow-pilgrims had passed to their reward; while a new generation had risen up around him. Great changes had taken place. There were some things that gave him grief, but others were full of hope and promise. Yet his zeal and activity remained unabated. His heart and hand were ready for every good work. For thirty years he had lived in the affection and undiminished confidence of his church. His influence was also lent to all the great questions that concerned the interest of this as well as the other colonies of New England. But new scenes and trials were now opening before him.

In 1667, the Rev. John Wilson, who had been associated with the distinguished Cotton and Norton, as pastor of the First Church in Boston, died. That was the oldest church except the one at Plymouth, and the most considerable one in the colonies. On the death of Mr. Wilson, Mr. Davenport was thought best fitted to succeed the eminent characters who had ministered there. In addition to this, his influence seemed called for at that time to resist the introduction into the churches of that region of what was then called the "Half-way covenant," by which the children of parents not pious, received baptism—an innovation which Mr. Davenport had so strenuously opposed in Holland. This question was now agitating the whole of New England.

In 1657, a synod had convened to discuss this question, and the party in favor of so far considering persons not convicted of scandalous practices as church members, as to allow them to have their children baptized, prevailed. The same decision prevailed at another synod, in 1662. Mr. Davenport was not a member of this synod, but he sent his written opinion, which, though the synod refused to hear it read, was "generally transcribed," and put within the reach of the members, and a report of concurrence in the views which he presented, was afterwards made by the minority.

On the 27th of September, (1667,) the call was made out, and a committee sent to New Haven to invite Mr. Davenport's removal to Boston. The well known opposition of their candidate to the innovation allowed by the "Synodists," awakened opposition on the part of some thirty prominent members of the Boston church, to Mr. Davenport's coming among them. This opposition had no effect in leading him to decline the call. He looked upon the application with favor, and felt it his duty to accept. His church, on the other hand, felt unwilling to part with one who had so long been their counselor and spiritual guide, and withheld their formal assent to his removal.

The importunities of the church at Boston, at last led to the decision, that while they would not take the responsibility of consenting to his removal, yet, if it was his determination to go, they would not oppose him. At this partial acquiescence in his own judgment, he felt at liberty to accept the call to Boston, and his removal from New Haven took place the last of April, just thirty years after the commencement of his ministry there. He arrived with his family at Boston, on the 2d of May.* He and his son, and their wives, were received into the church on the 11th of

* From John Hull's Diary,—"1668, 2d day, 3d month [May], at 3 or 4 in afternoon, came Mr. John Davenport to towne, with his wife, sonn, and sonn's family; was mett by many of the town. A great shower of extraordinary dropps of rain fell as they entered the end of the Town, but Mr. Davenport and his wife were sheltered in a coach of Mrs. Searls', who went to meet them.

"Dec. 9. Mr. Davenport and Mr. Allen were ordeyned." Communicated by Mr. Henry Davenport of Boston, to whom the writer is indebted for various collections from that city, obtained through him.

This gentleman's first ancestor in this country was Thomas Davenport, who settled at Dorchester, Massachusetts, in 1640, of whose numerous descendants he has gathered much information. From what part of England this Thomas Davenport, and also Captain Richard Davenport who arrived in America with Governor Endicott in 1628, came, has not been ascertained.—See New England Historical and Genealogical Register, vol. iv., pp. 111 and 351.

October, and on the 9th of December he was installed.

"His removal, under such circumstances," says Dr. Bacon, "occasioned much difficulty. The minority of the church in Boston charged him and the other elders with equivocation, because they communicated to the church, only those parts of the letters from New Haven, which seemed to imply a dismission, whereas, it was maintained, that if the whole had been read, it would have appeared that there was no dismission. Several letters were written, and messengers were sent from that church to this, in the hope of prevailing on this church [at New Haven] 'to declare their owning of the letter sent from them, to be a true dismission of Mr. Davenport.' Of that correspondence, nothing remains but a fragment of one of the letters from the New Haven church. That fragment is so full of reverent affection towards their pastor, even after he had torn himself away from them, and breathes so much of the Christian spirit, that it is well worthy of preservation. 'Though you,' say they, 'judge it the last expedient for your relief, and the remedy of some evils growing in the country, as also, we might do the same, if we had nothing before our eyes but his accomplishments and fitness for high service to God, in his church; but being so much in the dark about his way in leaving this church and joining to yours, that we are not without doubts and fears of some uncomfortable issue; we cannot, therefore, clearly act in such a way as is expected and desired. We are of the same mind as when we returned an answer to your first letter, thus expressing ourselves:—We see no cause, nor call of God, to resign our reverend pastor to the church of Boston by an immediate act of ours, therefore, not by a formal dismission under our hands. It is our great grief, and sore affliction, that we cannot do for him, whom we so highly esteem in love for his works' sake and profitable labors among us, what is desired, without wrong to our consciences. Anything that we have or are, beside our consciences, we are ready to lay down at his feet; such is our honorable respect to him, our love to peace, our desire of your supply, that we shall go as far as we safely can, in order to his and your satisfaction in this matter, having before us for our warrant, Acts xxi. 14: 'When he would not be persuaded, we ceased, saying, The will of the

Lord be done.' Therefore, to suppress what we could say touching that passage in our first letter, whereof such hold hath been taken, and what we have said in our last letter to you, of our reverend pastor's making null the liberty before granted, which, we doubt not, we are able clearly to demonstrate; yet, if this will satisfy (but not otherwise), we are content to wave and bury in silence, and leave both yourselves and him to make what improvement you see cause (without any clog or impediment from us upon that account), of the liberty before mentioned. 'As he hath been a faithful laborer in God's vineyard at New Haven, for many years, to the bringing home of many souls to God, and building up of many others, so it is, and shall be our prayer to God to lengthen his life and tranquillity in Boston, to double his Spirit upon him, assist him in his work, and make him a blessed instrument, of much good to yourselves and many others. The good Lord pardon, on all hands, what he hath seen amiss in these actings and motions, that no sinful malignity may obstruct or hinder God's blessing upon churches or church administrations. As himself and his son have desired, we do dismiss unto your holy fellowship Mr. John Davenport, junior, and Mrs. Davenport, elder and younger, desiring you to receive them in the Lord, as becometh saints, and imploring Almighty God for his blessing upon them from his holy ordinances in their communion, and walking with you. The God of all grace supply all your and our need, according to his riches in glory through Jesus Christ. Thus craving your prayers for us in our afflicted condition, we take our leave, and rest yours in the fellowship of the gospel.

NICHOLAS STREET,

In the name, and with the consent of the Church of Christ at New Haven.' "*

* His. Discourses, 143–145. The date of this letter was 12th October, 1668.

It may not be uninteresting in this place to add a list of the estimable men who have succeeded Mr. Davenport as pastors of the First Church in New Haven.

The Rev. Samuel Eaton, and Rev. William Hook, for a short time acted as teachers during the ministry of Mr. Davenport, both of whom returned to England, and after the restoration, were silenced for non-conformity. To these succeeded Rev. Nicholas Street, who was installed as Mr. Davenport's assistant, in 1659, and continued his associate in the ministry till Mr. Davenport's removal to Boston, when he had the sole charge of the church till his death, in 1674, when for eleven years there was no settled pastor.

Rev. James Pierpont was settled in 1685, and continued

Mr. Davenport was at this time more than seventy years of age. "What minister," asks the writer above quoted, "so far advanced in life, would now be called from one church to another, because of the eminency of his qualifications for usefulness? When was there ever another such instance of competition and controversy between churches for the enjoyment of the ministry of one who, always an invalid, had numbered more than three score years and ten? How rarely can you find a church who

sole pastor till his death, in 1714. Rev. James Noyes, son of Rev. James Noyes of Stonington, whose father was James Noyes, one of the early settlers of Massachusetts, was installed July 4, 1716, and continued their pastor till his death, 1761, when the Rev. Chauncey Whittlesey, who had been his associate, succeeded as sole pastor. Mr. Whittlesey died 1787, and was followed by Rev. James Dana, D.D., who was settled in 1787, and was dismissed in 1805. The Rev. Moses Stuart was ordained as pastor, March 5, 1805, and was dismissed in 1809, to accept a professorship in the Theological Seminary at Andover, Mass. On the 8th of April, 1812, the vacancy was supplied by the ordination of the Rev. Nathaniel W. Taylor, who was dismissed in 1822, to accept the Dwight professorship of Theology in Yale College. The Rev. Leonard Bacon, D.D., the present pastor, was installed in 1825, having now stood in that relation to this church for twenty-six years.

when a minister has torn himself away from them, retain for him so strong and reverent an affection?"

A portion of the church in Boston still protested against the views of Mr. Davenport, twenty-eight of whom withdrew and formed a new organization now known as the "Old South Church in Boston." An unhappy feeling long existed between these two churches, and the defection spread throughout all New England. It was not till within the last half century that the views of which Mr. Davenport was so long the champion triumphed.

Mr. Davenport's ministry, which had lasted nearly twenty years in England, and thirty in New Haven, was of short duration in Boston. At the time of his removal, his mental powers were in full vigor and the church there anticipated the enjoyment of his ministry for many years. But his services on earth were fast drawing to a close. He had labored among them in the Gospel but about two years, when on the 15th of March, 1670, he was suddenly seized with an apoplexy in which he was dismissed from a life of faithful and unremitted labor, and removed to his eternal rest. He died in the seventy-third year of his age, and was buried with every testimonial of respect in the tomb of the venerated Cotton.*

Mr. Davenport was a great scholar. From his early youth to his death he was devoted to study. "Those lucubrations of his which in London were protracted into the late hours of the night, were not discontinued when he had removed into a deeper wilderness than that which is now spread around the base of the Rocky Mountains." † He was "almost continually in his study and family, except some public work or private duty called him forth;" ‡ and he was so close and bent a student that it excited the attention of the wild Indians in his vicinity, who used to call him, according to their custom of applying significant or descriptive names, "*So-big-study-man.*" §

* This tomb is in the burying-ground of the Stone Chapel Church on Tremont Street. A broad slate stone monument marks the spot, on which are the following inscriptions: "Here Lye Intombed the Bodyes of the Famous Reverend and Learned Pastors of the First Church of CHRIST in Boston, viz. Mr. John Cotton, aged 67 years, Deceased, December 23d, 1652. Mr. John Davenport, aged 72 years, Deceased, March the 15, 1670. Mr. John Oxenbridge, aged 66 years, Deceased, December 28, 1674."

† Dr. Bacon. ‡ Church Records of New Haven.

§ Mather, Magnalia, III. 56.

While Mr. Davenport pursued an extensive range of study so as justly to merit the appellation of a universal scholar, yet his favorite study was Theology, in which he arrived at great attainments. The copious quotations from the Scriptures which abound in his sermons for proofs of doctrine and illustration of argument show a familiarity with the Sacred Writings almost unparalleled. In preparing for the pulpit he wrote out but part of his sermon and made but little use of his manuscript in public. Says one of his cotemporaries, "He was a person beyond exception and compare for all ministerial abilities, and that even in his latest years he was of that vivacity that the strength of his memory, profoundness of his judgment, floridness of his elocution were little if at all abated in him."* Another (Dr. Increase Mather), who in his youth, was wont to receive counsel from this aged divine, says, "He was a princely preacher. I have heard some say who knew him in his younger years that he was then very fervent and vehement as to the manner of his delivery, but in his later years he did very much imitate Mr. Cotton, whom, in the gravity

* Hubbard's History of Massachusetts, 602, 603.

of his countenance he did somewhat resemble. *Sic ille manus, sic ora ferebat.*"*

"Let us call up," says Dr. Bacon, "the shade of our ancient prophet.† I see him rising in his pulpit. The folds of his gown conceal in part the slenderness of his figure, worn thin with years of infirmity. The broad white bands falling upon his breast, starched and smooth,—the black round cap, from beneath which a few snowy locks show themselves,—the round face and delicate features, which, but for the short white beard might seem almost feminine,—the dark bright eye, which shows that age has not yet dimmed the fire within,—complete the venerable image. Every eye is fixed upon him. He names his text. As he reads it, all rise to show their reverence for the 'Scripture breathed of God.' After they have been seated again he proceeds. He unfolds his text historically and critically. He raises from it some one point of 'doctrine.' He 'proves' that doctrine by an induction of

* Magnalia III. 10.

† See Frontispiece. The original painting is in the Trumbull Gallery, Yale College, New Haven, and from a date on the canvas, seems to have been taken the year of his death.

instances from Scripture, or by the accumulation of proof-texts. He illustrates it, shows its connections with other truths, and justifies it to the understanding, by 'reasons' drawn from the nature of things, and evolving the philosophy of the subject. He closes, and applies his discourse with 'uses' or inferences drawn from his doctrine for 'instruction,' or 'comfort,' or 'admonition,' or 'exhortation,' till the last sands are falling in the hour-glass. Meanwhile the listening congregation knows no weariness. The weighty thought, the cogent argument, the flashing illustration, the strong appeal to affection or to hope, the pungent application, the flow of soul in the fervid yet dignified utterance — keep fast hold on their attention. 'They sit under the shadow of his doctrine,' says Hubbard, 'as it were with great delight, and find the fruit thereof sweet to their taste.'" *

It may further be added, Mr. Davenport was a most faithful patriot. He was engaged in all the great interests of the New England Colonies. His plans were laid, not for the good of the generation then existing alone—they embodied principles which were

* Historical Discourses, p. 149.

designed to develop their fruit for coming ages. But his efforts were more particularly directed to the welfare of the colony of which he and his associate, Eaton, were styled the Aaron and Moses.

Professor Kingsley, in speaking of these two men, says: "Mr. Davenport was a man of more native ardor than his associate, and possessed that fixedness of principle and firmness of resolve which fitted him to encounter opposition, and to embark in difficult and dangerous enterprises. The opinions of the Puritans, he adopted in their full extent; and persecution, as usually happens in the case of men of ardent temperament, instead of breaking his spirit, forced him to the extremes of his system. He thought that reformers were prone to linger, and even to halt in their course; and that after they had made a certain progress, their further improvement was hopeless. It was a saying of his, that as 'easily might the ark have been removed from the mountains of Ararat, where it first grounded, as a people get any ground in reformation, after and beyond the first remove of the reformers.'* He

* Mather's Magnalia, III. 53.

was roused, therefore, as we are told by Mather, 'to embark in a design of reformation wherein he might have opportunity to drive things in their first essay, as near to the precept and pattern of Scripture as they could be driven. With these views and feelings, he came to New England. If a part of his plan of a commonwealth proved to be impracticable, a part has stood the severe trial of time; and his success has been greater than that of most theorists in governments.

"I am aware that there has been an impression among some in this community, that Mr. Davenport was fond of power; that he was overbearing and arbitrary, and exercised a kind of dictatorship in the Colony. On what just foundation such an opinion rests, I have never been able to discover. That he had an extensive and commanding influence in all the colonial transactions; that he possessed those qualities of mind which fitted him to become a leader of others, and insensibly to mould them to his views, there can be no doubt; but there is no evidence that this ascendency was ever sought by him, or when possessed, was employed for unworthy purposes. Whatever pre-eminence he attained, was voluntarily conceded to long-tried and acknowledged intelligence, integrity and wisdom.

"If he had been influenced by a thirst for power, we might expect to find traces of it in the Colony laws; some valuable immunities of the clergy, some share granted them in the legislative or judicial departments of the government. But nothing of this character is to be found there. On the contrary, by the New Haven code, the clergy, so far from having any civil power, could not even perform the marriage ceremony, this being placed exclusively in the hands of the magistrates. The church which was formed under his advice and superintendence, was organized on principles strictly independent; a sort of spiritual democracy, in which, if there were any lords, they were 'lords brethren.' But what must place the question out of all doubt, whether Mr. Davenport assumed improper power in the colony, is the single fact that when he was invited to Boston in 1668, his removal was universally opposed by the people of the town. As he was determined to leave them, they appear to have silently acquiesced in the measure, but never to have given it their formal assent. This is not the mode in which mankind act when about to be relieved from even a moderately exercised tyranny."*

It is not alone as a scholar, a pulpit orator, the founder of a new commonwealth, or as a philanthropist, that we are called to admire the character of Mr. Davenport—but as a *Christian*. It was the reigning desire of his heart to see a pure Gospel church—a church composed of those who had a vital, experimental union with Christ, their living head, and for this, he deemed labor and suffering as of small account. He had that unwavering confidence in God, which led him to undertake whatever presented itself to him as *duty*, with an assurance that in the end the right would always succeed. It was this faith in God, which sustained him in the midst of the many difficulties and trials which marked his eventful life. The great question ever before his mind, was—*Is this right, and doth God require it?* That was to him the beginning and the end of all controversy. When assured of the divine command: "Lay this foundation; God doth require it;" he was ready at the loss of all things to yield obedience to the call.

* Historical Discourse, pp. 62–64.

Prayer was his strong hold—his mightiest weapon. Cotton Mather relates that "a young minister,* once receiving wise and good counsels from this good and wise and great man, received this among the rest, 'that he should be much in ejaculatory prayers; for, indeed, ejaculatory prayers—as arrows in the hand of a mighty man so are they,—happy is the man that hath his quiver full of them.' And it was believed that he himself was well used to that sacred skill of 'walking with God' and 'having his eyes ever towards the Lord' and 'being in the fear of the Lord all the day long,' by the use of ejaculatory prayers on the innumerable occasions which every turn of our lives does bring for these devotions. He was not only constant in more settled, whether social or secret, prayers; but also in the midst of all besieging incumbrances, tying the wishes of his devout soul to the arrows of ejaculatory prayers, he would shoot them away to the heavens, from whence he still expected all his help." †

Such was Mr. Davenport;—such were the fathers of New England. "And what," asks

* Supposed to be his father, Dr. Increase Mather.

† Magnalia, III. 54.

the author of the Historical Discourses, "do we claim for them? What for the Pilgrims of Plymouth,—what for the stern old Puritans of the Bay, and of Connecticut,—what for the founders of New-Haven? Nothing, but that you look with candor on what they have done for their posterity and for the world. Their labours, their principles, their institutions, have made New England, with its hard soil, and its cold long winters, 'the glory of all lands.' The thousand towns and villages,—the decent sanctuaries not for show but for use, crowning the hill-tops, or peering out from the valleys, — the means of education accessible to every family, — the universal diffusion of knowledge,—the order and thrift, the general activity and enterprise, the unparalleled equality in the distribution of property, the general happiness resulting from the diffusion of education, and of pure religious doctrine,—the safety in which more than half the population sleep nightly with unbolted doors,—the calm, holy sabbaths, when mute nature in the general silence becomes vocal with praise, when the whisper of the breeze seems more distinct, the distant waterfall louder and more musical, the carol of the morning birds clearer and sweeter — this is New England; and where will you find the like, save where you find the operation of New England principles, and New England influence? This is the work of our fathers and ancient lawgivers. They came hither, not with new theories of government, from the laboratories of political alchemists, not to try wild experiments upon human nature, but only to found a new empire for God, for truth, for virtue, for freedom guarded and bounded by justice. To have failed in such an attempt had been glorious. Their glory is, that they succeeded.

"In founding their commonwealths, their highest aim was the glory of God, in 'the common welfare of all.' Never before, save when God brought Israel out of Egypt, had any government been instituted with such an aim. They had no model before them, and no guidance save the principles of truth and righteousness embodied in the word of God, and the wisdom which he giveth liberally to them that ask him. They thought that their end, 'the common welfare of all,' was to be secured by founding pure and free churches, by providing the means of universal education, and by laws maintaining perfect justice, which is the only perfect liberty. 'The common welfare of all,' said Davenport, is that 'whereunto all men are bound principally to attend, in laying the foundation of a commonwealth, least posterity rue the first miscarriages when it will be too late to redress them. They that are skillful in architecture, observe, that the breaking or yielding of a stone in the groundwork of a building, but the breadth of the back of a knife, will make a cleft of more than half a foot in the fabric aloft. So important, saith mine author, are fundamental errors. The Lord awaken us to look to it in time, and send us his light and truth to lead us into the safest ways in these beginnings.'*

"Not in vain did that prayer go up to Heaven. Light and truth were sent; and posterity has had no occasion to rue the miscarriages of those who laid the 'groundwork' of New England. On their foundations has arisen a holy structure. Prayers, toils, tears, sacrifices and precious blood, have hallowed it. No unseemly fissures deforming 'the fabric aloft' dishonor its founders. Convulsions that have rocked the world have not moved it. When

* Discourse upon Civil Government, 14.

terror has seized the nations, and the faces of kings have turned pale at the footsteps of Almighty wrath, peace has been within its walls, and still the pure incense has been fragrant at its altar. Wise master-builders were they who laid the foundations. They built for eternity.

"Among those truly noble men, it is not easy to name one more strongly marked with bright endowments, and brighter virtues, or more worthy to be had in everlasting remembrance, than he for whom the quaint historian has proposed as his fit epitaph,—

'JOHANNES DAVENPORTUS,
In Portum delatus,

VIVUS, NOV-ANGLIÆ ET ECCLESIÆ ORNAMENTUM;
MORTUUS, UTRIUSQUE TRISTE DESIDERIUM.'" *

* Historical Discourses, 152–154.
This epitaph was written by Dr. Cotton Mather, and may thus be rendered:

JOHN DAVENPORT,
Borne into Port,

Living, the Ornament of New England and the Church;
Dead, an Irreparable Loss to Both.

EIGHTEENTH GENERATION.

Issue of Rev. John Davenport, (No. 68.)

(70.) I. John Davenport of New Haven, was born during the residence of his father in London, and was an only child. He accompanied his parents to America, in the year 1637. During his father's abode in New Haven, he does not appear to have been much engaged in public affairs, although Dr. Stiles, in his History of the Regicides, in speaking of the Courts of New Haven, about the year 1661, mentions him as one of the judges. He was not admitted a freeman at New Haven, till 15th of May, 1657. He was married, November 27, 1663, to Abigail, daughter of the Rev. Abraham Pierson of Branford, Conn., who was a sister of Rev. Abraham Pierson, the first Rector of Yale College. In 1668, he removed with his family to Boston, taking his letter of recommendation to the church there, from the church in New Haven. He was admitted freeman at Boston, in 1669. After his removal to Boston with his father, he was Register of Probate, from January 31, 1675, to August 17, 1676; but at the time of his death, which took place in the latter part of 1676, he is called a merchant. His wife survived him, and died at New Haven, July 20, 1718. Her grave is under the First (Center) Church.

The following is a fac-simile of his autograph:

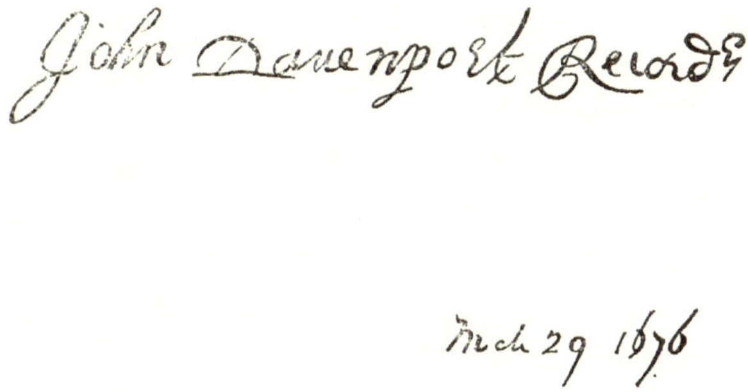

NINETEENTH GENERATION.

Issue of John Davenport, (*No.* 70.)

(71.) I. John Davenport, born at New Haven, June 7, 1665, and died August 31, aged eleven weeks.

(72.) II. Elizabeth Davenport, born at New Haven, October 7, 1666, who married Warham Mather in 1700.

[Warham Mather was the son of Rev. Eleazar Mather of Northampton, Mass., who died in 1669, leaving also another son named Eliakim, and a daughter Eunice, who afterwards married Rev. John Williams of Deerfield, who, with his family, was carried into captivity by the Indians, in 1704. Mrs. Williams was killed by the Indians, soon after they left Deerfield. Their mother's maiden name was Esther Warham, youngest child of Rev. John Warham of Windsor, Ct., who, after the death of Mr. Mather, married Rev. Solomon Stoddard, the maternal grandfather of President Edwards, by whom she had twelve children.

Warham Mather, after his marriage to Elizabeth Davenport, resided at New Haven, where for many years he filled the office of Judge of the Court of Probate.]

(73.) III. Rev. John Davenport of Stamford, who was born in Boston, and baptized by his grandfather, on the 28th of February, 1669. He graduated at Harvard College, in 1687, and commenced preaching in 1690. In 1691, he was invited to become an assistant to the Rev. Mr. James of East Hampton, Long Island.*

"APRIL 16, 1691. The town voted one hundred pounds for the support of the ministry. Sixty pounds to Mr. James, and forty pounds to Mr. Davenport; and Mr. Davenport to have his diet free."—*East Hampton Town Records.*

Mr. Davenport, for a time, waived this call, which—the way not seeming satisfactorily

* This ancient town was originally purchased by Theophilus Eaton, Governor of the Colony of New Haven, and Edward Hopkins, Governor of the Colony of Connecticut, in behalf of the proprietors, who had emigrated from Maidstone, county of Kent, England, and settled in Salem, Mass., and other towns in the vicinity of Boston, and who came and settled East Hampton, in 1648. On the payment of the stipulated sum, the writings were transferred from the original purchasers to the proprietors.

open for his settlement there—was soon after declined.

In 1693, Mr. Davenport was called to the work of the ministry in Stamford, Fairfield County, Ct. This town originally belonged to the Colony of New Haven, and was purchased of them by some of the inhabitants of Wethersfield, Ct., who settled there in 1641, the purchasers agreeing to join the New Haven Colony in their form of government. It derived its name from an ancient town in the county of Lincoln, England, from whence probably some of the first settlers originated.

The following extracts are transcribed from the town records of Stamford, both as a matter of interest in these modern times, and as showing the distinctness with which the people were wont to provide for the temporal wants of those who ministered unto them in spiritual things, whether single or "settled in a family:"

"A town meeting, orderly warned, the 10th day of March, 1693.—It having been formally voted our desire of Mr. John Davenport's coming to this place for a trial in the work of the ministry, and a committee appointed to signify their minds unto him upon that account; and Mr. Davenport being come (unto the Town):

at a full meeting being orderly warned, and also more fully by warrant added; therefore, for a further prosecution of that matter, with reference to their vote the 12th of September, 1692, doe now further order to a settlement in this place as a minister of the Gospel amongst us, and if upon trial they find his complying in judgement with what is mentioned in said vote, they have power to agree with him, and provide for his comfortable settlement, in respect of house and lands, and what else is needful for his encouragement, the committee have full power to doe according to their best discretion and the town's ability, and that the matter be forthwith attended.

"The names of the committee are—

"Capt. Selleck,
"Lieut. Bell,
"Wm. Ambler,
"Jon. Selleck, &c."

"July 17th, 1693.

"1st. At town meeting, orderly warned, the town by a unanimous vote doth give and grant to Mr. John Davenport, for his encouragement when he is sole (settled) minister in Stamford, a hundred pounds a year per anno, according to the committee's proposal to Mr. Davenport when he was last in Stamford.

"2d. It is voted that they give to Mr. Davenport ten pounds a year during Mr. Bishop's life, which makes seventy pounds a year: that is to say, ten pounds to be added to the sixty pounds, if Mr. Davenport doth settle in a family before Mr. Bishop's death.

"3d. The town per vote doth purpose and desire their committee to write and send what ye town hath voted to Mr. Davenport, and to send for him when and how they see most convenient.

"4th. The town per vote doth give and grant to Mr. John Davenport, when he is settled here in a family, his firewood, which is to be done in a general way, and not by rate, and to be done when the townsmen doe order a day or two in the year for it; further, it is understood that it is to be done by ye people of the town, all male persons from sixteen years and upwards."—*Town Records of Stamford.*

In 1694, Mr. Davenport was ordained as pastor of the church in Stamford, and on the 18th of April, 1695, he was married to Martha, widow of John Selleck, formerly a Miss Gould, by whom he had seven children.

The following is the minute of her death, copied from the records of the town:

"That Eminently pious and very virtuous Matron, Mrs. Martha Davenport, late wife to the Rev. John Davenport, Pastor of ye Church of Christ in Stamford, Laid down or Exchanged Her Mortall or Temporall Life, to putt on Immortality, and Doubtless was Crowned with immortal glory, on the first day of December, 1712." She was buried at New Haven.

The following extracts are given from "A Sermon preached at the Funeral of the Rev. John Davenport, late Pastor of the Church in Stamford, who died Friday, Feb. 5, 1731, in the 62d year of his age, and 36th of his ministry: And was decently interred on Monday following: By the Rev. Samuel Cooke, pastor of the Church in Stratfield [now Bridgeport].

"2 Kings ii. 12. '*My father, my father, the chariot of Israel and the horsemen thereof!*' Printed by J. P. Zenger, in New York, 1731, pp. 62."

Speaking of Mr. Davenport, on page 42 the author says, "He had the advantage of an accurate knowledge of those languages, wherein the Scriptures were given by Divine Inspiration, probably far beyond the compass of any of his survivors, within many scores of miles every way; and so could drink immediately out of the sacred fountain, those languages being almost as familiar to him as his mother tongue. [When he read his Bible in his family and in the pulpit, he did not make use of the English translation, but of the Greek and Hebrew original.] He was no less eminent in what did belong to him as the mouth of the people unto God. The spirit of grace and supplication rested upon him beyond the common measure. He was like Elijah, a man mighty in prayer: an Israel that was wont especially in cases of peculiar difficulty and emergency, to wrestle with God as a prince that would not be put off with a denial. . . . . He was a skillful and faithful vine-dresser in the Lord's vineyard, and an able laborer in his private and public dispensations. Witness his late painful and indefatigable labors, even in the time of his prevailing and fatal sickness; when nature was so weakened, that his thoughtful observers could not but look upon it with admiration, that he should appear in the pulpit, and with so much engagedness and fervor; not without some misgiving apprehensions within themselves, that his time of service was near expiring. He was a cloud richly fraught with the rains and dews of heavenly doctrines, and plentifully distilling the same here and there; and especially on this part of the Lord's vineyard. He was a watchman on the walls of God's Jerusalem here; and such an one as was eagle-eyed to discern the approaches of sin and danger and faithful to give warning thereof; whether men would hear or whether they would forbear.... The person whose exit now calls for our deep lamentation and mourning, was both our crown and our bulwark, our glory and our defence. Our crown is fallen from our heads, and our defence is departed. We have our chariot and horsemen taken away. Wo unto us, that we have sinned. It was many years since looked upon by the serious and judicious, as a special favor of Divine Providence, that a person of such distinction as we have now lost, was seated so near to the western limits of New England as a bulwark against any irruptions of corrupt doctrines and manners. Wo to us, our hedgewall in that respect is broken down... He was proof against the temptations of the smiles or frowns of others, to turn him out of the way to the right hand or to the left. What was many times in his mouth seemed to be always in his heart—*Magis amica veritas.* These things made him the object of the admiration of good men and the reverence of all."

Mr. Davenport for some time previous to commencing his labors in Stamford, taught the Hopkins' Grammar School in New Haven. He was a member of the Corporation of Yale College from 1707 till his death in 1731.

His second wife was Mrs. Elizabeth Maltby, daughter of John Morris, by whom he had two children. The following is the record of her death. "The ancient Madam, Mrs. Elizabeth Davenport, widow and relict of ye late Rev. Mr. John Davenport, died January 11, 1758."

(74.) IV. Abraham Davenport, baptized March 5, 1671, and died young.

(75.) V. Abigail Davenport, born in Boston, and baptized Sept 15, 1672, was married to the Rev. James Pierpont, of New Haven, (successor of Rev. John Davenport,) on the 27th of October, 1691. She died, Feb. 3, 1692. Her grave is under the First Church. Of Mr.

Pierpont, Dr. Bacon in his Historical Discourses, gives the following account.

["Mr. Pierpont was the younger branch of a noble family in England. It is believed, though the necessary legal proof seems to be wanting, that his son was the heir to the estates and the now extinct title of the earls of Kingston. In the latter part of 1684, he was invited to take the charge of the church in New Haven. In January, it was voted that a home-lot and house should be provided for Mr. Pierpont, which his people agreed to build by voluntary contributions. The lot was purchased and the building was immediately commenced. When it was finished it was one of the most commodious and stately dwellings in the town. For more than a century, it stood a monument of the public spirit of the generation by whose voluntary contributions it was erected. As the people were bringing in their free-will offerings of one kind and another, to complete and furnish the building, one man desiring to do something for the object, and having nothing else to offer, brought on his shoulder from the farms two little elm saplings and planted them before the door of the minister's house. Under their shade some forty years afterward Jonathan Edwards, then soon to take rank in the intellectual world, with Locke and Leibnitz, spoke words of mingled love and piety in the ear of Sarah Pierpont.*

* Jonathan Edwards, son of the Rev. Timothy Edwards, was born at East Windsor, Connecticut, October 5, 1703. He graduated at Yale College in 1720, before he was seventeen years of age. In 1724, he was appointed a tutor in Yale College, in which office he continued till he was called to settle in the ministry at Northampton, as an associate to his grandfather, (the Rev. Solomon Stoddard,) in 1726, where he continued in the pastoral office for more than twenty-three years. After his dismissal in 1750, he labored for some years among the Housatonic Indians, at Stockbridge, in Berkshire County. In 1758, he was called to the presidency of New Jersey College, where, soon after having entered upon the duties of his office, he suddenly died, March 22, 1758. His published works are numerous and he has justly been considered the most distinguished metaphysician and divine that America has ever produced. His wife, Sarah, daughter of the Rev. James Pierpont, of New Haven, was born January 9, 1710, married July 28, 1727, in her 18th year, and died in 1758.

The following account of this interesting person, when in her 13th year, was written on a blank leaf by Mr. Edwards, at the age of twenty. " They say there is a young lady in New Haven, who is beloved of that Great Being, who made and rules the world, and that there are certain seasons, in which this Great Being, in some way or other, comes to her and fills her mind with exceeding sweet delight, and that she hardly cares for anything, except to me-

Under their shade, when some sixty summers had passed over them, Whitfield stood on a platform, and lifted up that voice the tones of which lingered so long in thousands of hearts. One of them is said to be still standing before the mansion of the late Judge Bristol, in Elm Street; the tallest and most venerable of all the trees in this 'City of Elms,' and ever the first to be tinged with green at the return of Spring.

ditate on Him—that she expects after a while to be received up where he is, to be raised up out of the world, and caught up into Heaven; being assured that He loves her too well, to let her remain at a distance from Him always. There she is to dwell with Him, and to be ravished with His love and delight forever. Therefore, if you present all the world before her, with the richest of its treasures, she disregards it, and cares not for it, and is unmindful of any path of affliction. She has a strange sweetness in her mind, and singular purity in her affections; is most just and conscientious in all her conduct, and you could not persuade her to do anything wrong or sinful, if you would give her all this world, lest she should offend this Great Being. She is of a wonderful sweetness, calmness, and universal benevolence of mind; especially after this Great God has manifested himself to her mind. She will sometimes go about from place to place, singing sweetly; and seems to be always full of joy and pleasure, and no one knows for what. She loves to be alone, walking in the fields and groves, and seems to have some one invisible always conversing with her."

"The ordination of Mr. Pierpont took place on the 2d day of July, 1685, after he had been with the people eleven months as a candidate. On the 27th of October, 1691, he married Abigail Davenport, a granddaughter of his predecessor in the pastoral office. A little more than three months afterwards, on the 3d of February, she was taken from him by death. She died, as tradition tells us, of a consumption caused by exposure to the cold on the Sabbath after her wedding, going to meeting according to the fashion of the time, in her bridal dress.*

"Two years afterwards he was married at

* In Rev. James Pierpont's Almanac, of 1692, the following notes were inserted by himself on blank leaves. "Jan. 14, wife had fitts." "Feb. 1, we sent to Mr. Chauncey, of Strafford, to press him to come over, but he came not till 2 at night. He gave much encouragement and ordered friction of the lower parts which were utterly cold, whereupon her speech went away; he lodged in the house—he and I were called up between 2 and 3 o'clock in the night. Mr. Chauncey supposed no great hazard—I declared I thought it was our duty to resign this relation to the Lord whilst we had time, and to beg pardon ere we parted, which I endeavored in prayer.

" 3d, between 3 and 4, morning, my dear wife, Abigail, died of Histeric fitts.

" 4th, at night buried ! ! "

Communicated by Rev. Stephen Dodd, of East Haven.

Hartford, to Sarah Haynes, a granddaughter of Gov. Haynes, 'by Lieutenant-Colonel Allen, Assistant the 30th of May, 1694.' On the 7th of October, 1696, he was again bereaved. His second wife left one daughter, who bore the name of his first wife. This daughter afterwards became the wife of Rev. Joseph Noyes, pastor of the same church. His third wife was Mary Hooker, a granddaughter of the Rev. Thomas Hooker, the first pastor of the church in Hartford, to whom he was married on the 26th of July, 1698. This lady who survived him till November, 1740, was the mother of several children, one of whom, Sarah, became at an early age the wife of Jonathan Edwards, and was truly 'a help meet for him.'"

(76.) VI. Mary Davenport, born in Boston, and baptized the 17th of September, 1676. She was first married to Nathaniel Weed, of New Haven, who is spoken of as a practitioner of physic, and second to a Mr. Wade; of the same place.*

* New Haven received its present name in 1640, two years after Mr. Eaton and Davenport began their settlement. Designing the town for a commercial city, they laid out the place in a regular manner, dividing it into nine squares, the streets crossing each other at right angles.

TWENTIETH GENERATION.

Issue of Rev. John Davenport, (No. 73.)

(77.) I. Abigail Davenport, born July 14, 1696, and married to the Rev. Stephen Wil-

These squares were fifty-two rods on a side, separated by streets four rods in breadth. The central square was reserved for public purposes, and may vie with the public grounds of any city in the country. The surrounding squares have been divided into four, by streets running crosswise in the direction of the original ones. Besides these thirty-two squares, the town extends over considerable tracts beyond already covered with villas and houses. The city is much admired for its elegant appearance. Its beautiful elms and shade trees have a very striking effect. On the center square or green, represented in the accompanying engraving, are located three churches of various architecture, which are not excelled by any similar edifices in New England. First, on the right hand, stands the North Congregational Church, (Rev. Mr. Dutton's.) The building in the center with a tall spire, is the First Church, (Rev. Dr. Bacon's,) which occupies nearly the site of the original building, constructed for Mr. Davenport's society. Near this at the west, stands the State House, an edifice of the Doric order of architecture after the model of the Parthenon at Athens. On the left of the picture stands Trinity Church, (Episcopal,) a structure of much architectural taste and beauty. The buildings seen in the rear, pertain to Yale College. The present population of the city is about 20,000.

liams, D.D., of Springfield, Mass., July 3, 1718, by whom she had eight children, three of whom were ministers, the aggregate period of whose ministry was over a hundred and fifty years. Of these children, some further account will be given, under their appropriate head, in the next generation. She died August 26, 1766. The following account of Mr. Williams is principally drawn from Allen's Biographical Dictionary, and "The Williams Family History."

[Rev. Stephen Williams, D.D., minister of Springfield, Mass., and son of Rev. John Williams of Deerfield, Mass., was born May 14, 1693. In the night of February 28, 1704, when he was about nine years of age, his father's house was attacked by a party of Indians from Canada. The family were made captives. He, with his brothers (except Eleazar) and two sister, in the company of their parents, set out on a long and tedious march to the home of the Indians. In wading a river, on the second day, Mrs. Williams, his mother, who had scarcely recovered from a recent sickness, became nearly exhausted. She was unable to keep up with the rest. Her husband was not allowed to assist her, and she seemed on the point of fainting from weakness and fatigue. At this time, one of the Indians came up to her, and killed her with his hatchet. This woman was the granddaughter of the Rev. Richard Mather of Dorchester, the daughter of Rev. Eleazar Mather of Northampton, and sister of Rev. Dr. Increase Mather, President of Harvard College, and afterwards minister of Boston, who married Maria, the daughter of Rev. John Cotton, whose son was Rev. Cotton Mather of Boston.

After the death of Mrs. Williams, the surviving members of the family continued their journey of three hundred miles, till they reached Canada. Here they were retained in captivity, amid scenes of suffering, for about two years, when they were redeemed. Mr. Williams, the father, then returned to Deerfield, and was minister of that town till his death, June 12, 1729. His son, Stephen, graduated at Harvard College in 1713, and was ordained over the second church of Springfield, now Long Meadow, in the year 1718. He was married soon after his ordination, to Abigail Davenport, daughter of the Rev. John Davenport of Stamford, Ct. In 1745, he went to Louisburg as a chaplain under Sir William

Pepperell, and in 1755 to Lake Champlain, in the same capacity, under Sir William Johnson, and in 1756, under Major-General Winslow. He died June 10, 1782, in the 90th year of his age, and 66th of his ministry. His funeral was attended by his seven surviving children. His brother, Rev. Eleazar Williams, graduated at Harvard in 1708, and was settled at Mansfield, Ct. Another brother, Rev. Warham Williams of Waltham, Mass., who was also taken captive to Canada when but four years of age, graduated at Harvard College, and studied divinity with the Rev. Solomon Stoddard of Northampton, who married his maternal grandmother (Mrs. Esther Mather), relict of the Rev. Eleazar Mather, and daughter of the Rev. John Warham. He died June 22, 1751.]

(78.) II. John Davenport, born in Stamford, January 21, 1698, and was married by his father to Sarah Bishop,* September 6, 1722.

* Supposed to be a granddaughter of Rev. John Bishop, who was Mr. Davenport's predecessor.

The following circumstances are connected with Mr. Bishop's call to Stamford, about 1644: "The church there hearing that he was in the neighborhood of Boston, two brethren, George Slason and Francis Bell, were deputed to

He removed to what is now the North Society of Stamford, and was one of the original twenty-four members who were organized into a Congregational Church in New Canaan, on the 20th of June, 1733.* He deceased November 17, 1742, leaving fourteen children, the oldest of whom had not reached the age of nineteen when their father died, aged 44 years.

(79.) III. Martha Davenport, born February 10, 1700, was married to the Rev. Thomas Goodsell of Branford, October 6, 1731, by whom she had one child, Sarah, who married

go to Boston, and if he was to be found, to make known to him the wishes of the church. Although the country was full of hostile Indians, they went on foot, carrying their provisions, and succeeded at length in finding Mr. Bishop, 'to the eastward of Boston.' He accepted the call, and returned with them on foot, bringing his Bible under his arm, through the wilderness to Stamford. (This Bible is still in the possession of Mr. Noah Bishop, one of his descendants.")—*Historical Address by Rev. J. W. Alvord*, 1841. Published by Silas Davenport.

* The parish of Canaan was situated within the townships of Stamford and Norwalk, and was first incorporated in 1731. The church, in 1733, was organized with thirteen members from the Norwalk side, and eleven from the Stamford side. New Canaan was not incorporated into a township till 1801.

DAVENPORT PLACE,

ELM STREET NEW HAVEN CONN.

about 1760, Jeremiah Wolcott of Windsor, whose eldest daughter, Martha Davenport Wolcott, married Hezekiah Reynolds in 1778, who was the father of John Davenport Reynolds of Wallingford, and also of William Augustus Reynolds, who now owns, and resides upon the old Davenport place in Elm Street, New Haven.* Mrs. Goodsell died in 1796.

(80.) IV. Sarah Davenport, born July, 1702, and was married, first, to Captain William Maltby of New Haven, by whom she had three children—a son and two daughters. The son, Rev. John Maltby, graduated at Yale College in 1747, and for a number of years was the much loved pastor of a church in Bermuda, West Indies. He afterwards removed to Charleston, South Carolina, till, from impaired health, he removed to Hanover, N. H.,

* The accompanying engraving presents a view of the "Davenport Place," in Elm Street. The house occupied by its original proprietor was principally taken down, and rebuilt in its present form by the late Judge Pierpont Edwards, the father of Judge Ogden Edwards of New York, about seventy years ago. Some parts of the ancient dwelling appear in this mansion, and the cellar in which the regicides were concealed by Mr. Davenport, yet remains under the present building.

where he died in 1771. His monument is by the side of that of his step-father, Dr. Wheelock. One of the daughters died in youth, an example of patience and piety, and the other, Elizabeth, was married May 15, 1754, to Dr. Thaddeus Betts, a highly respected physician of Norwalk, Ct., who was the father of Judge William Maltby Betts, and the grandfather of Hon. Thaddeus Betts, Lieutenant-Governor of Connecticut, who represented his native state in the Senate of the United States, and who died at Washington in 1840, aged 52 years.

After the death of Captain Maltby, his widow married, in 1735, the Rev. Eleazar Wheelock, of Lebanon, Ct.

[Dr. Wheelock was born in 1711, and graduated at Yale College in 1733. He was settled at Lebanon, Ct., in 1735, where his labors were productive of much good. He was one of the most eloquent and successful ministers in New England. Dr. Trumbull describes him as "of a comely figure, of a mild and winning aspect; his voice smooth and harmonious, the best by far I ever heard. He had the entire command of it. His gestures were natural, and not redundant. His preaching and addresses were close and pungent, yet winning beyond all comparison; so that his audience would be melted into tears, even before they were aware of it." He became the founder of "Moor's Charity School for Christianizing the Indians;" which he afterwards removed to Hanover, N. H., where he became the founder of Dartmouth College, of which he was the first President, in 1770. After being at the head of the college for about nine years, he died in Christian peace, April 24, 1779.]

"Mrs. Sarah Wheelock was a woman of a meek and quiet spirit, active in duty, patient in trial, given to hospitality. So endeared was she to her husband by her natural and moral qualities, that her grave-stone bears the inscription, that her character was too estimable for an epitaph."*—*Memoir of her daughter, Mrs. Patten.*

(81.) V. Theodora Davenport, born Nov. 2, 1703, and died Feb. 15, 1712.

* The following inscription is from her monument, in the burying-ground at Columbia, formerly Lebanon: "Sacred to the memory of Sarah, the wife of ye Rev. Eleazar Wheelock, who died November 13, A.D. 1746, and in the 44th year of her age, and of a character too great and good to have anything said, worthy to be inscribed here."

On the grave-stone are also found the arms of Davenport.—*Communicated by Rev. Wm. Allen, D.D.*

(82.) VI. Dea. Deodate Davenport, of East Haven, born in Stamford, Oct. 23, 1706. He was married in 1730 to Lydia Woodward, daughter of the Rev. John Woodward.* He died Dec. 3, 1761.

(83.) VII. Elizabeth Davenport, born in Stamford, August 28, 1708, and was married to the Rev. William Gaylord, of Wilton, by whom she had two children, one of whom Martha, was married to Seth Taylor, of Norwalk, (now Westport.) Mrs. Gaylord died July 6, 1747, aged 38 years and 10 months.†

(84.) VIII. Hon. Abraham Davenport, of Stamford, born in 1715, and graduated at Yale College in 1732. He was married in Windham, Connecticut, by the Rev. Stephen White, on the 16th of November 1750, to Miss Elizabeth

* The Rev. John Woodward was graduated at Harvard College, in 1693; and ordained Pastor of the Church at Norwich, in 1699. He assisted in the Council that compiled the Saybrook Platform in 1708, and removed to East Haven in 1716, where he died the same year.

† The Rev. Mr. Gaylord was graduated at Yale College in 1730. He was re-married to Elizabeth Bishop, in 1753, by whom he had Aaron, Elizabeth, Samuel, Sarah, (who became the second wife of Dea John Davenport, No. 123,) Deodate and Moses.

Huntington, whose mother was a daughter of Rev. Timothy Edwards, of East Windsor, and the sister of Pres. Jonathan Edwards.

His first wife died December 17, 1773. He was re-married in Stamford, by the Rev. Dr. Wells, August 8, 1776, to Mrs. Martha Fitch.

"Mr. Davenport sustained many important offices in civil life, all of which he filled with honor to himself and fidelity to his country. He was for many years one of the Council of the State, and at the time of his death, was Judge of the Court of Common Pleas for the County of Fairfield, and Judge of the Court of Probate of Stamford. While he lived he was greatly respected, and his death was universally lamented. 'The righteous shall be had in everlasting remembrance.' "*

Of Colonel Davenport, Dr. Dwight in his Travels, (Vol. 3d, p. 497,) gives the following account :—

"In this town [Stamford], lived the Hon. Abraham Davenport, for a long time one of the Councillors of the State, and before that, of the Colony of Connecticut. This gentleman was the son of the Rev. John Davenport, and

* Tomb stone, Stamford.

the great-grandson of the Rev. John Davenport, the father of the New Haven Colony. Colonel Davenport was possessed of a vigorous understanding and invincible firmness of mind, of integrity and justice, unquestioned even by his enemies; of veracity exact in a degree, nearly singular; and of a weight of character which for many years decided in this County almost every question to which it was lent. He was early a professor of the Christian religion; and adorned its doctrines by an exemplary conformity to its precepts. He was often styled a rough diamond; and the appellation was, perhaps, never given with more propriety. His virtues were all of the masculine kind; less soft, graceful and alluring, than his friends wished; but more extensively productive of real good to mankind, than those of almost any man who has been distinguished for gentleness of character. It would be happy for this or any other country, if the magistracy should execute its laws with the exactness, for which he was distinguished. Colonel Davenport acquired property with diligence, and preserved it with frugality; and hence was by many persons supposed to regard it with an improper attachment. This, however, was a very erroneous opinion. Of what was merely ornamental, he was, I think, too regardless; but the poor found nowhere a more liberal benefactor, nor the stranger a more hospitable host. I say this from personal knowledge, acquired by a long continued and intimate acquaintance with him and his family. While the war had its principal seat in the State of New York, he took the entire superintendence of the sick soldiers, who were returning home; filled his own houses with them; and devoted to their relief his own time, and that of his family; while he provided elsewhere the best accommodations for such as he could not receive. In a season when an expectation of approaching scarcity had raised the price of bread-corn to an enormous height, he not only sold the produce of his own farms to the poor at the former customary price, but bought corn extensively, and sold this also, as he had sold his own. His alms were at the same time rarely rivalled in their extent.

"Two instances of Colonel Davenport's firmness deserve to be mentioned. The 19th of May, 1780, was a remarkably dark day. Candles were lighted in many houses; the birds were silent and disappeared; the fowls retired to roost. The Legislature of Connecticut was then in session at Hartford. A very general opinion prevailed that the day of Judgment was at hand. The House of Representatives being unable to transact their business, adjourned. A proposal to adjourn the Council was under consideration. When the opinion of Colonel Davenport was asked, he answered 'I am against an adjournment. The day of Judgment is either approaching, or it is not. If it is not, there is no cause for an adjournment: if it is, I choose to be found doing my duty. I wish therefore that candles may be brought.'

"The other instance took place at Danbury, at the Court of Common Pleas; of which he was Chief Justice. This venerable man after he was struck with death, heard a considerable part of a trial; gave the charge to the jury; and took notice of an article in the testimony which had escaped the attention of the counsel on both sides. He then retired from the bench; and was soon after found dead in his bed.

"To his friends Col. Davenport extended his acts of kindness, as if they had been his children. I say this from experience. Of his country and of all its great interests, he was a pillar of granite. Nothing impaired, nothing moved his resolution and firmness, while destined to support in his own station this valuable edifice.

"He was educated at Yale College, in which he took the degree of Bachelor of Arts in 1732. He died as he had long wished to die, in the immediate performance of his duty, November 20th, 1789, in the 74th year of his age."

(85.) IX. Rev. James Davenport, born in Stamford, 1716. He was educated at Yale College, where he graduated in 1732. He settled at Southold, Long Island, in 1738.

[Southold was the first settled town on Long Island, and originally extended from Brookhaven to Oysterpond-Point, including all the islands in that vicinity, and extending thence in a direct line to within a few miles of the Connecticut shore. Like East Hampton it was originally purchased by the magistrates of the New Haven Colony, and after being held by them for a number of years, was transferred to the actual settlers, who were principally emigrants from Norfolkshire, England; who had spent about two years in the New Haven Colony, and established themselves on this Island in 1640. Before they left New Haven, by the advice and aid of Governor Eaton and John Davenport, they were organized into a regular Church under a pastor, Rev. John Young, who accompanied them to the Island.]

Mr. James Davenport was the fourth pastor of this church, and remained there about two years, and was esteemed a pious, sound, and faithful minister. But in 1740, at the time Whitfield came to this country, and a season of great religious excitement prevailed, Mr. Davenport became carried away with enthusiastic impulses, aud without asking the approbation of his people, set out on an itineracy among the churches, leaving his own particular charge unprovided for.* He believed that the Lord was about to arise and have mercy upon Zion, for the time to favor her, yea, the set time was come, and that he was especially called to prepare the way of the Lord by calling the people to repentance.

Before leaving Southold, he assembled the people at his lodgings, and addressed them for twenty-four hours together. The effort overcame his strength and confined him for some days to his chamber.† He commenced his

* Prime's History of Long Island.

† The Great Awakening, by Rev. Joseph Tracy.

travels about the 1st of June, 1740. In the same month during the Session of the Presbyterian Synod, he was found at Philadelphia, preaching at Society Hill, with the Tennents and others.

In the autumn, he joined Whitfield, who wrote in his journal, October 30, on arriving at New York:—"To add to my comfort, the Lord brought my dear brother Davenport, from Long Island, by whose hands the blessed Jesus has of late done great things." Having parted, they met again November 5, at Baskinridge, New Jersey, where Davenport had been preaching to about three thousand people in the parish of the Rev. Mr. Cross. Here Whitfield remained for one or two days, and set out accompanied by Mr. Davenport to Philadelphia. After a perilous journey, in which they twice narrowly escaped drowning, they arrived in Philadelphia on Saturday eve, the 8th.* Mr. Davenport was particularly a favorite with Whitfield, and also with the Tennents.

"The Rev. Andrew Crosswell in a pamphlet in his defence," says Tracy, "produced numerous testimonies in his favor; for example:—'Mr. Whitfield declared in conversation that he

* The Great Awakening.

never knew one keep so close a walk with God as Mr. Davenport. Mr. Tennent, in my hearing, affirmed Mr. Davenport to be one of the most heavenly men he ever was acquainted with. Mr. Pomeroy, who is acquainted with both, thinks he doth not come one whit behind Mr. Whitfield, but rather goes beyond him, for heavenly communion and fellowship with the Father and with the Son, Jesus Christ. Mr. Parsons of Lyme told me the other day, [this was July 16, 1742,] that not one minister whom he had seen was to be compared to Mr. Davenport, for living near to God, and having his conversation always in Heaven.* Mr. Owen, also, of Groton, said that the idea he had of the Apostles themselves scarcely exceeded what he saw in Mr. Davenport. In brief, there is not one minister in all Connecticut, that is zealously affected in the good cause of God at this day, but instead of slighting him is apt to think more highly of him than we ought to think of men, and to receive him almost as if he was an angel from Heaven." † "This is the statement," adds Mr. Tracy, " of

* "Parsons, however, did not approve of all his measures, as appears by his own statements."

† Great Awakening, pp. 230–231.

an honest partisan—so far as a partisan can be honest; not false, but too highly colored. Davenport had certainly produced wonderful effects, and collected a large tribute of veneration. He rode—to use language of a more modern date—'on the very top wave of the spirit of the age.' More than any other man, he embodied in himself and promoted in others, all the unsafe extravagances into which the revival was running; and those whose zeal outran their knowledge, saw in him what they proudly hoped soon to become."

After leaving Mr. Davenport at Philadelphia, we lose sight of him till the next Spring or Summer, when we find him again pursuing his travels in Connecticut, and in other parts of New England.

Among other places he visited East Hampton, Long Island. Rev. Dr. Beecher, in giving the history of that town in a sermon in 1805, remarks: "The revival of religion in 1741–2, was the first general revival ever witnessed in the town. It commenced apparently by the instrumentality of the famous Mr. Davenport, who was the means of doing both good and evil. The novelty of his conduct thoroughly aroused the attention of the people and brought them within the reach of those alarming truths, which like a torrent he poured upon them. The effect was great. They were pricked in the heart, and cried out, 'Men and brethren, what shall we do to be saved?' But his rashness in some degree obscured the glory of his work: but notwithstanding the unpleasant circumstances attending the revival, there were about one huudred persons who to appearance were made partakers of a new life, in consequence of which, about sixty persons were added to the church, soon after the settlement of Dr. Buel."

His proceedings were constantly of the most extravagant character. "Endowed," says Dr. Bacon, "with some sort of eloquence, speaking from a heart all on fire, and accustomed to yield himself without reserve to every enthusiastic impulse, he was able to produce a powerful effect upon minds prepared by constitution or by prejudice to sympathize with him.

"New Haven seems to have been one of the principal theaters of his efforts. The celebrity of his father, and of his more illustrious ancestor, and his numerous connections here, his mother being a native of New Haven, afforded him of course a favorable introduction."* He came to that place during the year 1741, and commenced preaching. He gained considerable influence among many members while occupying the pulpit there. He was censorious and uncharitable in his public addresses, and even publicly declared his belief that the pastor of the church,—the Rev. Mr. Noyes, was an unconverted man. The result of his measures was unhappy upon the church, as many led away by the extraordinary excitement of the times, became dissatisfied with their pastor and their former connection, and withdrew from the old church and effected a new organization, which is now known as the North Church.

In the Summer of the same year, Mr. Davenport visited Stonington, Connecticut. "Here it was said, near one hundred persons were struck under conviction by his first sermon, and about that number converted in eight days, including about twenty Indians; and that many were left under 'hopeful con-

* Historical Discourses, pp. 212–214.

victions.' * From Stonington he visited Westerley, Rhode Island, where, according to the account of the Rev. Joseph Park, then laboring there as a missionary from the London Society, a large number of conversions took place, and among the number were many Indians, who connected themselves with the church, and by their subsequent lives evinced the genuineness of the change that had been wrought in them. †

Throughout the whole country a religious zeal hitherto unknown was spreading, and many were led into various extravagancies. Among these, Mr. Davenport was foremost. He adopted the method of calling in question the piety of ministers, and his measures generally tended to produce disaffection in many churches. He gave himself up to "impulses" and the most enthusiastic proceedings, till carried away with the excitement of the times, he

* The Great Awakening, p. 235.

† Among the Indians converted through Mr. Davenport's labors, was one afterwards known by the name of Rev. Peter John, who was for many years a faithful and successful preacher of the Gospel, among the Shinnecock tribe on Long Island. Through his zeal and piety, several churches of the native Indians were gathered. He died about the beginning of the present century, at the advanced age of 88, and was succeeded in the ministry by his grandson.

seems to have become almost insane, and was so treated by his opposers, although, as has been observed, it would be difficult to tell which was most bewildered, he or the General Assembly of Connecticut, that sought to restrain him, and that, at their late session, had passed a law, in most flagrant violation of the rights of conscience, repressing, by civil penalties, the practices of itinerants and exhorters.

The last and most extravagant of these public proceedings of Mr. Davenport, was at New London, where he was invited in the Spring of 1743, to organize a church. To cure the people there of their idolatrous love of worldly things, he called on them to collect their ornaments, consisting of jewels, rings, &c., and also their clothes, that they might be committed to the flame, and even added to the list a number of books—the works of Beveridge, Flavel, &c.

From this time, Mr. Davenport seems to have withdrawn from his public career, and through the efforts of his personal friends, the Rev. Drs. Williams and Wheelock, of Lebanon —the latter of whom had married his sister— he became convinced that in his course he had committed many errors, and voluntarily published a full and most ingenuous confession of the extravagances into which he had been led. This confession will be found in the Appendix.

Mr. Davenport was formally dismissed from Southold, L. I. in 1746, and afterwards settled at Hopewell, N. J., where he usefully labored for some years, and died in 1755.

TWENTY-FIRST GENERATION.

Issue of Abigail Davenport, (No. 77.)

(Who Married Rev. Stephen Williams, D.D.)

(86.) I. John, born March 8, 1720, and was married January 22, 1747, to Ann Colton, by whom he had nine children, died March, 1772.

(87.) II. Stephen, born January 26, 1722, was graduated at Yale College in 1742, and ordained at Woodstock, Second Society, Nov. 1747. He married, October 18, 1748, Miss Martha Hunt, sister of the Rev. John Williams, of Deerfield, by whom he had six children. He died April 1795, having been in the ministry nearly fifty years.

(88.) III. Eunice, born September 1, 1723, and married May 1, 1753, Mr. William Stebbins, by whom she had one child, Stephen William Stebbins, who was born June 6, 1758, who graduated at Yale College, and was a settled minister at Stratford, for 29 years. He married Miss Eunice Street, daughter of the Rev. Nicholas Street, of East Haven, by whom he had a son, Rev. William Stebbins, who was settled at West Haven, and a daughter, Ann, who is is the present wife of the Rev. Richard S. Storrs, D.D., Braintree, Mass. Mrs. Stebbins died in 1805.

(89.) IV. Warham, born January 7, 1726, graduated at Yale College, in 1745, was ordained at Northford, a parish in Branford, Connecticut, June 30, 1750, and was married Nov. 13, 1752, to Ann Hall, daughter of the Rev. Samuel Hall, of Cheshire. Their children were, Warham, who married Ann Wilford; Samuel Hall, Jonathan Law, Davenport who married Mary Atwater; Ann, who married first the Rev. Jason Atwater, second Rev. Lynde Huntington, and after his death, Rev. Mr. Barker; William Augustus, Lucy, Abigail, who died young; Abigail, who married Stephen Maltby, Eunice K. Cooke, Samuel, and Sarah who married Dr. Pynchon. The Rev. Dr. Williams, father of the above, married again to Mrs. Whiting, widow of Colonel

William Whiting, of New Haven. Dr. Williams died April, 1788. He was in the ministry about forty years, and for many years was a member of the Corporation of Yale College.

(90.) V. Samuel, born May 31, 1729, and was married February 14, 1760, to Miss Lucy Burt, daughter of Deacon Nathaniel Burt. One of their daughters, Sarah, born 1765, was married to the Rev. Richard Salter Storrs, who succeeded her grandfather, Rev. Dr. Williams, as pastor of the Church at Long Meadow. Mr. Storrs was the father of the Rev. Richard S. Storrs, D.D., of Braintree, Mass., who is the father of the Rev. Richard S. Storrs, pastor of the Church of the Pilgrims, Brooklyn, N. Y. One of the sons, Samuel Williams, born Sept. 23, 1774, now (1851) lives on the old place at Long Meadow, formerly occupied by his grandfather, Rev. Dr. Stephen Williams.

(91.) VI. Davenport, born May 11, 1731, and died at Sheffield, Oct. 8, 1758, as he was returning from the army in which he held a lieutenant's commission.

(92.) VII. Martha, born May 1733, and was married January 4, 1759, to Mr. Reynolds, a son of Rev. Peter Reynolds, of Enfield, Ct., by whom she had several children. She was afterwards married to Deacon Ely, of Long Meadow.

(93.) VIII. Nathan, born Oct. 28, 1735, was graduated at Yale College, in 1756, and ordained at Tolland, April 30, 1760. He married, Oct. 20, 1760, Miss Mary Hall, daughter of Captain Eliakim Hall, of Wallingford, Ct. Dr. Williams died, April 15, 1829, in the 94th year of his age, and 66th of his ministry. His wife, Mrs. Mary Williams, died March 9, 1838, aged 95 years and 4 months.

TWENTY-FIRST GENERATION.—Continued.

Issue of John Davenport, (No. 78.)

(94.) I. John Davenport of Stamford, born January 15, 1724. He resided at Davenport Ridge on lands which he inherited from his grandfather, the Rev. John Davenport of Stamford, and which continue in the family to the present day. At the age of eighteen, he became a professor of the Christian religion, by uniting with the church at New Canaan, March 7, 1742. He was married to Deborah Amblar, June 2, 1748, "by Jonathan Maltbie, Esq., one of his Majesty's Justices for the County of Fairfield." Died June 23, 1756, aged 32 years.

(95.) II. Joseph Davenport, born August 9, 1725, and was married to Hannah Amblar, by Abraham Davenport, Esq., July 5, 1753. Mrs. Davenport died March 15, 1769.

(96.) III. Nathan Davenport, born January 15, 1727.

(97.) IV. Gould Davenport, born Sept. 6, 1728, died Jan. 26, 1752.

(98.) V. Deodate Davenport, born Jan. 5, 1730, and was married to Lydia Raymond, by Abraham Davenport, Esq., June 16, 1757. Mrs. Davenport died March 19, 1773. Married again to Mrs. Elizabeth Jones, September 28, 1774. He died March 10, 1808, aged 78 years.

(99.) VI. Martha Davenport born Feb. 20, 1731, and married to John Crissey, by Abraham Davenport, Esq., April 7, 1757.

(100.) VII. Eleazar Davenport, born March 15, 1732.

(101.) VIII. Thaddeus Davenport, born February 3, 1734.

(102.) IX. Elizabeth Davenport, born April 1, 1735.

(103.) X. Silas Davenport, born May 13, 1736, and married to Miss Mary Webb, in Stamford, by Rev. Mr. Wells, March 7, 1765.

(104.) XI. Hezekiah Davenport, born Jan.

14, 1738, and was married at the Cramp Ponds, (Yorktown,) by the Rev. Mr. Sackett, to Ruth Ketchams, Dec. 7, 1763. He was a Lieutenant in the army in the war of the Revolution, and fell at Ridgefield, on his return from the battle of Danbury, in 1777. Mrs. Davenport died in 1775.

(105.) XII. Josiah Davenport, born August 6, 1739.

(106.) XIII. Stephen Davenport born April 9, 1741.*

TWENTY-FIRST GENERATION.—Continued.

Issue of Sarah Davenport, (No. 80.)

(Who Married Rev. Eleazar Wheelock, D.D.†)

(107.) I. Theodora, who married Alexander Phelps, of Hebron, Connecticut, afterwards of Oxford, N. H., whose son Rev. Davenport Phelps, an Episcopal minister, died at Pultneyville, N. Y., 1818, aged 58 years.

(108.) II. Ruth, who married Rev. William Patten, D.D., of Halifax, Mass.

The following notice of Mrs. Patten and her descendants, is principally drawn from her me-

* Omitted XIV., Sarah Davenport.

† The children by a former husband are given under No. 80.

moir written by her son, the Rev. William Patten, D.D., of Hartford, Ct.

Ruth Wheelock, daughter of the above-mentioned Sarah, and granddaughter of the Rev. John Davenport, of Stamford, Connecticut, was born March 4, 1740. When young, she was an intelligent and docile child, and great attention was paid to her education. Her mind early and rapidly matured. At the age ot eighteen, she was considered one of the most accomplished and interesting of young women. At this early age, (June 9, 1758,) she became the wife of the Rev. William Patten, pastor of a church in Halifax, Plymouth County, Mass.

[Mr. Patten's early developments were not less remarkable than those of his wife. When five years of age, he is said to have composed a sermon on the first verse in the Bible, the sentiments and connection of which excited the surprise of his friends. He entered Harvard College, when about twelve years of age, graduated at sixteen; taught school and studied Theology under Rev. Mr. Havens of Dedham, Massachusetts; was licensed to preach, engaged to supply the pulpit in Halifax, for two or three Sabbaths, and before that time expired, received a unanimous call to settle over them as a pastor, and was installed Feb. 2, 1757, seven weeks before he was nineteen years of age, and married Ruth Wheelock, before he had reached the age of twenty years. Dr. Patten died January 16, 1775, in the 37th year of his age.]

Mrs. Patten survived her husband for a long time, and lived an example of devoted piety, usefully engaging herself in the work of her Master. She died December 5, 1831, aged 91 years and 9 months, having been a professor of the faith of the Gospel, for 77 years. Their son, Rev. William Patten, graduated at Harvard College, in 1780, and received the honorary degree of D.D., at Brown University. He was settled in the ministry at Newport, R. I., in 1786, where he preached about 48 years. He married Hannah Hurlbut, of New London. They had several children, one of whom is William Patten, Esq., a lawyer of Providence, R. I. Ruth W. who married Frederick W. Hotchkiss, of Hartford. Joseph, a lawyer in New York. Mary Ann, who married C. S. Halsted, of Brooklyn, N. Y. George W. a Captain in the U. S. Army; and Floride.

(109.) III. Rev. Ralph, who graduated at Yale College in 1765, and was an assistant of his father, but in consequence of feeble health was disqualified from becoming a pastor, and finally for any useful labors.*

TWENTY-FIRST GENERATION.—Continued.

Issue of Dea. Deodate Davenport, (No. 82.)

(110.) I. Sarah Davenport, of East Haven, born July 7, 1731; who married John Mix.

(111.) II. Martha Davenport, born May 26, 1733, and was married to Gold S. Silliman, of Fairfield, by whom she had one son, William, who married a daughter of Dr. Allen, and afterwards a Miss Jennings. [Mr. Silliman

* There were two or three other children who died young.

By a subsequent marriage, Dr. Wheelock had several children, one of whom, Hon. John Wheelock, LL. D., was born at Lebanon, Ct., January 28, 1754, entered Yale College, but graduated with the first class of four persons, at Dartmouth, in 1771. He succeeded his father as President of Dartmouth College, in 1779, which office he held for 36 years. He married Maria, the daughter of Gov. Suhm, of St. Thomas, whose only daughter, Maria Malleville, married the Rev. William Allen, D.D., of Northampton, Mass., formerly President of Bowdoin College, and author of the American Biographical Dictionary. Two other daughters of Dr. Wheelock married Messrs. Woodward and Ripley, both Professors in Dartmouth College.

graduated at Yale College in 1752. He was a General in the army in the war of the Revolution, and was taken by the British, just before the burning of Fairfield, and carried a prisoner to Long Island. His second wife was Mrs. Rebecca Noyes, (widow of the Rev. Joseph Noyes,) by whom he was the father of Mr. Gold S. Silliman, of Brooklyn, N. Y., and also of Professor Benjamin Silliman, M.D., LL.D. of Yale College.]

(112.) III. William Davenport, born in 1734, and died Sept. 17, 1742.

(113.) IV. John Davenport of East Haven, born 1738, and was married to Anna Pierpont, in 1780, and afterwards to Mrs. Phebe Todd, but had no children. Died January 9, 1820, aged 82 years.

(114.) V. Deacon Samuel Davenport of East Haven, born 1740, and was married in 1766, to Mary Street. He died July 9, 1810. Mrs. Davenport died December 21, 1803, aged 66 years.

(115.) VI. Roswell Davenport, born 1742, died September 19, 1749.

(116.) VII. Lydia Davenport, born 1746, married Samuel Holt.

TWENTY-FIRST GENERATION.—CONTINUED.

Issue of Hon. Abraham Davenport, (No. 84.)

(117.) I. Hon. John Davenport of Stamford, born Jan. 16, 1752, and graduated at Yale College in 1770. He was married to Mary Silvester Wells, daughter of the Rev. Dr. Noah Wells, by Abraham Davenport, May 7, 1780. He was Major of the militia in this section of the State, in the war of the Revolution. In 1799, he was chosen a Representative Member of the American Congress, to fill the vacancy occasioned by the death of his younger brother, (Hon. James Davenport,) of which he continued for 18 years a member, during the Presidency of the elder Adams, and also of Presidents Jefferson and Monroe. He was punctually at his post from the opening to the adjournment of each session of Congress, and answered to his name when called to vote on all subjects. Having declined a re-election in 1817, he spent the remainder of his days in the bosom of his family. He died in Christian peace, Nov. 28, 1830. His wife survived him, and died in Brooklyn, N. Y., June 28, 1847, at the advanced age of 93 years.

(118.) II. Abraham Davenport, born Oct. 21, 1753, died October 25, 1754.

(119.) III. Elizabeth Davenport, born Sept. 16, 1756, and was married by the Rev. Dr. Wells, to James Cogswell, M.D., of Preston, August 8, 1776. They had one daughter, Alice, who became the wife of the Rev. Samuel Fisher, D.D., of Greenbush, N. Y., who is the father of the Rev. Samuel Ware Fisher, who recently succeeded the Rev. Dr. Beecher, as pastor of the 2d Presbyterian Church, Cincinnati, Ohio.

"Elizabeth, wife of James Cogswell, M. D., departed this life, Nov. 15, 1779.*

* Dr. Cogswell was the son of Rev. James Cogswell, D.D., of Hartford, Ct., who was born Jan. 6, 1720, and died Jan. 2, 1807, having been for sixty years a laborious and faithful minister of the Gospel. He had also a brother, Mason F. Cogswell, M.D., who died in 1830, aged 69 years, who had a daughter named Alice, who though de. prived of hearing and speech, was distinguished for her intellectual attainments and loveliness of character. She died December 30, 1830, aged 25 years. The American Asylum for the Deaf and Dumb at Hartford, under Providence, owes its origin to the father's tenderness towards his child, and his sympathy for her fellow-sufferers, and will long stand an enduring monument to his memory.—*Connecticut Historical Collections.*

Dr. James Cogswell afterwards married Mrs. Abigail

(120.) IV. Hon. James Davenport, born October 12, 1758, and graduated at Yale College in 1779. He was married to Abigail Fitch, by Abraham Davenport, Esquire, May 7, 1780. Mrs. D. died Nov. 1782, aged 22 years. Married second, to Mehitabel Coggshall, by the Rev. William Lockwood, of Milford, Ct., Nov. 6, 1790. He was a member of the State Legislature, and Judge of the Court of Common Pleas. In 1796, he was chosen a Representative Member of the American Congress, during the Presidency of General Washington. He died suddenly, August 3, 1797. He was a member of the Corporation of Yale College from 1793 to the time of his death.

Of Mr. Davenport, President Dwight, in his Travels, vol. iii. p. 500, says: "Few persons in this country have been more, or more deservedly, esteemed than the Hon. James Davenport. His mind was of a structure almost singular. An infirm constitution precluded him to a considerable extent, from laborious study, during his early years; and, indeed, throughout most of his life. Yet an unwearied attention to useful objects, a critical observa-

Loyd, and had several children, James, John, Sarah, and Harriet.

tion of everything important which fell under his eye, and a strong attachment to intelligent conversation, enabled him by the aid of a discernment almost intuitive, to accumulate a rich fund of valuable knowledge. With respect to conversation he was peculiar. The company of intelligent persons he sought with the same eagerness and constancy, as the student his books. Here he always started topics of investigation, fitted to improve the mind, as well as to please; and in this way, gathered knowledge with the industry, and success, with which the bee makes every flower increase the treasures of its hive. I never knew the value of intelligent conversation, and the extent of the contributions, which it is capable of furnishing to the stock of knowledge possessed by an individual, exhibited more clearly, and decisively, than in his example. At the same time, his own conversation was so agreeable, and intelligent, and his manners so engaging, that his company was coveted by all his numerous acquaintance. His life, also, was without a stain; and on his integrity, candor, and justice, his countrymen placed an absolute reliance. With these qualifications, it will not be a matter of wonder, that at an early period of his life, he was employed by the public in an almost continual succession of public business; or that he executed every commission of this nature honorably to himself, and usefully to his country. He died in the thirty-ninth year of his age, of a paralytic stroke, brought on by a long continued, and very severe, chronic rheumatism. Few persons have been more universally, or deeply, lamented."

(121.) V. Huntington Davenport, born April 18, 1761, and "departed this life on the evening following the 22d of October, 1769."

TWENTY-FIRST GENERATION.—Continued.

Issue of Rev. James Davenport, (No. 85.)

(122.) I. Rev. John Davenport, born at Freehold, N. J., August 11, 1752, and graduated at Princeton College in 1769, and received the honorary degree of A.M., at Yale College in 1785. He studied Theology with Drs. Bellamy and Buel, and was ordained at Mattatuck, a parish in the town of Southold, L. I., June 4, 1775, and served the congregation there as a stated supply for two years. He was an amiable and excellent man, and labored for some time in different parts of the Island,

and was dismissed from the Presbytery of Suffolk, April 12, 1786. While at Mattatuck, he was married to Mrs. Elizabeth Barker, the widow of his predecessor, the Rev. Nathaniel Barker, by the Rev. John Storrs, Dec. 18, 1775, with whom, notwithstanding the great disparity in their ages, he lived happily for many years. He was the first minister upon Long Island, that refused to administer baptism upon the indulgent plan. He was settled at Bedford, N. Y., and afterwards at Deerfield, N. J., August 12, 1795, and dismissed from feeble health in 1805. In 1809 he returned to the State of New York, and died at Lysander, July 13, 1825. He had no children.—*Prime's His. L. I., Allen's Bio. Dic.*

(123.) II. James Davenport. No children.

(124.) III. Elizabeth Davenport, married a Mr. Kelsey, of Princeton, but had no children.

Issue of John Davenport, (No. 94.)

TWENTY-SECOND GENERATION.

(125.) I. Dea. John Davenport, born in Stamford, May 24, 1749, and was married by the Rev. Dr. Wells, June 4, 1772, to Prudence Bell, daughter of Jesse Bell, of Stamford.*

* Another daughter of Mr. Bell married Mr. Water-

She died, December 23, 1794, aged 43 years. Married 2d, to Sarah Gaylord, daughter of the Rev. William Gaylord, of Wilton, August, 1795. Mr. Davenport was one of the early members of the church organized in North Stamford, of which he was an esteemed officer at the time of his death, which occurred Feb. 6, 1820. Mrs. D. survived him, and died Feb. 11, 1846, aged 87 years.

(126.) II. Sarah Davenport, born Jan. 7, 1751, and was married by the Rev. Dr. Wells, to Monmouth Lounsbury, of Stamford, April 16, 1770, died about 1819.

(127.) III. Stephen Davenport, born March 9, 1752, was a school-teacher. Not married. Died about 1777.

(128.) IV. Rhoda Davenport, born Jan. 4, 1754, and was married to Thaddeus Huested, Nov. 19, 1775.

bury, the father of Gideon Waterbury, of New York, who was the father of the Rev. J. B. Waterbury, D.D., of Boston. One of Dr. Waterbury's sisters, Harriet, married the Rev. John Scudder, M.D., and another, Catharine, became the wife of the Rev. Myron Winslow, both Missionaries at Madras, in India.

TWENTY-SECOND GENERATION.—CONTINUED.

Issue of Joseph Davenport, (No. 95.)

(129.) I. Hannah Davenport, born May 19, 1755.

(130.) II. Deborah Davenport, born Jan. 30, 1757.

(131.) III. Martha Davenport, born Oct. 18, 1759. Married Mr. Scofield.

(132.) IV. Gould Davenport, born Oct. 5, 1762, was a school-teacher. Married and removed to Ohio.

(133.) V. Joseph Davenport, born March 28, 1765, died Oct. 28, 1766.

Issue of Deodate Davenport, (No. 98.)

(134.) I. Lydia Davenport, born April 3, 1758. Married Peter Bishop. Died Jan. 7, 1837, in the 80th year of her age.

(135.) II. Sarah Davenport, born Feb. 13, 1760. Married David Webb, of Ohio, by whom she had a son Nathan, and others.

(136.) III. Samuel Davenport, born April 3, 1762, and died December 30, 1775.

(137.) IV. Mary Davenport, born June 2,

1764, and was married to Dea. Isaac Benedict,* of New Canaan, August 19, 1794; by whom she had one child, Lorana, born December 7, 1795, who married Emory Whitlock.

[Dea. Isaac Benedict held several public offices in the community where he resided, and was for some time a soldier in the war of the Revolution. He died May 17, 1841, in the 90th year of his age. A sermon was delivered on the occasion of his death, by the Rev. T. Smith, from Gen. 35: 29. "And Isaac gave up the ghost and died, and was gathered into his people, being old and full of days."†]

* Dea. Benedict's first wife was Jane Raymond, by whom he had Isaac, who married Fanny Hopkins; Gould married Betsey Foot; Samuel R. (died young); Abigail married William Davenport; Obadiah married Clarissa Bingham; Lewis married Mary Scribner; Lorana (died young); and Rev. Amzi who graduated at Yale College, in 1814, and married Martha, daughter of General Solomon Cowles, of Farmington.

† Dea. Benedict was descended from Thomas Benedict, who came from Nottinghamshire, England, to Massachusetts, in 1638, and who finally settled with his family in Norwalk, Connecticut in 1665. All his direct ancestors, for one hundred and fifty years, held the office of Deacon in the Church of Norwalk.

His father was Dea. Nathaniel Benedict of Norwalk, who died in 1806, in the 90th year of his age, and whose

(138.) V. Deodate Davenport of Stamford, born June 2, 1766, and married to Abigail Handford, Sept. 25, 1788. Died Oct. 29, 1839. Mrs. D. died Sept. 6, 1848, in her 80th year.

character is thus described in an article written by the Hon. Roger Minot Sherman, and published in a newspaper at the time of his death:

"Dea. Nathaniel Benedict died in Norwalk, on the morning of the 2d of April, 1806, after a shock of the palsy, with which he lingered about twelve days, in the 90th year of his age. On the 3d, his remains were followed to the grave by a large concourse of friends and relatives, among whom were his twelve surviving children, and many of his more remote posterity. He has left ninety-one grandchildren, and eighty-eight great-grandchildren, the whole number of his descendants now living, being 191.

"For about thirty-two years he sustained the office of Deacon of the First Congregational Church in that town. Deacon Benedict was one of those venerable personages by whom what remains of the pious habits of our forefathers have been transmitted to the present generation. His long life has been eminently exemplary, and years to come will feel its happy influence. Every morning and evening witnessed his devotions. His Sabbaths were faithfully appropriated to public worship and religious family instructions. An amiable, cheerful disposition, a sound mind improved by a good degree of reading and much reflection, and adorned with a bright constellation of Christian graces, comprised his character. At his funeral, an appropriate sermon was delivered by the Rev. Dr. Burnett, from Prov. xiv. 32: 'The wicked is driven away in his wickedness; *but the righteous hath hope in his death.*'"

(139.) VI. Nathan Davenport, born Aug. 8, 1768, and married to Polly Smith, Sept. 14, 1800. Died May 18, 1817.

(140.) VII. John Davenport, born Jan. 11, 1771, and married Elizabeth Keeler, of Wilton, April 2, 1795. He removed to Charlton, N. Y., where he died, Jan. 4, 1834.

(141.) VIII. Elizabeth Davenport, born March 20, 1773, and died May 30, 1792.

(142.) IX. Abigail Davenport, born July 28, 1775. Married to Lebbeus Reed, Oct. 1795. Mr. Reed died at Spencertown, N. Y., April 22, 1851.

(143.) X. Betsey Davenport, born Oct. 12, 1777. Married Charles Knapp. Died July 28, 1825.

(144.) XI. Ann Davenport, born Nov. 14, 1779. Married Thomas Warren. Died Sept. 22, 1831.

(145.) XII. Clarissa Davenport, born April 25, 1782. Married to Samuel Raymond, June 1804. (There were two other children who died in infancy.)

TWENTY-SECOND GENERATION.—CONTINUED.

Issue of Silas Davenport, (No. 103.)

(146.) I. Nancy Davenport, born Dec. 21, 1765, and married to David Maltby, of Stamford, by Hon. James Davenport, Nov. 19, 1786. Died in 1815.

(147.) II. Abraham Davenport of Stamford, born October 30, 1767, and married to Polly Brown, October 26, 1793. Died in 1845.

(148.) III. Mary Davenport, born March 17, 1770. Died March 21, 1848.

(149.) IV. Ebenezer Davenport, born May 9, 1773. Married Jerusha Aulstine. Died at Flatbush, N. Y., 1833. No issue.

(150.) V. Rufus Davenport of New York, born in Stamford, October 18, 1775, and married to Antoinette Cable, October 23, 1827. Mrs. Davenport died April 28, 1832.

(151.) VI. Charles Webb Davenport, born February 9, 1778. Married Amelia Fitch. Died in Illinois in 1843.

(152.) VII. Catharine Davenport, born February 24, 1783. Married James Palmer. Died in 1813.

TWENTY-SECOND GENERATION.—CONTINUED.

Issue of Lieut. Hezekiah Davenport, (*No.* 104.)

(153.) I. Pruella Davenport, born August 25, 1764. Married a Mr. Dikem. Died February 28, 1809.

(154.) II. Martha Davenport, born 1766. Died November 3, 1807.

(155.) III. Abigail Davenport, born 1768. Died November 24, 1798.

(156.) IV. William Davenport, born in Stamford, September 17, 1770. Married, 1st, by the Rev. Amzi Lewis, to Theodora Davenport, November 17, 1799. Mrs. Davenport died October 29, 1809. Married, 2d, to Nancy Hoyt, June 17, 1810. She died September 28, 1838. Married, 3d, by the Rev. Dr. Todd, of Stamford, to Anna Tuttle, September 26, 1840. Mr. Davenport died November 13, 1850, aged 80 years.

(157.) V. Elizabeth Davenport, died young.

(158.) VI. James Davenport, died young.

(159.) VII. Isaac Davenport, died young.

TWENTY-SECOND GENERATION.—CONTINUED.

Issue of Dea. Samuel Davenport, (No. 114.)

(160.) I. Sarah Davenport, born in East Haven, January 31, 1767. Married Ira Smith, in 1784.

(161.) II. Roswell Davenport, born in East Haven, April 28, 1768, and married to Esther Heminway, 1793. Resides at Erie, Pa.

(162.) III. Hezekiah Davenport, born in East Haven, December 11, 1769, and married Philena Pierpont. Mrs. Davenport died October 29, 1827.

(163.) IV. Martha Davenport, born December 16, 1771. Married to Eli Potter, of East Haven, in 1793. Died in 1841.

(164.) V. Mary Davenport, born December 16, 1771. Married to John Woodward, of East Haven, in 1794. He died August 26, 1819.

(165.) VI. Street Davenport, born in East Haven, January 28, 1775, and married to Nancy Maria Shults, April 19, 1827. Resides at Townsend, Ohio.

TWENTY-SECOND GENERATION.—Continued.

Issue of Major John Davenport, (No. 117.)

(166.) I. Elizabeth Huntington Davenport, born March 4, 1781. Married to the Hon. Peter W. Radcliffe (Judge) of Brooklyn, N. Y., October 1, 1799. Died May 28, 1850. No issue.

(167.) II. John Alfred Davenport of Brooklyn, N. Y., born in Stamford, June 24, 1783. Graduated at Yale College in 1802. Married Eliza M. Wheeler, February 10, 1806.

(168.) III. Mary Wells Davenport, born in Stamford, September 12, 1785, and married to James Boorman, of New York, November 10, 1810.

(169.) IV. Theodosia Davenport, born Jan. 31, 1789. Died February 8, 1810.

(170.) V. Dea. Theodore Davenport of Stamford, born January 26, 1792, and married by the Rev. Dr. Spring, to Harriet Grant Chesebrough, of New York, February 25, 1834.

(171.) VI, Rebecca Ann Davenport, born July 7, 1795. Died January 15, 1817.

(172.) VII. Matilda Davenport, born in Stamford, April 17, 1798, and married to the

Rev. Peter Lockwood, now of Binghamton, N. Y.*

TWENTY-SECOND GENERATION.—CONTINUED.

Issue of Hon. James Davenport, (*No.* 120.)

(173.) I. Betsey Coggshall Davenport, born January 27, 1781, and married to Charles W. Apthorp, of Boston.

(174.) II. Abigail Fitch Davenport, born November 17, 1791. Married to Rev. Philip Melancthon Whelpley, Pastor of the First Presbyterian Church, New York.

[Rev. Mr. Whelpley was the son of the Rev. Samuel Whelpley, formerly of Berkshire county, Massachusetts, but subsequently of New York. At about the age of eighteen, he publicly professed his faith in Christ by uniting with the Presbyterian Church in Newark, New Jersey, under the pastoral charge of Rev. Dr. Richards. Having pursued a course of study with his father, he was licensed to preach by the Presbytery of New Jersey, at the age of nineteen. Before he was twenty years of age, he was chosen Pastor of the First Presbyterian Church in New York.

* Rev. Mr. Lockwood graduated at Yale College in 1817.

"Mr. Whelpley possessed pulpit qualifications of the highest order. He was gifted with a very pleasing countenance, aspect, and figure; his voice was sonorous, clear, and flexible in its tones, his gesture was simple, grave, and appropriate. Indeed it is not easy to conceive of one naturally better qualified for the pulpit orator. While he did not discountenance these advantages by neglect, his heart was too truly touched by the love of souls to value them if separated from a simple declaration of the glorious Gospel of God our Savior; but for mere oratory in the pulpit none could feel more entire compassion than he."* In the month of March, 1824, he suddenly ruptured a blood vessel, and the hemorrhage was so great that his life was considered in imminent danger; from this he but partially recovered till on the 17th of the following July (1824), he was called from a station of eminent usefulness to his crown and reward in Heaven. He died in the 30th year of his age.]

(175.) III. Mary Ann Davenport, born in Stamford, November 11, 1793, and was married

* Memoirs of the Rev. Mr. Bruen, p. 181.

to the Rev. Matthias Bruen of New York, Jan. 2, 1823.

[The Rev. Mr. Bruen was descended from John Bruen, Esquire, of Bruen Stapleford, (near the original seat of the Davenports,) in the County of Chester, one of whose sons, Obadiah Bruen, was among the earliest Puritan emigrants to New England, his family having been much persecuted in the reign of Charles I., for their friendship to the celebrated Mr. Prynne, at the time of his imprisonment in the castle of Chester. He was a patentee of the Colony of Connecticut, from Charles II. in 1662, and was Recorder of New London until the year 1667, when he, with the Rev. Abraham Pierson of Branford, bought of the Indians for themselves and their associates, the now flourishing city of Newark, then called New-work, in New Jersey. In this place his descendants have since continued to reside.

The Rev. Mr. Bruen, whose father was Matthias Bruen, was born in Newark, N. J., April 11, 1793. He graduated at Columbia College in 1812, soon after which he commenced the study of Theology, with Dr. John M. Mason, of New York. In 1816, he travelled in Europe with his distinguished preceptor. In the beginning of 1819, being invited to preach in the American Chapel of the Oratoire at Paris, he was ordained in London, and then passed six months in Paris.

In 1822, he was employed as a missionary in the city of New York, but refused to receive any compensation. During his labours in New York, he collected the Bleecker Street Congregation. Of this people he became the stated pastor, and continued such till his death, Sept. 6, 1829, aged 36 years.

Mr. Bruen engaged earnestly in various benevolent institutions. He was agent and corresponding secretary of the Domestic Missionary Society, and when it was changed into the American Home Missionary Society, he still assisted by his counsels. Bible, Sabbath-School, Tract, and Foreign Mission Societies, engaged his efforts, and in the Greek cause he cheerfully co-operated. He was accomplished in manners, in literature, and in the knowledge of mankind. Though possessed of eminent qualifications, he felt it his highest honor to lay all his distinctions at his Master's feet, and devote his life to the glory of God and the good of mankind.

He published a Sermon at Paris on the death

of a young lady from New York, and sketches of Italy.—*Memoirs of Bruen and Am. Bio. Dictionary.*]

Mrs. Bruen now resides at Newport, R. I.*

(176.) IV. Frances Louisa Davenport, born November 10, 1795, and married the Rev. Thomas H. Skinner, D.D., formerly pastor of the Mercer Street Presbyterian Church, New York, and now Professor of Pastoral Theology in the Union Theological Seminary in the same city.

TWENTY-THIRD GENERATION.

Issue of Dea. John Davenport, (No. 125.)

(177.) I. John Davenport, born October 27, 1773, and was killed by a fall from a horse, at the age of 11 years.

(178.) II. Ralph Davenport, born 1775, died 1779.

(179.) III. Theodora Davenport, born Sept. 27, 1779, and married to William Davenport,

* Mrs. Bruen's present residence at Newport stands upon the site occupied by her maternal ancestors, two hundred years ago—her mother being a direct descendant of the Hon. John Coggshall, who was first President of the Colony of Rhode Island in 1647, under the patent granted to Roger Williams, by the Earl of Warwick.

son of Lieutenant Hezekiah, Nov. 17, 1799. Died Oct. 29, 1809.

(180.) IV. William Davenport of New Canaan, born in Stamford, March 25, 1781, and was married by the Rev. Justus Mitchell, to Abigail Benedict, daughter of Dea. Isaac Benedict, Sept. 12, 1802. She died Oct. 9, 1839, aged 59 years.

Mrs. Davenport was a woman of much native energy, blended with great mildness and gentleness of character. Her piety was of a cheerful cast, lightening every burden of life, sustaining the heart under trial, sanctifying affliction, and rendering the future ever bright and joyous through the power of divine faith and love. Precluded by feeble health for the most part of her life from public efforts of charity, her benevolence often exhibited itself in plans of doing good to those around her and who came under her immediate influence. But it was in the private circle of *home* that her virtues shone most brightly, and where the happy influence of her serene and cheerful piety was most apparent. With a strong faith in the promises of God to parental faithfulness, she labored diligently and prayerfully to in spire her children with honorable and right impulses, and to train them up for usefulness and for heaven.

The closing scene of her life showed most strikingly the power of Divine grace to impart peace and joy to the dying believer. After weeks of painful suffering, which she bore with Christian resignation, she sank to rest while reclining in the arms of the writer. To her may aptly be applied the lines of one of our sweetest female poets :

> " And thus she stood,
> Clad in that panoply of faith and prayer,
> Serenely on the verge of three score years—
> Prompt at her Master's call, and ripe for heaven:
> Then leaning on the breast of filial love
> Took her last peaceful sleep.
> So beautiful,
> The pure in heart go forth to meet their God."

Mr. Davenport was again married July 28, 1842, to Mrs. Catharine M. Isaacs, of Brooklyn, N. Y., in which place he now resides.

(181.) V. Sarah Davenport, born March 5, 1783, and married to Jonathan Bates, of Darien, June 24, 1804. She died February 17, 1839.

(182.) VI. James Davenport of North Stamford, born February 2, 1787, and married to Martha Warren, February 6, 1810. Died Oct. 27, 1845.

(183.) VII. Julia Ann Davenport, born Nov. 30, 1794, and married to Jotham Hoyt, Jan. 4, 1817.

(184.) VIII. John Gaylord Davenport, born March 6, 1799, died April 1, 1799.

(185.) IX. Elizabeth Davenport, born Oct. 4, 1802, died April 12, 1818.

TWENTY-THIRD GENERATION.—Continued.

Issue of Sarah Davenport, (No. 126.)

(Who Married Monmouth Lounsbury.)

(186.) I. Betsey.
(187.) II. Sally.
(188.) III. William.
(189.) IV. Monmouth.
(190.) V. Nancy.
(191.) VI. Polly.
(192.) VII. Jemima.
(193.) VIII. Prudence.
(194.) IX. Deborah.
(195.) X. Tamor.
(196.) XI. John Davenport.

Issue of Rhoda Davenport, (No. 128.)

(Who Married Thaddeus Huested.)

(197.) I. Shadrach.
(198.) II. Deborah.
(199.) III. Catharine.

TWENTY-THIRD GENERATION.—CONTINUED.

Issue of Lydia Davenport, (No. 134.)

(Who Married Peter Bishop.)

(200.) I. Samuel, born Nov. 21, 1782.
(201.) II. Polly, born Jan. 23, 1785.
(202.) III. Betsey, born March 26, 1787.
(203.) IV. David, born March 6, 1790.
(204.) V. Elsa, born Feb. 11, 1795.

TWENTY-THIRD GENERATION.—CONTINUED.

Issue of Deodate Davenport, (No. 138.)

(205.) I. Samuel Davenport of Wilton, born July 9, 1789. Married Susan Betts, Oct. 30, 1811.

(206.) II. Handford Davenport, of New Canaan, born March 10, 1791, and married by the Rev. William Bonney, to Hannah St. John, daughter of Col. Enoch St. John, Sept. 10, 1817.

(207.) III. Polly Davenport, born Aug. 31, 1793. Died March 18, 1796.

(208.) IV. Polly Davenport, born June 19, 1796. Married to Amzi Scofield, Nov. 25, 1819.

(209.) V. Abigail Davenport, born May 21, 1798. Died Nov. 1, 1825.

(210.) VI. Thaddeus Davenport of North

Stamford, born April 2, 1800. Married Pelinda Lyon, Feb. 9, 1831.

(211.) VII. Joseph Davenport of North Stamford, born Jan. 3, 1803. Married to Julia Young, Sept. 15, 1824.

(212.) VIII. Darius Davenport of North Stamford, born Dec. 8, 1805. Married to Susan Betts, of Wilton, Jan. 9, 1832.

(213.) IX. William Henry Davenport of Brooklyn, N. Y., born Oct. 27, 1807, and married to Ellen Maria Burdett, May 6, 1835. Mrs. D. died Oct. 1, 1846, aged 29, and was buried at Greenwood Cemetery, Brooklyn, N. Y.

TWENTY-THIRD GENERATION.—Continued.

Issue of Nathan Davenport, (*No.* 139.)

(214.) I. George A. Davenport of Wilton, born Jan. 31, 1808, and married to Mary Sturges. Is Judge of the Probate of Norwalk.

(215.) II. James Smith Davenport of Wilton, born Sept. 5, 1811. Married Mary Olmstead, April 6, 1840.

(216.) III. Mary Ann Davenport, born Dec. 16, 1813. Married to Matthew Smith, Oct. 8, 1833. Mr. S. died July 1, 1841, in the 32d year of his age.

Issue of John Davenport, (No. 140.)

(217.) I. Elizabeth Davenport, born Sept. 7, 1796, and married to William Wheeler, March 5, 1822.

(218.) II. Sally Davenport, born Dec. 27, 1799, and was married to Jeremiah Ward, March 20, 1824. Died August 19, 1826.

(219.) III. Lewis Davenport, born Sept. 18, 1803, and married to Griswold Maxwell, Jan. 20, 1826.

(220.) Amzi Davenport of Charlton, N. Y., born April 9, 1807, and was married to Mary E. Hall, April 9, 1833. Mrs. D. died Feb. 7, 1842. Married, 2d, to Thirza Redfield, Sept. 15, 1842.

TWENTY-THIRD GENERATION.—Continued.

Issue of Abigail Davenport, (No. 142.)

(Who Married Lebbeus Reed.)

(221.) I. Darius.

(222.) II. Eliza.

(223.) III. William.

Issue of Betsey Davenport, (No. 143.)

(Who Married Charles Knapp.)

(224.) I. Samuel, married Eliza Burchard.

(225.) II. Eliza, married Isaac Sterling.

(226.) III. Betsey.

Issue of Ann Davenport, (No. 144.)

(Who Married Thomas Warren.)

(227.) I. Ephraim Chauncey, born March 13, 1808. Married Elmira Burr, Louisa Taylor, and Julia B. Warner.

(228.) II. Joseph Davenport, born Oct. 2, 1809. Married Maria Jesup.

(229.) III. John, born Feb. 19, 1813. Married Caroline Hoyt.

(230.) IV. Elizabeth, born May 16, 1818. Married Charles Olmstead.

TWENTY-THIRD GENERATION.—Continued.

Issue of Clarissa Davenport, (No. 145.)

(Who Married Samuel Raymond.)

(231.) I. Ann, born Feb. 12, 1805. Married Charles Raymond, of Norwalk.

(232.) II. Clarissa, born March 26, 1806. Married Nathan Comstock, of Wilton.

(233.) III. Sally, born Nov. 25, 1807. Married John Webb, of Stamford.

(234.) IV. John, born July 17, 1809. Married Elisha Raymond, of Norwalk.

(235.) V. Harriet, born Nov. 4, 1812.

(236.) VI. William, born July 26, 1814. Married Joanna Morton.

Issue of Nancy Davenport, (No. 146.)

(Who Married David Maltby.)

(237.) I. William Davenport.
(238.) II. Mary Catharine.
(239.) III. James Rufus.
(240.) IV. John Robert.
(241.) V. Rev. Ebenezer Davenport.
(242.) VI. Albert Silvester.

TWENTY-THIRD GENERATION.—CONTINUED.

Issue of Abraham Davenport, (No. 147.)

(243.) I. Julia Davenport, born June 5, 1795, and married to John Burrall, of Norwalk, by whom she had one son, Samuel Davenport Burrall, born Sept. 16, 1834.

(244.) II. James Silas Davenport, born November 3, 1797, and died 1846.

(245.) III. Samuel Abraham Davenport, born Dec. 24, 1799, and died Dec. 28, 1821.

(246.) IV. Elizabeth Davenport, born Jan. 5, 1802, and married Charles Burrall, of New York. She died Dec. 3, 1826.

(247.) V. Mary Davenport, born March 14, 1804.

(248.) VI. Harriet Davenport, born Feb. 28, 1806. Died Feb. 6, 1827.

(249.) VII. Ebenezer Charles Davenport,

born October 9, 1809. Died September 15, 1841.

(250.) VIII. Catharine Brown Davenport, born Jan. 6, 1812. Died Jan. 25, 1814.

(251.) IX. William B. Davenport, born June 27, 1820. Married Frances Potter, of Providence, R. I. by whom he had one son, William A. Brown Davenport, born Feb. 24, 1847.

Issue of Rufus Davenport, (No. 150.)

(252.) I. Rufus C. Davenport, born Sept. 11, 1828. Died Jan. 9, 1832.

(253.) II. George F. Davenport, born Feb. 26, 1830, and graduated at the University of New York, in 1847. Is now a lawyer in New York.

(254.) Antoinette Cable Davenport, born Jan. 4, 1832. Died Aug. 16, 1832.

TWENTY-THIRD GENERATION.—Continued.

Issue of Charles Webb Davenport, (No. 151.)

(255.) I. Charles Webb Davenport of Cambridge, Illinois, born March 22, 1818, and married to Electa Moore, May 21, 1843.

(256.) II. Thomas Fitch Davenport, of Illinois, born Feb. 6, 1820, and married to Elizabeth Lloyd, June 22, 1848.

(257.) III. Amelia Lewis Davenport, born May 18, 1822, and married to Mahlon Lloyd, Dec. 30, 1844.

(258.) IV. Mary Elizabeth Davenport, born Dec. 16, 1824, and married to J. Hannaman, Dec. 11, 1844.

(259.) V. Rufus Adolphus Davenport, born Jan 23, 1826. Died Sept. 5, 1833.

(260.) VI. Theodore Silas Davenport, born March 29, 1830.

(261.) VII. Edward Adolphus Davenport, born April 11, 1833.

Issue of Catharine Davenport, (No. 152.)
(Who Married James Palmer.)

(262.) I. James, born July 18, 1812, who was adopted by his uncle Eleazar Davenport, and bears the name of James Davenport. He married Catharine Eliza Bennett, Oct. 23, 1843.

TWENTY-THIRD GENERATION.—Continued.

Issue of William Davenport, (No. 156.)

(263.) I. Hezekiah Ralsea Davenport of Brooklyn, N. Y., born in Stamford, Feb. 24, 1801, and was married by the Rev. Dr. Milnor, of New York, to Mary Rapelyea, Sept. 22, 1834.

(264.) II. Mary Ann Davenport, born in

Stamford, April 23, 1803, and married by Rev. Henry Fuller, to Ralph Hoyt, Feb. 28, 1827. Mr. H. died Oct. 28, 1839.

(265.) III. Adolphus Davenport, born Feb. 9, 1805. Died Oct. 15, 1826.

(266.) IV. Silas Davenport of Brooklyn, N. Y., born March 16, 1811, in Stamford, and married in New Haven, by the Rev. Mr. Cleveland, to Betsey Ann St. John, March 28, 1836.

(267.) V. William Davenport of North Stamford, born April 22, 1813, and married to Clarissa Rockwell, Feb. 3, 1834.

(268.) VI. Sarah Davenport, born June 10, 1815, and married to John F. Randall, June 10, 1838, by whom she had one son, John Edward, who died young.

(269.) VII. Emily Davenport, born Sept. 7, 1817, was married to Harvey D. Sanderson, Feb. 4, 1836.

TWENTY-THIRD GENERATION.—Continued.

Issue of Sarah Davenport, (No. 160.)

(Who Married Ira Smith.)

(270.) I. Polly, married Urial Lindsley, M.D.

(271.) II. Enos, married Asena Thompson.

(272.) III. John, died young.

(273.) IV. Davenport, died young.

(274.) V. Hezekiah, died aged 19 years.

(275.) VI. Nancy, married Levi Thompson.

(276.) VII. Lorinda, married P. A. Williams, M.D.

(277.) VIII. Fanny, married George Dudley.

(278.) IX. Sarah, married John Stonell.

(279.) X. Isaac, married Polly Williams.

(280.) XI. Lura, married Dr. Williams.*

Issue of Roswell Davenport, (*No.* 161.)

(281.) I. John Davenport, born April 5, 1794. Died June 6, 1815.

(282.) II. William Davenport, of Erie, Pa., born Nov. 28, 1796, and married to Phylance Tracy, October 16, 1823.

(283.) III. Mary Davenport, born August 26, 1803, and married to Aaron Waldo, Nov. 1819.

(284.) IV. Nancy Davenport, born Dec. 24, 1815, and married to Enos Lyon, in 1836.

Issue of Hezekiah Davenport, (*No.* 162.)

(285.) I. Perlina Street Davenport, born July 31, 1804, and married to Warren Parker, 1827, and died in 1829.

* There were two others who died young.

(286.) II. James Percival Davenport, born Nov. 22, 1807, and removed to South America.

(287.) III. Henrietta Edwards Davenport, born Jan. 4, 1810, and married Lucius Walker, of New York, Jan. 9, 1837.

(288.) IV. Nancy Vere Davenport, born May 15, 1812, and married to Jacob T. Bond, of Brooklyn, N. Y., March 14, 1836.

(289.) V. Augusta Davenport, born June 22, 1814, and married to Leonard Currier, Sept. 10, 1834.

(290.) VI. Frances A. Davenport, born Jan. 5, 1817, and married to Edward B. Hayes, of New York, Nov. 20, 1839.

(291.) VIII. Samuel Breck Davenport, of East New York, born April 5, 1819, and married to Mary Ophelia Hunt, May 16, 1841.

(292.) VIII. John Gould Davenport, born June 16, 1822, and married to Roxanna Wilcox, August 28, 1844.

(293.) IX. Jane Davenport, born May 17, 1825, died Feb. 23, 1837.

Issue of Street Davenport, (No. 165.)

(294.) I. Sullivan Shults Davenport, born 1828.

(295.) II. Mary Hetty Davenport.

TWENTY-THIRD GENERATION.—CONTINUED.

Issue of Martha Davenport, (No. 163.)

(Who Married Eli Potter.)

(296.) I. Charlotte, born 1796.

(297.) II. Eliza, born 1799.

(298.) III. Edward, born 1802.

(299.) IV. Lyman, born 1805.

(300.) V. Amanda, born 1809. Died 1836.

Issue of Mary Davenport, (No. 164.)

(Who Married John Woodward.)

(301.) I. Eliza, born May 9, 1802.

(302.) II. John, born August 18, 1807. Died 1821.

(303.) III. Lyman, born Jan. 12, 1810.

(304.) IV. Laura, born Jan. 12, 1810.

(305.) V. Roswell, born Jan. 2, 1811.

(306.) VI. Emeline, born May 5, 1814.

TWENTY-THIRD GENERATION.—CONTINUED.

Issue of John A. Davenport, (No. 167.)

(307.) I. Julia Matilda Davenport, born Dec. 26, 1806. Died June 22, 1826.

(308.) II. Rev. John Sidney Davenport, born in Stamford, Sept. 26, 1808. Graduated at Yale College in 1833. Married to Elizabeth

S. Leverett, July, 1836. Is now a settled minister (Episcopal) at Oswego, N. Y.

(309.) III. Theodosia Davenport, born Nov. 8, 1810, and married to Russell C. Wheeler, October 23, 1833. Mr. W. died August 13, 1847.

(310.) IV. Rev. James Radcliffe Davenport, born Nov. 15, 1812. Graduated at Yale College in 1830. Married to Mehitabel W. Newell, Sept. 7, 1836. Is now a settled minister (Episcopal) at Albany, N. Y.

(311.) V. Mary Davenport, born Aug. 7, 1814. Married to Josiah W. Wheeler, Oct. 15, 1835.

(312.) VI. Elizabeth Davenport.

TWENTY-THIRD GENERATION.—Continued.

Issue of Dea. Theodore Davenport, (No. 170.)

(313.) I. Mary Caroline Davenport, born Nov. 9, 1836.

(314.) II. Robert Chesebrough Davenport, born Sept. 1838. Died May 2, 1843.

(315.) III. John Davenport, born Aug. 28, 1840.

(316.) IV. James Boorman Davenport, born December 19, 1842.

(317.) V. Richard Tigbe Davenport, born Feb. 27, 1846. Died Feb. 8, 1847.

(318.) VI. Helen Matilda Davenport, born March 9, 1849.

Issue of Matilda Davenport, (*No.* 172.)

(Who Married Rev. Peter Lockwood.)

(319.) I. John Davenport,* born Oct. 9, 1825. Died December 20, 1844.

(320.) II. Theodore, born June 30, 1827. Died May 8, 1831.

(321.) III. Radcliffe Boorman, born May 6, 1829.

* John Davenport Lockwood was born in Stamford, at the house of his maternal grandfather, Hon. John Davenport. At the age of seven years he gave evidence of a change of heart, and made a public profession of his faith in Christ, by uniting with the church under the charge of his father. He was remarkable from the first dawning of his boyhood for an early maturity of talent, from which, in connection with his manifest piety, his friends indulged the hope that he might become a minister of the Gospel, and an ornament to the Church. In the Fall of 1844, he became a member of Yale College, where he suddenly died, December 20, 1844, and was interred in the burying ground of New Haven. A marble monument to his memory was "erected by his class-mates."—*Memoirs of John D. Lockwood, by his Father.*

(322.) IV. James Boorman, born May 31, 1831. Died June 3, 1831.

(323.) V. Mary Elizabeth, born Feb. 28, 1835.

(324.) VI. Anna Matilda, born October 1, 1837.

(325.) VII. Theodosia Davenport, born July 28, 1839.

TWENTY-THIRD GENERATION.—Continued.

Issue of Betsey C. Davenport, (No. 173.)

(Who Married Charles W. Apthorp.)

(326.) I. Mary Mehitabel, married Rev. Horace Bushnell, D.D.

(327.) II. Elizabeth Cogswell.

(328.) III. Frances Louisa.

(329.) IV. Emily Sophia, married Mr. Sampson, of New York.

(330.) V. Catharine, married Dr. Head.

Issue of Abigail F. Davenport, (No. 174.)

(Who Married Rev. P. M. Whelpley.)

(331.) I. James Davenport.

(332.) II. Philip Melancthon, died young.

(333.) III. Philip Melancthon.

Issue of Mary Ann Davenport, (No. 175.)

(Who Married Rev. Matthias Bruen.)

(334.) I. Mary Ann Lundie, died young.
(335.) II. Frances Davenport.
(336.) III. Mary Lundie.

TWENTY-THIRD GENERATION.—CONTINUED.

Issue of Frances L. Davenport, (No. 176.)

(Who Married Rev. T. H. Skinner, D.D.)

(337.) I. Mary Ann Davenport.
(338.) II. Frances Davenport.
(339.) III. James Davenport.
(340.) IV. Helen.

TWENTY-FOURTH GENERATION.

Issue of William Davenport, (No. 180.)

(341.) I. Isaac Gould Davenport, born Jan. 17, 1804, and married to Hannah Wilson, Oct. 12, 1831. Died in New York, April 28, 1839.

(342.) II. John William Davenport, born July 22, 1807. Died at New Canaan, May 26, 1826.

(343.) III. Theodore Davenport, born Jan. 15, 1810, and died August 20, 1830.

(344.) IV. Lewis Benedict Davenport, born June 24, 1812. Was a school-teacher for several years. Died at New Canaan, Dec. 17, 1836.

(345.) Mary Jane Davenport, born March 7, 1814.

Miss Davenport was a person of much benevolence of character. She early devoted herself to the service of Christ. Her heart was warmly enlisted in the cause of Sabbath-Schools and Missions. For several years she was engaged in the profession of teaching, to which she devoted herself with a perseverance and zeal seldom witnessed. She sought not only to train the intellect of her pupils, but also to bring them to the knowledge of Christ. These labors for their spiritual welfare are still gratefully remembered by some who enjoyed her instructions. In the Spring of 1836, while teaching in Darien, the scarlet fever broke out among her pupils. She continued her labors in the school by day, and watched with some who were sick at night. She took the disease, came to her home in New Canaan, where in less than a week she passed to her eternal rest, April 25, 1836.

(346.) VI. Amzi Benedict Davenport, born in New Canaan, Ct., Oct. 30, 1817, and was married in Brooklyn, N. Y., May 2, 1842, by the Rev. William B. Lewis, to Frances Maria Isaacs. Mrs. D. died June 9, 1848, and was buried at Greenwood.

Married, 2d, in Brooklyn, by the Rev. Dr. Dwight, Oct. 30, 1850, to Jane Joralemon Dimon. For fifteen years he has been engaged as principal of a private school,—now the Willoughby-Street Academy, Brooklyn, N. Y.

(347.) VII. Julius Davenport, born in New Canaan, Ct., May 26, 1821, and married to Mary Ann Bates of New York, by Rev. J. W. M'Lane, June 4, 1846. For several years he has had charge of a private school, in Brooklyn, N. Y.

(348.) VIII. Harriet Abigail Davenport, born in New Canaan, May 23, 1824, and married to Elisha Comstock, of Norwalk, by the Rev. Theophilus Smith, Oct. 3, 1842.

Issue of Sarah Davenport, (No. 181.)

(Who Married Jonathan Bates.)

(349.) I. John Davenport, born Jan. 19, 1806. Married Sarah Bell.

(350.) II. Charles Augustus, born Sept. 24, 1807. Married Polly Tuttle.

(351.) III. Theodore, born Aug. 5, 1809.

(352.) IV. Sally Elizabeth, born May 1, 1811. Married William H. Bates.

(353.) V. Julia, born June 11, 1814. Married Carmi Betts.

(354.) VI. Walter Henry, born Oct. 26, 1817. Married Sarah L. Clock.

(355.) VII. Frances, born Aug. 27, 1819. Died July 27, 1820.

(356.) VIII. Fanny.

TWENTY-FOURTH GENERATION.—Continued.

Issue of James Davenport, (No. 182.)

(357.) I. John Davenport, born April 9, 1811.

(358.) II. George Davenport of North Stamford, born March 24, 1813, and married to Amanda Fuller, by her father, Rev. Henry Fuller, Nov. 25, 1841. Mrs. D. died July, 1843. Married, 2d, to Charlotte Warner, March, 1850.

(359.) III. James Augustus Davenport of Green Point, N. Y., born July 20, 1818, and married to Martha Ann Meeker, of Norwalk, November 4, 1839.

(360.) IV. Isaac Lewis Davenport, born June 10, 1821, and married to Emily J. Andreas, Dec. 3, 1846.

(361.) V. Silvester Davenport, born Feb. 24, 1824, and married Dec. 22, 1847, to Ann H. Strong.

Issue of Julia Ann Davenport, (No. 183.)

(Who Married Jotham Hoyt.)

(362.) I. John Willis, born Oct. 30, 1820.

(363.) II. Mary Bell, born Sept. 27, 1822. Died Nov. 13, 1843.

(364.) III. Amelia, born Oct. 22, 1823.

(365.) IV. Charles Edward, born May 5, 1825.

(366.) V. Louisa Maria, born Dec. 1, 1826.

(367.) VI. Julia Augusta, born April 17, 1829.

(368.) VII. Emily Cordelia, born July 26, 1835.

TWENTY-FOURTH GENERATION.—CONTINUED.

Issue of Samuel Davenport, (No. 205.)

(369.) I. Charles Augustus Davenport of Wilton, born August 26, 1812, and married to Sarah Maria Gaylord, Oct. 16, 1831.

(370.) II. Sarah Louisa Davenport, born April 11, 1816. Died Nov. 8, 1826.

(371.) III. John Davenport, born May 28,

1822, and married to Sarah Elizabeth Whitney, Sept. 1846.

Issue of Polly Davenport, (*No.* 208.)

(*Who Married Amzi Scofield.*)

(372.) I. Amzi Lewis, born March 6, 1821. Married Mary Lockwood.

(373.) II. Cyrus, born Jan. 22, 1823.

(374.) III. William Wallace, born March 2, 1825.

(375.) IV. Abigail Louisa, born March 2, 1827.

(376.) V. Henry, born April 16, 1829.

Issue of Thaddeus Davenport, (*No.* 210.)

(377.) I. William Henry Davenport, born Nov. 27, 1833.

TWENTY-FOURTH GENERATION.—CONTINUED.

Issue of Joseph Davenport, (*No.* 211.)

(378.) I. Emily Susan Davenport, born Oct. 23, 1825, and died May 16, 1835.

(379.) II. William Young Davenport, born March 30, 1830.

(380.) III. Caroline Davenport, born May 15, 1837.

(381.) IV. George B. Davenport, born April 6, 1839, and died April 18, 1844.

(382.) V. Edward Sherman, born Sept. 13, 1843.

Issue of Darius Davenport, (No. 212.)

(383.) I. Caroline Davenport, born Feb. 20, 1833. Died March 15, 1834.

(384.) II. Horace Davenport, born Sept. 22, 1835. Died May 19, 1837.

(385.) III. Sarah Davenport, born Nov. 20, 1839.

(386.) IV. Burrall Davenport, born Feb. 23, 1849. Died June 15, 1850.

Issue of William Henry Davenport, (No. 213.)

(387.) I. William Henry Davenport, born April 6, 1840.

(388.) II. Sarah Ellen Davenport, born Sept. 17, 1841.

(389.) III. Ellen Maria Davenport, born Aug. 16, 1846.

TWENTY-FOURTH GENERATION.—CONTINUED.

Issue of George A. Davenport, (No. 214.)

(390.) I. Mary Davenport.
(391.) II. Abby Davenport.

Issue of James S. Davenport, (No. 215.)

(392.) I. Charles Oscar Davenport, born July 31, 1842.
(393.) II. George Alfred Davenport, born Feb. 14, 1849.

Issue of Mary Ann Davenport, (No. 216.)

(Who Married Matthew Smith.)

(394.) I. Sereno Newton, born Feb. 11, 1836.
(395.) II. Eugene Davenport, born April 24, 1839.

Issue of Elizabeth Davenport, (No. 217.)

(Who Married William Wheeler.)

(396.) Julia Emeline, born Feb. 22, 1825, and died Nov. 13, 1846.
(397.) II. Sarah Elizabeth, born May 16, 1828, and married to Joseph S. Condé, Dec. 22, 1847.

Issue of Amzi Davenport, (No. 220.)

(398.) I. Ann Eliza Davenport, born Feb. 5, 1835.

(399.) II. Mary Elizabeth Davenport, born Feb. 1, 1842. Died Feb. 8, 1842.

TWENTY-FOURTH GENERATION.—Continued.

Issue of Charles W. Davenport, (No. 255.)

(400.) I. Mary Esther Davenport, born Jan. 21, 1845.

(401.) II. Priscilla A. Davenport, born Feb. 17, 1847.

(402.) III. Charles Silas Davenport, born March 5, 1849.

Issue of Thomas F. Davenport, (No. 256.)

(403.) I. Thomas Willett Davenport, born in Illinois, April 22, 1849. Died Sept. 21, 1849.

(404.) II. Thomas Arthur Davenport, born Dec. 31, 1850.

Issue of Amelia L. Davenport, (No. 257.)

(*Who Married Mahlon Lloyd.*)

(405.) I. Charles, born October 9, 1841. Died August 1, 1842.

(406.) II. Florence, born May, 1844.

(407.) III. Isabel, born November 1, 1849.

Issue of Mary E. Davenport, (No. 258.)

(Who Married J. Hannaman.)

(408.) I. Calista, born January, 1846. Died September, 1846.

(409.) II. Charles, born September 23, 1848.

Issue of James Davenport, (No. 262.)

(410.) I. Rufus Davenport, born December 12, 1844.

(411.) II. Mary Davenport, born November 30, 1847. Died October 9, 1848.

(412.) III. James Davenport, born September 29, 1849. Died March 16, 1851.

TWENTY-FOURTH GENERATION.—Continued.

Issue of Hezekiah R. Davenport, (No. 263.)

(413.) I. Mary Theodora Davenport, born August 3, 1835, and died August 13, 1836.

(414.) II. Frances Victoria Davenport, born May 29, 1837, and died February 16, 1838.

(415.) III. Ralsa Adolphus Davenport, born in New York, December 29, 1838.

(416.) IV. Phebe Cortelyou Davenport, July 9, 1841.

(417.) V. John Rapelyea Davenport, born in Brooklyn, Feb. 20, 1844.

(418.) VI. Mary Frances Davenport, born Aug. 4, 1846, and died Jan. 30, 1847.

(419.) VII. Caroline Augusta Davenport, Jan. 16, 1848.

(420.) VIII. William Lawrence Davenport, born Aug. 28, 1850.

Issue of Mary Ann Davenport, (No. 264.)

(Who Married Ralph Hoyt.)

(421.) I. Adolphus, born Aug. 4, 1828. Is a lawyer in New York.

(422.) II. Theodora.

TWENTY-FOURTH GENERATION.—CONTINUED.

Issue of Silas Davenport, (No. 266.)

(423.) I. Sarah St. John Davenport, born Nov. 30, 1837, and died Oct. 23, 1838.

(424.) II. William St. John Davenport, born in Brooklyn, Aug. 16, 1840.

(425.) III. Sarah Elizabeth Davenport, born June 24, 1843.

(426.) IV. Silas Augustus Davenport, born in Brooklyn, June 27, 1846.

(427.) V. Anna Maria Davenport, born Jan. 27, 1851.

Issue of William Davenport, (No. 267.)

(428.) I. Mary Ann Davenport, born in North Stamford, Dec. 9, 1834, died April 5, 1850.

(429.) II. Charles William Davenport, born March 31, 1836, and died May 9, 1838.

(430.) III. William Webster Davenport, born in North Stamford, Jan. 16, 1839.

(431.) IV. Emily Clarissa Davenport, born March 20, 1841.

(432.) V. Henry Adolphus Davenport, born March 26, 1845.

Issue of Emily Davenport, (No. 269.)

(Who Married Harvey Sanderson.)

(433.) I. Adolphus Davenport, born January 18, 1837.

(434.) II. Emily Texiana; died young.

(435.) III. Isabella.

Issue of William Davenport, (No. 282.)

(436.) I. Mary Davenport, born October 5, 1824.

(437.) II. Fanny Davenport, born December 11, 1826, and married to William A. Galbraith, of Erie, Pa., May 25, 1846.

(438.) III. Sarah Davenport, born March 5, 1829.

(439.) IV. William R. Davenport of Erie, born July 31, 1831.

(440.) V. Samuel A. Davenport, born January 15, 1834.

(441.) VI. Helen Sophia Davenport, born January 3, 1839.

(442.) VII. Marilla P. Davenport, born June 12, 1842.

TWENTY-FOURTH GENERATION.—CONTINUED.

Issue of Henrietta Edwards Davenport, (*No.* 287.)

(*Who Married Lucius Walker.*)

(443.) I. Aldace Atwood, born June 30, 1838.

(444.) II. Alice Henrietta, born February 10, 1841, died April 12, 1845.

(445.) III. Edna Minerva, born October 23, 1843.

(446.) IV. Lucius Pierpont, born March 29, 1848.

Issue of Nancy Vere Davenport, (*No.* 288.)

(*Who Married Jacob T. Bond.*)

(447.) I. James Davenport, born February 8, 1838, died March 23, 1840.

(448.) II. Leonard Currier, born August 8, 1840.

Issue of Augusta Davenport, (No. 289.)

(Who Married Leonard Currier.)

(449.) I. Frances Augusta, born January 25, 1836.

(450.) II. Mary Jane, born Jan. 29, 1838.

(451.) III. Henrietta Edwards, born June 15, 1840, died March 25, 1845.

(452.) IV. Julietta Davenport, born June 15, 1840.

(453.) V. Sarah M., born Feb. 6, 1842.

Issue of Samuel B. Davenport, (No. 291.)

(454.) I. James Percival Davenport, born February 11, 1842.

(455.) II. Augustus Pierpont Davenport, born February 23, 1844.

(456.) III. Adalaide Virginia Davenport, born July 10, 1846.

(457.) IV. Emma Davenport, born June 13, 1848, and died February 23, 1849.

(458.) Street L. Davenport, born April 27, 1850, and died March 25, 1851.

Issue of John Gould Davenport, (No. 292.)

(459.) I. Franklin Edwards Davenport, born May 21, 1845.

(460.) II. Elmira M. Davenport, born September 7, 1847.

(461.) III. John Pierpont Davenport, born December 4, 1850.

TWENTY-FOURTH GENERATION.—Continued.

Issue of Rev. John S. Davenport, (No. 308.)

(462.) I. Julia Matilda Davenport, born January 21, 1839.

(463.) II. Martha Davenport, born January 21, 1840.

(464.) III. James Davenport, born December 17, 1841.

(465.) IV. Elizabeth Davenport, born December 27, 1843.

(466.) V. John Sidney Davenport, born June, 1846.

Issue of Theodosia Davenport, (No. 309.)

(Who Married Russell C. Wheeler.)

(467.) I. John Davenport, born August 28, 1834.

(468.) II. William, born August, 1836.

(469.) III. Julia Davenport, born November 10, 1844.

(470.) IV. Theodosia Mary, born September 21, 1847.

Issue of Rev. James R. Davenport, (*No.* 310.)

(471.) I. Anna W. Davenport, born February, 1838.

(472.) II. John Alfred Davenport, born February 16, 1840.

(473.) III. Mary Boorman Davenport, born February, 1845.

(474.) IV. Russell Wheeler Davenport, born November, 1849.

Issue of Mary Davenport, (*No.* 311.)

(*Who Married Josiah W. Wheeler.*)

(475.) I. Mary Boorman, born June, 1837.

(476.) II. Elizabeth Davenport, born Jan. 1839.

(477.) III. William, born July, 1847.

TWENTY-FIFTH GENERATION.

Issue of Isaac Gould Davenport, (*No.* 341.)

(478.) I. Isabella Augusta Davenport, born in New York, August 1, 1832, and died November 12, 1832.

(479.) II. Isabella Augusta Davenport, born July 25, 1833, and died December 17, 1844.

(480.) III. John William Davenport, born in New York, July 1, 1835, and died February 26, 1838.

(481.) IV. Mary Jane Davenport, born January 31, 1838. Died young.

(482.) V. John William Davenport, born January 12, 1839.

TWENTY-FIFTH GENERATION.—Continued.

Issue of Amzi Benedict Davenport, (No. 346.)

(483.) I. John Isaacs Davenport, born in Brooklyn, N. Y., May 16, 1843.

(484.) II. Albert Barnes Davenport, born in Brooklyn, N. Y., April 3, 1845.

(485.) III. Frances Maria Davenport, born February 27, 1848, and died at New Canaan, Ct., August 13, 1848. Buried at Greenwood.

Issue of Julius Davenport, (No. 347.)

(486.) I. William Bates Davenport, born in New York, March 10, 1847.

(487.) II. Julius Bates Davenport, born in New York, June 24, 1849.

Issue of Harriet A. Davenport, (No. 348.)

(Who Married Elisha Comstock.)

(488.) I. George William, born in New Canaan, November 22, 1845.

(489.) II. Frances Maria, born October 26, 1848. Died January 9, 1849.

(490.) III. Sarah Elizabeth, born November 24, 1849.

TWENTY-FIFTH GENERATION.—Continued.

Issue of James A. Davenport, (No. 359.)

(491.) I. Charles Francis Davenport, born May 5, 1841.

(492.) II. Ralsey Davenport, born February 10, 1843.

(493.) III. Emma Louisa Davenport, born December 17, 1846.

(494.) IV. Jane Amanda Davenport, born September 13, 1848.

Issue of Isaac Lewis Davenport, (No. 360.)

(495.) I. Sarah Andreas Davenport, born October 16, 1847.

TWENTY-FIFTH GENERATION.—CONTINUED.

Issue of Charles A. Davenport, (No. 369.)

(496.) I. Sarah Louisa Davenport, born in Wilton, August 5, 1832.

(497.) II. Emily Davenport, born June 18, 1834.

(498.) III. John Gaylord Davenport, born November 24, 1839.

Issue of John Davenport, (No. 371.)

(499.) I. Samuel Davenport, born in Wilton, Oct. 15, 1847.

(500.) II. Thomas Davenport, born Sept. 3, 1849.

APPENDIX.

EXTRACT FROM

"THE SAINT'S ANCHOR-HOLD *in all Storms and Tempests. Preached in Sundry Sermons; and published for the Support and Comfort of God's People in all times of Trial.* By JOHN DAVENPORT, B.D., *sometime Minister of St. Stephens', Coleman Street, London, and Pastor of a Church of Christ in New Haven, in New England.* HEB. vi. 18, 19, 20.—'Lay hold upon the hope set before us; which hope we have as an anchor to the soul, &c.' London: 1661. Reprinted: 1701."

LAM. 3 : 24.—" *The Lord is my portion, saith my soul, therefore will I trust in him.*"

THIS book is, according to the judgment of a godly, learned writer,* an abridgment of all Jeremiah's sermons, from the thirteenth year of Josiah, unto the fourth of Jehoiakim; and that book which God commanded Jeremiah to write, and to cause Baruch to read publicly, upon the day of a fast, kept in the ninth month of the fifth year of Jehoiakim, which afterward Jehudi read unto the king, sitting by a fire in his winter-house, who was so far from repenting, that, when he had read three or four leaves of it, he cut it with a penknife, and cast it into the fire, till all was consumed, and rejected the intercession of some of his princes, that he would not burn it, and he commanded to lay hold on Jeremiah and Baruch; but God hid them. (See the story at large in Jeremiah, 36th chapter.) Where-

* Mr. Broughton.

upon the Lord commanded Jeremiah to write the book again, with additions, which the same writer thinks was this chapter, which consists of a threefold alphabet in the Hebrew. The prophet having discharged his offices, in laboring to convince the Jews of their sins, and to bring them to repentance; when he found not the success he desired, he falls to lamenting and weeping for their pride and obstinacy in sin, and teacheth them also how to lament their own misery in captivity; and, because there was among them a basket of good figs, he teacheth them how to exercise faith and hope in the midst of their sorrows. Among other passages, my text has a tendency thereunto, which admits a double consideration:—I. As a part of a lamentation. II. As an expression of a free spirit. Accordingly I shall handle it, first, as a part of a lamentation. In verses 17, 18, you may see their deep dejection and despondency: "I said my strength and my hope is perished from the Lord." In verses 19, 20, 21, you see how from the good fruit of their affliction in humbling them, they gather *hope.* In verses 22, 23, they can see mercy in God toward them in their affliction. In my text, they are as men that find rest after their dangers and tossings at sea, by casting anchor upon firm ground, in a safe harbor.

The Doctrine, note, I collect from the words so considered, is this:

Doctrine—Though it may be the case of true believers to be greatly dejected for a time, yet, even then, God doth support their spirits, and quicken their faith and hope in him.

To clear this point, we must prove two things; First, that it may be the case of true believers to be greatly dejected for a time. This may be abundantly confirmed, both by the Scriptures in the examples of Job, David,

Hezekiah, Asaph, Heman, and of Christ himself, in the garden, and on the cross, and by reasons of sundry sorts.

Reason I.—From God himself sometimes withholding the light of his countenance from true believers. Then it is with them as it is with the earth, which would be covered with darkness, coldness, and deadness, if the light and influence of the sun were withdrawn from it. He is "the God of all comfort" (2 Cor. 1 : 3); without him no true comfort can be had. Sometimes he creates darkness in the soul; then it is filled with fear, and amazement, and disquietment. And thus he doeth for holy and good ends. First, to confirm believers to Christ, as members to their head (Rom. 8 : 29). Secondly, to inform them where their "life is hid," viz., "with Christ in God" (Col. 3 : 3), and that Christ "the last Adam was made a quickening Spirit" (1 Cor. 15 : 45); that thereby he may quicken his people in God, who quickeneth the dead, when themselves had not only a sentence of death in their bodies, as Paul had (2 Cor. 1 : 9), but also a sense of death in their souls, as Heman had (Psalm 88 : 5). Thirdly, to reform them. Partly, for correction for their unthankfulness for former comforts received from him, and for their not improving them unto the ends for which he gave them. As a father, when he seeth his child doth but play with the candle, which he afforded him to work by, takes it from him, and leaves him in the dark. Partly, for prevention of spiritual pride (2 Cor. 12 : 7); of spiritual wantonness and self-confidence (Psalm 30 : 6, 7); of carnal security (Cant. 5 : 6); and sundry other distempers.

Reason II.—From Satan, that envious one, who, as in the beginning sought to cast Adam out of Paradise, and to bereave him of his happiness in communion with God, so now, finding believers in the kingdom of grace, which consists in righteousness and peace and joy in the Holy Spirit, when he cannot deprive them of their righteousness, will endeavor to disturb their peace, and damp their joy; knowing that when they perform duties uncomfortably, they do them weakly, and but by halves. To this end, *First,* he strives to hide from them those promises that might comfort them, when they have most need and use of them, and he sometimes prevails herein (Heb. 12 : 5). *Secondly,* he suggests any word that may terrify them, and presents to their memory and thoughts former sins, to amaze them. *Thirdly,* he presents all things to them in false glasses; the comforts of God in a diminishing glass, that God may seem to them less merciful, less gracious than he is, and the promises of God less free, less general than they are; that all the consolations of God may seem small things to them (Job 15 : 11). But he presents to them their sins in a multiplying glass, that they may seem more and greater than they are; their sins as unpardonable; their miseries as intolerable, incurable; their state as desperate. *Fourthly,* he useth his instruments to deal with them as the Philistines did with Isaac, whose wells they stopped up, to make unprofitable to them wells of salvation, from whence believers might draw waters of consolation. Thus he used Saul to banish David from the ordinances, and wicked men to insult and reproach him; saying, where is now thy God (Ps. 42 : 3)? So others, to twit them in their religion, when they are in distress, saying, Where are now your prayers, your hearing, reading, meditating, conferring, your conscientious and exact walking, your confidence in God? You live more dejected than others, and are as fearful as others, to die. Thus, they thrust, as it were, swords and daggers into their bones to kill their comforts, as David there complaineth, verse 10.

Reason III.—From themselves. *First*, Sin presseth down their spirits, and hinders their cheerful progress in a Christian course, as weight doth runners in a race (Heb. 12 : 1). Sorrow in the heart pulls it down, especially when guilt of sin is added to it. When the shoulder is out of joint it cannot bear its own pain, much less other burdens. So it is with the soul; a wounded spirit who can bear (Prov. 18 : 14)? *Secondly*, Their spirit sometimes suffers from their bodies, by sympathy; as in melancholy, which so darkens their imagination that everything seems dark to them, and so sours their spirits that everything seems bitter to them, and so fills them with fears and suspicions that everything affrights them. *Thirdly*, Sometimes passion so prevaileth in them, that the higher faculties of the soul are subjected to the affections which so bemist the understanding that it cannot judge of things according to right reason; the conscience becomes suspensive and wavering, and the memory, like a leaking vessel, lets the grounds of comfort run out, and be forgotten. *Fourthly*, Sometimes spiritual gifts of grace are not exercised, but as the body grows listless when some dull humor seizeth, faith is oppressed by unbelief, hope with fears; they do not put forth themselves to wrestle with God, and stir up themselves to take hold on him, but yield unto every temptation and discouragement. Thus you see, that it may be the case of believers to be greatly dejected for a time.

The second thing to be cleared, is, that though it be thus with true believers, for a time, yet then God will do two things for them.

First, He will secretly support them, so that they may say as Paul did, in 2 Cor. 4 : 8, 9, "We are troubled on every side, yet not distressed; we are perplexed, but not in despair; persecuted, but not forsaken; cast down, but not destroyed." God dealt with the basket of good figs in captivity, as Christ did with Peter, who first let him see his own weakness, in the water, then quickened him to cry unto him for help, and then stretched forth his hand and withheld him (Matt. 14 : 30, 31). So the Lord left the church so far that they complained, my hope is perished from the Lord; yet speedily raised them up in sight of his mercy, to trust and hope in him. In like manner he supports believers.

Reason 1.—From God's unchangeableness in his love; and unchangeableness in doing them good (Isa. 64 : 5; and 40 : 27, 28, 29, 31).

Reason 2.—From God's faithfulness in his covenant and promises (Isa. 54 : 8, 9; Ps. 37 : 24; Heb. 13 : 5). He will quicken their faith to look unto himself for relief and comfort, in such times (2 Chron. 20 : 12; Ps. 121 : 1, 2; Jon. 2 : 3, 4), for these reasons:

Reason I.—From the efficacy of the spirit of faith in them. As the needle in the compass being touched with the loadstone, though it may be removed and shaken this way and that, for a time, yet resteth not till it point to the north; so the soul, being touched by the Spirit of Grace, though it may be forced by temptation from its bent for a time, yet it hath no rest till it stand Godward. They may by temptations be as sheep driven from mountain to mountain, and forget their resting place (Jer. 50 : 6). But the spirit of faith in them will cause them to return unto God, and to say as David (Ps. 116 : 7): "Return unto thy rest, O my soul." Believers are like Noah's dove, that finding no rest for the soles of its feet, in the deluge, returned unto the ark. Other men will, like the raven, be soon satisfied with other things.

Reason II.—From the suitable operation of God's Spirit in them unto the end of God's afflicting them. God's end in afflicting his children is to drive them from all other things unto himself. For he corrects them for their good. (Heb. 12 : 10.) And it is good for them to draw near to God. (Ps. 73 : 28.) When afflictions work us thereunto, it is from the Spirit's sanctifying operation in them. For, *first*, afflictions cannot work thus of themselves, but rather set men further off from God by discontentment with his Providence, because it crosseth their carnal affections. And, *secondly*, The Soul itself is apt to misgivings in such cases, and to have hard thoughts of God. And, *thirdly*, Satan takes such occasions to breed and increase a distance and division between the soul and God. Therefore, it must be from the sanctifying operation of God's Spirit in them, and with them, when they work this good (Rom. 8 : 28).

Use I.—For instruction.

1. Here we may see the difference between believers and others, in their dejected condition. *First*, Believers have the spirit of faith in them, whereby the Soul, though it may be overborne by passion and temptation for a time, yet will work itself into freedom again, as oil will be uppermost. The spirit, as a spring, will be cleansing itself more and more, from that mud that is in it. But the heart of unbelievers is like a standing pool, where that which is cast into it rests. They are like the sea, where trouble and unquietness are in their proper place (Isa. 57 : 20). True rest and peace are forever separated from sin and any soul, till the breach between God and the soul be made up by faith in Christ.

Secondly, Believers have an interest in God, and he in

them, through Jesus Christ. Hence they are kept, as in a garrison, by his mighty power, through faith unto salvation (1 Pet. 1 : 5), through the intercession of Christ (Luke 22 : 3), by the Spirit of Christ, dwelling with them, and who shall be in them, and abide with them, forever; so that they shall not be left comfortless (John 14: 16, 17, 18). Hereupon Paul triumphed in Rom. 8 : 35, &c.; where he puts the question about persons, and answers about things; neither shall separate them from the love, which either Christ bears to them, or they to Christ. Sin cannot separate them from Christ's love to them, because he hath more than conquered it, by his own power. Tribulation cannot separate believers from the love they bear to Christ, because they shall more than conquer it, by the power of Christ. It is not our hold of God and Christ; but God's and Christ's hold of us, that keeps us to him. The root bears us up, not we the root (Rom. 11 : 18). This Asaph acknowledged unto God, when his feet were almost gone, his steps had well nigh slipped; saying, nevertheless I am continually with thee, thou hast holden me by my right hand (Ps. 73 : 2, 23). But unbelievers are "without Christ, and without God in the world" (Eph. 2 : 12). Therefore when their creature comforts fail them, they are as a ship tossed in the sea without a pilot, and without an anchor, which soon is bulged upon rocks, or falleth upon quicksands, having no God to guide or support them.

2. Hence we may learn how to carry ourselves towards afflicted, dejected Christians. Judge mercifully and wisely of poor weaklings (Ps. 41 : 1). Men are apt, through want of wisdom and love, to misapprehend the causes of their dejectedness. It is the less to be wondered at, that a heathen king misinterpreted the dejected countenance of Nehemiah (Neh. 2 : 2), seeing godly Eli miscensured

Hannah, as a distempered woman, when she was in bitterness of spirit (1 Sam. 1 : 14, 15), and Job's friends misjudged him for his afflictions, and men generally misconstrued Christ's sufferings (Isa. 53 : 4, 5). They are not always the best that are merriest, nor they the merriest in the heart that are so in the face. Nor are they always of the weakest faith or spirit, who are sometimes dejected, as we see Joshua was, in Josh. 7th. Therefore be not rash or harsh in censuring the dejected ; but rather work with God for their support and comfort. Two things are required hereunto ; knowledge and goodness (Rom. 15 : 14). The first will make you able, the second willing, to be helpful to such. Labor to abound in both. First, in knowledge both of the word (Col. 3 : 16), and of the temper of the party, that you may speak to them suitably and seasonably (Isa. 56 : 4). Second, in goodness, to pity them, to pray for them, and to set them in joint. (Gal. 6 : 1).

3. As for yourselves, beware that you misjudge not your own estate towards God, under such dejections, but know that, if ever you had any clear testimony of God's love to you in Christ Jesus, the love of God toward you is unchangeable, it is an everlasting love (Jer. 31 : 3). Therefore hold the confidence and rejoicing of your hope firm unto the end (Heb. 3 : 6), and say with the Church in Mich. 7 : 8—" When I sit in darkness the Lord will be a light unto me."

Use II.—For admonition.

Take heed of placing your comfort too much in the creature, which being subject to change and inconstancy, will be apt to breed disquietment. Vexation inseparably follows vanity, when vanity is not apprehended to be where it is. In what degree any are lifted up in expectation of satisfying good from creatures, or overjoyed with the comforts of them, in that degree they are dejected in the disappointment of their hope, and distressed in the loss of creature contentments. Inordinacy of affections embitters all afflictions. Hence arise those bitter complaints; I had settled my contentment and hope in such a friend, or relation, but now they are gone, and with them all my joy is gone. Woe is me, I am undone! Therefore Agar prayed wisely in Prov. 30 : 8—"Remove far from me vanity and lies," *i. e.*, vain and false apprehensions, whereby the affections are too strongly fixed upon things that are vain and lying, promising that contentment which they cannot yield. Confidence in vanities makes them idols, and makes the heart vain like the things it relies upon (Ps. 115 : 8). They shall find continual disquietment who walk in a vain shadow (Ps. 39 : 6). The best remedy against this is, by dwelling in the secret place of the Most High, to abide under the shadow of the Almighty (Ps. 91 : 1, 2).

LAM. 3 : 24.—"*The Lord is my portion,*" *&c.*

THE words having been considered as they lie in the context as a part of a lamentation, we proceed to handle them, as in my text they hold forth the expression of a free spirit; that is, of a spirit set at liberty from those sad perplexities, wherein it hath been entangled and held under deep dejection and despondency. The text thus considered, containeth the anchor-hold of a tossed, afflicted spirit, wherein three particulars are to be noted. 1st. An assertion, "*The Lord is my portion;*" 2d. A proof of it,

"*Saith my soul;*" 3d. A consectary, or inference from the premises, "*Therefore will I hope in him.*" I will speak only of the first at this time: "*The Lord is my portion.*" Now, a part, or portion, is not to be taken here in a mathematical or common use of that word, as denoting a part of a whole, as it is frequently in Scripture, when that part of estate which parents give their children is called their portion (Gen. 31 : 14); and that part of the spoil, which is the soldier's share, is their portion (Gen. 14 : 24); and that *dimension* of food which is allowed unto any is called their portion (Deut. 18 : 8); and the alms given to the poor is called their portion (Eccl. 12 : 2). For God is not parted or divided, and distributed among his people, so that one hath one part of him, another, another part of God; but every one hath whole God, wholly, as the whole sun shines to every one; in which respect, God is called a sun (Ps. 84 : 11). Therefore, God is said to be his people's portion, not in a comparative, but in an absolute sense, God himself is theirs, a suitable and all-sufficient good to them. They have not only gifts and all good things from him, but himself also to be their God, in the covenant of grace, through Jesus Christ. He is their portion, though *not formally*, yet in two senses. First, *objectively*, as he is their ultimate end, and chief good. Second, *casually*, as he gives, together with himself, in Christ, all good to them. The Doctrine, note, shall be this:

Doctrine. All true believers have such a blessed interest in God as renders him their portion. It is the voice of faith, to say, "*The Lord is my portion:*" others may say, The Lord is an all-sufficient portion; but only believers can say, The Lord is *my* portion. Because only faith interests a man in God, and appropriates him to him. This, faith does by a double act. *First*, by a direct act whereby true believers see in God those properties which are required in a satisfying portion. They are three: 1. *all-sufficiency*; 2. *perpetuity*; 3. *safety in placing his happiness and full contentment there*. All these, the Scriptures declare to be in God alone. 1. A sufficiency (Gen. 17: 1; Ps. 84: 11); 2. Perpetuity. It tells us, that he is without shadow of change (James 1: 17), and that he will never fail nor forsake his people (Heb. 13: 5); 3. Safety in placing all our contentment and happiness in him alone (Ps. 144 : 15). *Second*, by a reflected act of faith, a believer seeth his peculiar right and interest in God as his portion. Hence David saith: "The Lord is the portion of mine inheritance, and of my cup" (Ps. 16:5); and "thou art my portion, O Lord" (Ps. 119:57); and Asaph, "Whom have I in heaven but thee, and there is none upon earth that I desire besides thee." And again; "God is the strength of my heart, and my portion forever" (Ps. 73 : 25, 26). To clear this, two things must be added: 1st, The grounds, whereupon the saints have claimed this interest in God, as their portion; 2d. The use they have made of God, under this notion and relation. For the first, their title unto God as their portion, is founded: 1st, in God's voluntary and free donation of himself to them, in the covenant of grace, whereby both they become his portion (Deut. 32 : 9), "*The Lord's portion is his people*," and he becomes their portion. "The portion of Jacob is the former of all things; the Lord of Hosts is his name" (Jer. 10 : 16). An act so done, by one that is *sui juris*, is a strong binding act, as Peter argued in the case of Ananias (Acts 5: 4). It was free and deliberate, and therefore exceedingly dishonorable to break it. God stands much upon his honor in this (Ps.

89 : 34), "My covenant will I not break." And (Ps. 111 : 5) "he will ever be mindful of his covenant."

2d. This donation is confirmed sundry ways: 1st. By oath (Ps. 89 : 35), "Once have I sworn by my holiness." Again; in Ps. 105 : 9—"he remembered his oath unto Isaac." The covenant of grace, whereby God gives himself to be his people's God and portion, Micah saith, God hath unto our fathers from the days of old (Micah 7 ult). Which also Zechariah declares to be *performed* when he sent Christ (Luke 1 : 73). 2d. By seals: as circumcision is called a seal of the righteousness which is by faith (Rom. 4 : 11); because it eternally sealed the covenant whereby God becomes the God of his people (Gen. 17 : 7, 11). So it is with both the sacraments of the New Testament, by parity of reason. 3d. By marriage unto Christ (Hosea 2 : 19, 20). Agreements upon marriage are firm, because upon rational consideration. A consideration inserted adds weight to a deed and covenant. The consideration is, that we shall be joined unto the Lord Jesus, and then all the promises of God in him are yea and amen to us, in him (2 Cor. 1 : 20). And Christ's God and Father is our God and portion (John 20: 17). 4th. By a recovery after judgment, if I may so speak, when, after they are fallen into God's displeasure, and returned to him, with repentance for and from their sins, and renewing their faith in Christ, they have renewed their taking hold of the covenant, and have pleaded it with God, and their plea hath been accepted. Thus did Moses for Israel after they had sinned in the matter of the golden calf (Ex. 32 : 10, 13), and the Israelites for themselves (Isa. 63 : 10, 16, 17, 19). The second thing to be shown is, what use the saints have made in their right and interest in God as their portion.

They have made use of him thus, both for themselves and others. 1st. *For themselves.* 1. To glory in God; "this God is our God" (Ps. 48 ult). 2. "To delight themselves in the Lord," in confidence of his goodness to them, in the midst of temptations (Ps. 37: 4). Whence followeth a rolling of themselves upon him in all their ways and difficulties, verse 5; and a patient waiting upon God in delays, with hope of a good issue—verse 7. 2d. *For others*, whether they be friends or enemies, or of a middle sort. I. Friends. A poor believer can pleasure his richest friends out of this, his portion, his God. This is a prophet's, and a righteous man's reward (Matt. 10 : 41). Thus Paul abundantly recompensed all his friends and well-wishers out of his portion (Phil. 4 : 19). "My God shall supply all your need, according to his riches in glory by Jesus Christ." II. Enemies. In Jesus Christ, all believers have sufficient help from God against all sorts of enemies, and can, in a holy manner, challenge them to do their worst, and triumph over them, before the battle, upon this assurance, "My God will help me; therefore, I shall not be confounded" (Isa. 50 : 7, 8, 9). Other men are strong in men, in arms, in shipping, in fortifications, &c. A believer hath all in God; he is "strong in the Lord, and in the power of his might" (Eph. 6 : 10). III. A middle sort. Laban fared the better for Jacob; Potiphar, Pharaoh, and all Egypt, for Joseph; the Sodomites for Lot; the mariners, and all that were in the ship, for Paul (Acts 27 : 24); the world, for the saints; for the holy seed are the props that shore up the places where they live, that the wrath of God doth not overwhelm them (Isa. 6 : 13.)

Use I.—*For Instruction:* Hence we learn to behold and admire the excellence and happiness of every true believer in his portion. The All-sufficient God is their portion ; his greatness, power, mercy, grace, goodness, faithfulness, forgiveness, justice, all are for them ; and that they may possess him as their portion, He gives them his Son to be theirs, through faith, and with him all things (1 Cor. 3 : 21, 22, 23). Thus, " The brother of low degree is exalted " (James, 1 : 9). He hath the best portion that God can give, and upon the best assurance that God can make (Heb. 6 : 18). Hence David calls such, "the excellent ones" (Ps. 16 : 3). He had conversed with rich men, great men, wise men, after the flesh ; yet he called none of them excellent ones ; he well knew that the righteous is more excellent than his neighbor (Prov. 12 : 16).

USE II.—*For Exhortation* : 1. Generally to all, to make out for this portion. To this end wait upon God in his ordinances, with thirsty souls ; it will not be in vain (Isa. 55 : 1, 2, 3 ; Prov. 8 : 34. 35). For thereby, either it shall be cleared unto you, that the Lord is your portion, or the Lord will become your portion. And he is so unto them, in whom faith is wrought in Christ by the Spirit, in the ministry of the Gospel. They that can say to Christ with Thomas, "My Lord and my God" (John 20 : 28), may also say to God, with David, in Ps. 142 : 5, " O Lord, thou art my refuge and my portion in the land of the living." This is the privilege of those who answer God's call by joining to him in covenant. So saith the Lord : " I entered into covenant with thee, and thou becamest mine" (Ezek. 16 : 8) ; and again, in Hos. 2 : 23, " I will say unto them which were not my people, Thou art my people, and they shall say, Thou art my God."

To persuade you thereunto, consider, 1,—Every man desires to have the best for his portion in other things, in houses, land, food, apparel, cattle. But this portion is simply, absolutely the best. This Christ teacheth in Luke 16 : 12. This he calls our own, those "another man's." When a man views houses, or surveys land, or tells money for another man, his heart is not so affected with them, as when he views, surveys, tells for himself. Propriety draws and engages the heart, to that wherein a man hath a property, though it be but mean and worthless, and carrieth the heart after it; much more, when propriety and a most worthy property meet together; as David found this to be, Ps. 4 : 6, 7. 2d, The misery of those that have not this portion (Eph. 2 : 12). Little, or rather no cause, have such to bless themselves in their worldly portions and possessions, as worldly men are apt to do (Ps. 49 : 18). For they "have their portion only in this life," which is but a vapor. But believers are happy in their portion in God, both in and after this life: for they "shall behold his face in righteousness, and shall be satisfied when they awake in his likeness" (Ps. 17 : 14, 15). Attend, therefore, in time, to the counsel of Christ, in Rev. 3 : 17 : 18.

2. Especially to believers, to behave themselves as it becomes those who have God for their portion. That you may so do, first, professedly avouch God to be your portion (Deut. 26 : 17). This is done in three ways. First, When you set your love upon him, with such an esteem of him as is meet for such a portion. "Where a man's treasure is, there will his heart be also" (Matt. 6 : 21). Let God be your treasure. When you look upon all things in the world, single out those which you account most amiable, desirable; then ascend in your thoughts to heaven, and contemplate all the excellencies there; the rivers of pleasure, the blessed fellowship of saints in glory; each of them as dear to one another as if all relations of husbands

and wives, of parents and children, and friends, were in every one of them; yet let God and Christ be above them all. So did Asaph (Ps. 73 : 25). So will every one that knows God's name aright (Ps. 91 : 14). "Because he hath set his love upon me, therefore will I deliver him, I will set him on high because he hath known my name." Secondly, When you are content to part with all to enjoy him alone. A maid will say of a man whom she loves: I will have him, though I beg my bread with him. A man will lay out his estate in suit for his own. Thirdly, When you live in the world with affections free from worldly engagements, as pilgrims, whose hearts are at home when their feet are travelling abroad. Again, possess, use, and enjoy God as your portion.—Thus, 1st, Live upon God as the Israelites in Canaan did upon their lots and inheritance; live upon God's favor in Christ (Ps. 30 : 5), and upon his promises (Isa. 38 : 16). Live by the faith of the Son of God (Gal. 2 : 10), fetching all your comforts thence. 2d, Walk with God (Gen. 5 : 24), and work in God (John 3 : 21). Marry in the Lord, live unto the Lord, exalting his ends and rules in all things. 3d, Cast all your care upon him (1 Peter 5 : 7). You may try men in smaller things, before you trust them with greater; especially if they be strangers. But it is dishonorable to God, if you do not, at the first, trust him with all you are, and have. When men's hearts sink in every danger, it is from a defect, either of faith or in faith. See how Christ reproveth Peter (Matt. 14 : 30, 31). David's first recourse was to God, and whatever means he used, he looked up to him (Ps. 5 : 3). 4th, Live contentedly, when you enjoy God in his ordinances, without covetousness (Heb. 13 : 5), and without discontentedness, because of outward afflictions or wants. David, as he was the sweet singer of Israel, so expressed a sweet frame of spirit, in 2 Sam. 23 : 5, "He hath made with me an everlasting covenant, ordered in all things, and sure; this is all my salvation and all my desire," &c. 5th, Make up all your happiness in God. A worldly man, when he views his houses, lands, cattle, barns filled with corn, &c., his heart is cheered like that rich fool in Luke 12 : 19; but see the vanity of that joy in the answer of God to him, verse 20. But a true believer hath true cause of rejoicing in his portion, having such an estate in God, and Christ, and the covenant, that he shall want nothing (Ps. 23 : 1). His down-lyings and up-risings, himself and his children, are well provided for. What though his estate lieth not in lands, or monies, or plenty of corn or cattle? he hath that which is better for his portion. A believer is a citizen of heaven; there is his inheritance; things on earth are added to him, only *pro viatico*, while he is travelling thitherward.

[The foregoing extract comprises about one-eighth part of the matter contained in "The Saint's Anchor Hold," upon the same subject, and is here introduced to show the spirit and style of the preacher, "in whose heart" (remark the Rev. Messrs. Hooke and Caryl in their introductory epistle to the work) "the *text* had been written by the Spirit of God, long before these discourses were penned by their author."]

LETTERS AND EXTRACTS.

[TO THE Rev. W. Davenport Bromley, of England, my special acknowledgments are due for obtaining the following Letters of Rev. John Davenport to Lady Vere. Having heard that such Letters existed in the British Museum, and Mr. B. having kindly offered further to assist me in my researches—just as the work was going to the printer, the 18th of March, 1851,—I wrote to him, expressing my desire, if possible, to secure copies of at least a portion of them. The 2d of May found me in the receipt of the Letters, which, after a whole day's search, were found (*Catalogue Ayscough*, "LETTERS OF DIVINES, MUSEUM BRITANNICUM BIBL., BIRCHIAN: 1275, PLUT. CVII. D.") and copied by Mr. Bromley. Their arrival was nearly at the time the printing had proceeded to the point where the Letters are inserted. As reference has already been made to the Appendix, they are here introduced, independent of the previous arrangement of this portion of the book.

Lady Mary Vere (as I gather from Wood, and others) was the daughter of Sir John Tracy, Kt. of Tuddington, County of Gloucester. Her husband was Horatio, Lord Vere, baron of Tilbury, the son of John de Vere, the fifteenth Earl of Oxford. During the reign of Charles I. he went into Holland as commander of a regiment sent to join with the united princes of Germany. He is characterized by Fuller in his "Worthies," as "of an excellent temper; it being true of him what is said of the Caspian Sea, that it doth never ebb nor flow, observing a constant tenor, neither elated with success nor depressed by defeat." He died the 2d of May, 1635, and was interred near his brother Sir Francis Vere, in Westminster Abbey. Between Lady Vere and Mr. Davenport there appears to have existed a warm friendship, evidently growing out of a similarity of religious views and feelings, and their mutual trials. But the Letters will amply speak for themselves.

A. B. D.

Rev. John Davenport to Lady Vere.

To the truly noble and worthy the Lady Vere, these be directed in Hague.

COLEMAN STREET, [LONDON,] *Jan.* 18, 1627.

MADAM:

A LINE to me from your Honor would have been to me good news from a far country. Mr. More was a welcome messenger, when he gave me assurance of your safe arrival after so dangerous and troublesome a voyage. He that delivered you on the sea will preserve you also on the land. How safe are you, Madam, that are hid under his wings, and held in his hands. In nothing be careful, but in all things let your requests be made known unto God, with prayers and supplications, and giving of thanks. Keep a record of special mercies, they will much strengthen you against future fears. I hope to wait on your Honor in England again, ere long, if that be true which I wrote to my lord. If not, yet while I live I hope to meet you daily in presenting our offerings and sacrifices at the door of the sanctuary. Be confident of this, that I am ever mindful of your Honor, making mention of you in my secret prayers, night and day. I beseech your Ladyship that I may still enjoy the benefit and assistance of your prayers, which I am sure have been accepted, and will still prevail with our All-sufficient God, through the medium of our Lord and Savior. Good Madam, let me prevail with you to take the encouragement which God gives you;—set a higher price on your prayers. Use and enjoy that interest which you have in God's favor through Christ. If earthly men can give good things to their children, what good thing can your heavenly Father deny you? only believe steadfastly; ask in faith, and waver not. You have an unjust judge granting the request of a strange widow; a sleepy man satisfying the importunate desire of his neighbor, when he comes unceasingly; and will not the righteous God who is faithful in his promises, grant the petitions of his children, whose prayers are always in season to him who commandeth them to pray always? Hagar was a bond-woman cast out of the church—she prayed not, but wept; she looked not up to God, but upon her Ishmael—that scoffing Ishmael; yet God heard and helped her. Will he not much more regard Sarah, who leaves her own country and father's house, to go with Abraham, in obedience to God, when she seeketh his face by prayer for herself and family, wherein God's name is called upon? Doubtless He will hear when she prayeth, and before she speaketh He will answer. Here stay up your heart, good Madam, and rejoice in the Lord. Many prayers must be denied and refused if you want anything that is good. But that I may not tire you with too much scribbling for conclusion or these rude lines written in too much haste, let me entreat your ladyship to present my service to my Lord Horton, and his good lady; excuse my not writing to them at this time by the haste of this bearer, Mr. Robert Hyrick, whom I presume to recommend to your notice, beseeching you to remember my Lord of his promise to hasten his preferment, with whom also I join Mr. Humfrey, who still waiteth in the city, expecting resolution from your Honor, how to dispose of himself. If I had but a little more time I would have written to Mr. Balinford and Mr. Sedgwick, to whom I desire to be affectionately remembered.

I rest your honorable Ladyship's much obliged,

John Davenport.

Rev. John Davenport to Lady Vere.

LONDON, *June* 30, 1628.

MADAM,

SINCE my recovery out of a dangerous sickness, which held me for a week or fortnight before Shrove-tide, to as long after Easter, (for which I return most humble and hearty thanks to the God of my life, the Father of mercies), I have had divers purposes of writing to your Honor, only I delayed in hope to write somewhat concerning the event and success of our *High Commission* troubles. But I have hoped in vain, for to this day we are in the same condition as before delayed to the finishing of this session in Parliament, which now is inhappily concluded without any satisfying contentment to the King or commonwealth. Threatenings were speedily revived against us by the new bishop of London, Dr. *Laud*, even the next day after the conclusion of their session. We expect a fierce storm from the enraged spirit of the two bishops. Ours, as I am informed, hath a particular aim at me upon a former quarrel, so that I expect ere long to be deprived of my pastoral charge in Coleman Street. But I am in God's hand, not in theirs, to whose good pleasure I do contentedly and cheerfully commit myself. If it be his will to have me laid aside as a broken vessel of no use, his will be done, and blessed be his name that he hath served himself of me hitherto. If otherwise he be graciously pleased to continue me in my station and ministry, he is able to keep that which I have committed to him, and I will wait on his goodness, however things succeed on earth. If he will not deliver me out of the mouth of the lions, yet he will deliver me from every evil work, and will preserve me to his heavenly kingdom. In the midst of these troubles the Lord hath not left me without many comforts, among which, the remembrance of your former favors, and the assurance of the present help of your prayers which I know prevail much with God, through Jesus Christ our Lord, doth exceedingly comfort me. I rejoice much when I hear of your health by your noble and worthy son-in-law, in whom I account your Honor and his Lady, your virtuous daughter, very happy as in one whom I am persuaded will far exceed the most of our nobility in the truest worth.* But much more did I rejoice to hear from him the continuance of your resolution to do God all the service you can in your place, whereunto the good hand of God I am confident hath brought you for some special end. The whole country looks upon your personal carriage, and upon your ordering of your family. Concerning your remove from the Hague, Dr. Sibbs and I have had some conference. We both agree in this conclusion, that in case absolute necessity do not enforce, you should not remove your dwelling both in respect of the benefit your family may have by being members of a congregation besides their help at home and in respect of the help and encouragement the ministry and cause of Religion at the Hague may have by your continuance and example. The glory that may redound to God,

* Her son-in-law here referred to, I suppose to have been Thomas, Lord Fairfax, who after leaving College spent some years in martial discipline under the command of Lord Vere, and who married Anne, one of his daughters, by whom he had Mary and Elizabeth; the first of whom was married to George Villiers, Duke of Buckingham, Nov. 19, 1657. Lord Fairfax was one who warmly espoused the parliamentary side in the civil wars, and contributed much to the gaining of the celebrated battle of Naseby. He was shipped in 1648 to the Hague. At the restoration of Charles II. he was formally reconciled to that monarch. He died in 1676. A. B. D.

and the good that may accrue to your family by your continuance there, will recompence the loss you sustain in your outward estate, but if this be not sufficient, we desire that you should propose the question with your own opinions and reasons more fully; and we will endeavor to satisfy your Ladyship by a more full answer. Mr. Sedgwick wrote to me for a prayer for Sir Edward Vere.* I have one in readiness for him if that I may hear an answer of what I wrote to Mr. Sedgwick, to whom and to Mr. Balinford, I desire heartily to be remembered. I confess myself indebted to Mr. Balinford for answer to his line, which I hope to satisfy ere long. I wrote letters to my Lord and to your Ladyship, by Mr. Hyrick, but never heard what became of them or him. I find a great miss of you, Madam, in the midst of my troubles, but I am not worthy to enjoy such a friend: sometimes I think I placed too much content in the enjoyment of such a friend, yet again I check myself fearing I did not prize you enough. I was not thankful enough to you, nor to God for you. The Lord enable me now to pay my debts to my noble Lord and your good Ladyship, by fervent and frequent prayers for you both. I hope ere long to be in Norfolk with my Lord Horton. My wife doth often make mention of your Ladyship. With most hearty —— of my esteem, I rest your honorable Ladyship's ———

—— DAVENPORT.

[Endorsed "Mr. Davenport, afterwards of New England, author of Power of Congregational Churches."]

* Obadiah Sedgwick took the degrees at Magdalen Hall, Oxford, about 1620, and afterwards became Chaplain to Lord Vere, with whom he went into the low countries.

Sir Edward Vere, was the son of John Vere, the sixteenth Earl of Oxford, and the nephew of Horatio, Lord Vere. A. B. D.

Rev. John Davenport to Lady Vere.

[EXTRACT.]

MADAM,

THE report of that great breach which it has pleased the Divine Providence to make in that family wherein you are so much interested, did at first somewhat astonish me, but after some recollections —— my thoughts —— affected me with sorrow and pity; for the public loss wherein the whole land suffereth by the fall of such a pillar, whose wisdom and public spirit made him of singular use not to Norfolk only, in his prudent management of his government, but to the whole realm in his strong compliance with the best affected patriots in Parliament for the promoting any profitable proposals and motions for the good of the whole nation. With pity and compassion to his good Lady and the tender branches whose loss I would rather wail than express, knowing how sensible love maketh us of that comfort which is more dear to us than our eyes, and more useful than our hands, and which we would choose rather to enjoy in the want of all outward things than to want in the enjoyment of all things; nor can I look aside from your Ladyship, Madam, when I remember how fearful you were because of the infection in these parts, lest by your coming hither any infection or sickness by any of yours might be brought into the family, in which respect the Lord hath dealt mercifully for the help of your spirit, that this sad accident befell not at your first coming hither, nor till half a year was past. * * * *

[Mr. Bromley adds in a note "The rest of this letter continues on the same subject," but does not give the date. In the numbering however, it is placed before the following line which he extracts from Letter No. 4, to Lady Vere, dated Dec. 26, 1629. "I will not fail to solicit Sir Maurice Abbot, on your business concerning Hales." Mr. B. also says that "John Davenport complains that his letters have been opened and read."]

Rev. John Davenport to Lady Vere.

To the Right Honorable and Very Noble Lady, the Lady Vere, these be delivered at the Hague.

Most Noble and much Honored Lady,

In the midst of my disappointments and tossings to and fro, it is some comfort that I have assurance of the continuance of your favor towards me, and of your remembrance of me in prayer. I know that love which you have been pleased so freely to cast upon me will quicken you to all diligence and industry in any way and cause which may conduce to the procuring of my liberty, but hitherto it hath pleased God to leave me in much darkness and many difficulties, to unbottom me wholly of the creature, and to reveal himself now clearly and fully in all issues and events that befall me. Be not troubled, much less discouraged, good minds, at any rumors you meet with concerning my present way. The persecution of the tongue is more fierce and terrible than that of the hand. At this time I have sense of both; but I can say that it is for thy name's sake, O Lord, that I bear this reproach; but the injurious surmises of those by whom I should be comforted and supported, many that profess religion in a higher strain than some others, doth most afflict me. I pray God it be not laid to their charge. The truth is, I have not forsaken my ministry, nor resigned my place, much less separated from the Church, but am only absent a while to wait upon God in the settling and quieting of things for light to discern my way, being willing to lie and die in prison, if the cause may be advantaged by it, but choosing rather to preserve the liberty of my person and ministry for the service of the Church elsewhere, if all doors are shut against me here. What I now do or suffer, is not caused by any guilt of any practice or action done or intended by me, which may expose me to any just censure of authority, much less by a desire of ease, as some give out, having gotten a great estate; least of all, by referring to my own private benefit, any thing committed to my trust for the public good. My estate, although not in any present want, is not able to maintain me without a calling. In the business of the Feoffees, I have given up my account on oath. The Lord God knoweth that I am so far from gaining by the business in my outward estate, that I am out of purse on my own particular, for the advancement of it. The only cause of all my sufferings is the alteration of my judgment in matters of conformity to the ceremonies established, whereby I cannot practise these, as formerly I have done, wherein I do not censure those who do conform; nay, I account many of them faithful and worthy instruments of God's glory, and I know that I did conform with as much inward peace as now I do forbear. In both, my uprightness was the same, but my light different. In this action, I walk by that light which shineth unto me. Let no man say the matters be small, and what need I be scrupulous in these things. That which the apostle speaketh, Rom. xiv., was but a small matter; yet you see how heavy a doom he passeth upon him that doth it, doubting of the lawfulness of it. I have been taught by my God and Saviour to allow no commandment of the Lord small, and to despise a man's way, that is too despicable and slight a thing to be stood upon. You know what an evil it is; but these things are not small, neither in themselves, nor in the consequences of them, but I have not time to be large, only thus much I thought good to present to your Honor, in way of account for the present, hoping, if God will give me an opportunity, to make a large and full apology for the satisfaction of all men. Any that know me, might have suspended their opinions and censures till they had heard from myself the reason of my actions. With much advice, of many ministers of eminent weight and worth, I have done all which I have done hitherto, and with desire of pitching on that way wherein God might be most glorified. In his due time, he will manifest it. Mr. Harris, I know fully, and I do heartily love. He is a very worthy man; of a very gracious heart, humble, mild and gentle spirit; a man not at all taken notice of by the bishops. He is weak and sickly, but you need not be discouraged by that, for it is a lingering weakness whereby he might hold out long; but his spirit is very active in good. He is very fit for your occasions in all respects. You shall be very happy in him, if you can have him, for he is one of a thousand. It is not in the bishop's power to take from you what is settled on your nobility and others by Magna Charta—the right and power of entertaining chaplains. The good Lord strengthen your inward man with the joys of his spirit.

Your Honorable Ladyship's most obliged,

JOHN DAVENPORT.

MADAM—

I pray send by this bearer
2 or 3 sheets of gilded paper.
I am about to write to my Lord Keeper.

Rev. John Davenport to Lady Vere.

To the Right Honorable Lady Vere, these present in Hackney.

July 21, 1635.

[EXTRACT.]

[Complaining of distractions by the unquiet spirit of Mr. Paget]—who, to all his former injuries, addeth this; that he hath now published a tedious book in English, full of reproaches and slanders against me, wherein he doth also injury to Mr. Parker, Dr. Ames, and Mr. Forbes, who are at rest, and Mr. Hooker, who is far absent, and to the best members of his own church, whom he brandeth several ways, which will give the prelates too much advantage, and open the mouths of enemies against the truth; this I am now constrained to answer for the truth's sake, notwithstanding all my former weakness; but our God is strong, in whom I trust that he will strengthen me to write with such a spirit as I ought. Help me with your prayers, and if any speak of Mr. Paget's book, let them know that I am about to answer it. It may be of good to prevent prejudice in the *Queen*, if your Honor, when you are pleased to write to her and Lady Lewiston, take notice of their favor to me, and pray them not to be prejudiced by any suggestions against me from that book, or otherwise, till they may peruse my answer. This I ask, not for any use I have of the Queen's favor, but that I may not be hindered from receiving good from my ministry, which yet she well esteemeth.

Another letter, directed as above,

Dated ROTTERDAM, 25 *Dec.*, 1632–[5?]

[EXTRACT.]

But what can a poor Pilgrim, a banished man do? That which is wanting in this condition, shall not be wanting in prayer to God, or letters to yourself as to the knowledge of your condition, as necessity, I shall minister occasion. I ever remain in unfeigned thankfulness and faithfulness.

Your Honorable Ladyship's most obliged,
in the Lord Jesus,
JOHN DAVENPORT.

To the Right Honorable the Lady, the Lady Mary Vere, These, Hackney.

NEW HAVEN, 13*th* 9*th month* [*Nov.*], 1647.

[EXTRACT.]

The Lord's controversy with his people is not yet ended, but his hand is stretched out still, and worse things are yet for to come, till the slaughter of the witnesses shall be finished, which I suppose is not yet passed. When I seriously compare the description of that time, as it is in Rev. xi., with the providence of God which has passed upon his people at this day, yet I believe that the light which is now discovered in England concerning church order and government, will never be wholly put out, though I expect that contrary principles will prevail for a time with the generality, and sundry in reputation for godliness, they be more renewed in the spirit of their mind to prove, &c., what is that perfect will of God whereby a full and exact conformity to heavenly rules and patterns will be hindered and overborne by such as plead for conforming to this world.

Your Honorable Ladyship's ever obliged,
to serve you in the Lord,
JOHN DAVENPORT.

NOTE A.

[Many autograph letters of Mr. Davenport to Governor Winthrop are still preserved in the Winthrop family, at New Haven. Most of these have been published by Dr. Bacon, in his Historical Discourses, and also in the Third Series of the Collections of the Mass. Historical Society. In the latter, the original orthography is retained. A few of these will here be introduced, extracted from the above-named works, and also one to the Rev. John Cotton, now in the possession of Mr. J. W. Thornton, of Boston, which has never before been published.]

I.

The Rev. John Davenport and Gov. Eaton, "To the much honored the Governor, Deputy, and Assistants, &c.," of Massachusetts.

It may please the worthy and much honored Governor, Deputy, and Assistants, and with them, the present court, to take knowledge that our desire of staying within this patent was real and strong, if the eye of God's providence (to whom we have committed our ways, especially in so important an enterprise as this, which, we confess, is far above our capacities) had guided us to a place convenient for our families and for our friends. Which as our words have often expressed, so, we hope, the truth thereof is sufficiently declared by our almost nine months' patient waiting in expectation of some opportunity to be offered us, for that end, to our great charge and hindrance, many ways.

In all which time, we have, in many prayers, commended the guidance of our apprehensions, judgments, spirits, resolutions and ways, into the good hand of the only wise God, whose prerogative it is to determine the bounds of our habitations according to the ends for which he hath brought us into these countries; and we have considered, as we were able, by his help, whatsoever place hath been propounded to us, being ready to have, with contentment accepted (if by our stay any public good might be promoted) smaller accommodations, and upon dearer terms (if they might be moderately commodious) than, we believe, most men, in the same case with us, in all respects would have done. And whereas a place for an inland plantation, beyond Watertown, was propounded to us, and pressed with much importunity by some whose words have the power of a law with us, in any way of God, we did speedily and seriously deliberate thereupon, it being the subject of the greatest part of a day's discourse. The conclusion was, that, if the upland should answer the meadow ground in goodness and desirableness (whereof yet there is some ground of doubting) yet, considering that a boat cannot pass from the bay thither, nearer than eight or ten miles distance, and that it is so remote from the bay and from any town, we could not see how our dwelling there would be advantageous to these plantations, or compatible with our conditions, or commodious for our families or for our friends.

Nor can we satisfy ourselves that it is expedient, for ourselves, or for our friends, that we choose such a condition, wherein we must be compelled to have our dwelling-houses so far distant from our farms, as Boston or Charlestown is from that place, few of our friends being able to bear the charge thereof (whose cases, nevertheless, we are bound to consider), and some of them that are able, not being persuaded that it is lawful for them to live continually from the greatest part of their families, as in this case, they would be necessitated to do. The season of the year, and other weighty considerations, compelled us to hasten to a full and final conclusion, which we are at last come unto, by God's appointment and direction, we hope in mercy, and have sent letters to Connecticut for a speedy transacting the purchase of the parts about Quillypieck, from the natives which may pretend title thereunto; by which act we are absolutely and irrevocably engaged that way; and we are persuaded that God will order it for good unto these plantations, whose love so abundantly above our deserts or expectations, expressed in your desire of our abode in these parts, as we shall ever retain in thankful memory, so we shall account ourselves thereby obliged to be anyway instrumental and serviceable for the common good of these plantations as well as of those, which the Divine Providence hath combined together in as strong bond of brotherly affection, by the sameness of their condition, as Joab and Abishai were, whose several armies did mutually strengthen them both against several enemies—2 Sam 10 : 9, 10, 11; or rather they are joined together as Hippocrates his twins, to stand and fall, to grow and decay, to flourish and wither, to live and die together. In witness of the premises we subscribe our names,

JOHN DAVENPORT.
THEOPH. EATON.

The 12th day of the 1st Month [March], Anno 1638.

II.

To his worthily much honored friend, John Winthrop, Esq., these present in Pequot.

HONORED SIR,—

By Joseph Alsop we did expect your arrival with your family here, and your abode with us this winter. But instead of yourself I received your lines, whereby I understand that your real purpose of transporting your family, was, contrary to your expectation, utterly disappointed. If you knew how much of our hopes of enjoying you with us comforted us, you would easily apprehend how much the frustration of them damped us. And if Mrs. Winthrop knew how welcome she would be unto us, she would neglect whatsoever others may suggest to discourage her from coming to us. And because I understood by Joseph Alsop how boisterously some of your plantation opposed your voyage, with your family, to us ward, and intimated that the vessel was rotten and your lives would be endangered by the voyage, I signified in a letter which I sent to you by Higby, that on the Lord's day after his departure from Pequot, which was the next day after the date of your letter to me, as I remember, Joseph Alsop gave public thanks in the congregation for his safe and comfortable passage. And that you might know what preparation was made for your comfortable being in your house this winter, I showed in the same letter how careful and active my wife hath been to procure hands to prepare your house, whereby your well is cleansed, and a new pump set up, and the rooms are made warm, and tables, with some chairs, are provided. The twenty loads of wood you mentioned are ready, and some already laid in. The rest wait but for your coming. Also thirty bushels of wheat, and fifty pounds of candles; which together with other things, I signified that you may see, and Mrs. Winthrop also, how earnestly your coming to us is expected and desired. You will now receive some farther intelligence from Mr. Goodyear, concerning the iron-work, unto which there is a great forwardness among the people generally, which it seems is somewhat checked by your absence at this time. Sir, I thank you for the books you sent me to read, which I am diligently perusing. My wife took care of your apples that they may be kept safe from the frost, that Mrs. Winthrop might have the benefit of them. Now the Lord pave your way to us, and make your journey safe, comfortable and prosperous; in whom I rest,

Yours, exceedingly obliged,

John Davenport.

New Haven, *the last of the* 9*th*, '55, [30*th Nov.* 1655.]

Sir, I forgat to give you notice, that my wife hath provided for Mrs. Winthrop a cleanly, thrifty maid servant, sister Beckley's daughter, whom she kept from a service at Connecticut, where she was much desired, in expectation of your coming.

III.

To the right worshipful John Winthrop, Esq., these present in Hartford.

Honored Sir,—

A report that you was gone to the Bay, put me from my purpose of sending the enclosed, till I might certainly know where my letter might find you. I have now received intelligence by John Thomas, that you are at Hartford, and that Mrs. Winthrop hath been very ill and in great danger of her life, but is now, by the mercy of God, recovered. Blessed be his name for this mercy to her and to yourself and yours, in her recovery. But withal he saith that yourself are very ill, and have taken physic this day, and that he staid three hours to understand how it wrought, and is informed that it wrought well. This giveth us some ground of hope that God will graciously bless the means for restoring your health, whose life we account exceeding precious, and a blessing to many. He who hath given you a merciful heart to others in their sickness, hath promised that you also shall obtain mercy. We are not wanting to you in our prayers, since we heard of your state, which was but this night; nor shall we cease from praying for your life and health, till we know that our petition is answered for your good. Be pleased to let us hear from you by the first opportunity, how it is with you. My wife desireth to send something suitable to your present condition, but knoweth not what till she hear further concerning you. At present she sends you a few fresh raisins, and a little liquorice, and your own unicorn's horn, which she hath kept safe for you, since you sent it for Mrs. Eaton. My wife is ashamed to send so few raisins, but she hath no more so good. Were it not I am loth to trouble you with many lines, I should write much more concerning other matters, and particularly to return thanks for your mindfulness of me for a vent for some of my horses, by Mr. Adis, concerning which I hope to have an opportunity of speaking with you ere long. The Lord Jesus be with you, and bless means for your recovery. With presenting my service and my wife's and son's to Mrs. Winthrop and yourself, and our love to yours, I rest, sir,

Your much obliged,

JOHN DAVENPORT.

NEW HAVEN, *the* 20*th d. of the* 5*th m.* [*July*], 1658.

IV.

To the Right Worshipful, his much honored friend, John Winthrop, Esq., these present in Hartford.

HONORED SIR,—

These few lines are to congratulate your return to your family, as I hope in health, and to give you an account of my negotiation with ours about the iron-work, the issue whereof is according to your mind, as the enclosed to Capt. Clarke from our governor will show, which I send enclosed that it may more speedily be conveyed to him by land, than we can expect it will be by sea. The Lord also bless the intended marriage of your eldest daughter to Mr. Newman for many comforts to you both, and to your family, and to themselves! Be pleased to present mine, my wife's, my son's, humble service to Mrs. Winthrop, together with yourself, with many thanks to her for her great kindnesses to us when we were at Hartford. In great haste, I must *manum de tabula.* The Lord Jesus dwell with you and yours in peace and loving kindness! In whom I rest,

Yours obliged,

JOHN DAVENPORT.

NEW HAVEN, *the* 22*d of the* 8*th*, '58 [22*d Oct.* 1658.]

V.

To the Honored John Winthrop, Esq., Governor of Connecticut colony, these present in New London.

HONORED SIR,—

Your quick departure from Hartford, after my son's return home from thence, denied me an opportunity of expressing our due thanks for your loving entertainment of so bold a visitor, whereof he speaketh much, and yet is not satisfied with what he hath spoken, thinking it falls short of what he should speak, to express your and Mrs. Winthrop's kindness to him. Sir, you know that the affections of parents are apt to sympathize with their children, and to take contentment in what they find to be justly pleasing and comfortable to them. Hence it is that I desire to take this first overture for conveyance of these few lines in way of thankfulness from us, both to yourself (as I have already done to Mrs. Winthrop by J. Latimer) for the same; and to let you know that I have received a large letter from Mr. Blinman, dated Aug. 22, whereby I understand that God hath brought him to Newfoundland, in safety and health, and maketh his ministry acceptable to all the people there except some Quakers, and much desired and flocked unto. He hath made choice of a ship for Barnstable to his content, the master being godly. After these passages, and his notifying to me the lady Kirk's respectful and loving mention of me, whom, she saith, she hath heard in London, he addeth to what I had heard from England, that a fine of 5*l.* is put upon any that shall name the last protector. 2. That the Lord Henry is sent for out of Ireland, and out of his place. 3. That four are sent from England, and four from France, and four from the States, to see whether they can compose matters between Swede and Dane. 4. That 30,000*l.* is demanded for the old protector's funeral, which the parliament refused to pay. Some urged that those that had the mourning clothes should pay for them, that the commons might not be charged. 5. That the last protector was like to be apprehended for the debt, but withdrew; whereupon the parliament gave him six months' liberty to come to terms with creditors. 6. That Mr. Hugh Peters is distracted, and under sore horrors of conscience, crying out of himself as damned, and confessing heinous actings. He concludes, "For the truth hereof, *sit fides penes auctorem.*" 7. That there is an ambassador gone for Spain. Lastly, That the fleet in the West Indies have taken an almost incredible mass of treasure in some Spanish towns there. Reported by a ship in the harbor where Mr. Blinman lies, that met a frigate at sea, going home for. I shall not add at present, but my desires for your safe journey to the Bay and speedy return to your family, and then to New Haven,—and my wife's, with our son's respectful and most affectionate salutations and humble service.

Yours, exceedingly obliged,

JOHN DAVENPORT.

NEW HAVEN, *the 28th d. of the 7th m.* [*28th Sept.*] 1659.

VI.

To the Right Worshipful John Winthrop, Esq. Governor of Connecticut Colony, these present in Hartford.

HONORED SIR,

Yesterday, Mr. Gilbert and Deacon Myles brought unto me a letter written by yourself to sergeant Whitehead, about your house, which, it seems, was an answer to a letter sent by I know not whom, nor when, to yourself, in the name of the townsmen, and with their consent, that they might purchase the house for the town. From Brother Herriman's discourse with my wife, I understand that himself and Brother Wakeman had speech with you, to promove that motion. All this was done and written without my knowledge and my wife's and son's. They did not, nor any from or for them, make it known unto me in the least, that such a letter or message should be sent unto you. Two of the brethren who were not townsmen, spake with me formerly about their fear of losing the governor for want of an house, and propounded yours, concluding from your own words that you would not dwell here, though if there had been any ground of hope of the contrary, they would not have propounded it. This I add, that I may do them right. My advice was, that they would not send to you about it; and to stay them from so doing, I told them that I heard you purposed to come hither shortly, (for so Daniel your man had reported,) and did think that they would wait for that. These things I thus particularly relate, that you may see that I had not the least hand in what they have done, nor consent to it, nor knowledge of it. When the forenamed showed me your letter, and enquired what I would do in reference to the power and trust you was pleased to commit to me about alienating your house, I told them, as I had said unto yourself before, that I must desire to be excused from acting in that business, and did refuse it, and do still pray you to waive me in that employment, who shall in other things deny you nothing that I am fit to do, if I may really pleasure you thereby. My son also hath refused to act in that matter. Had a letter been brought to us to subscribe, for inviting you to bring your family when you shall find a convenient time, and to come and dwell in your house, and the sooner the welcomer, &c., we should have signed that with both our hands. What is done I have not yet heard, therefore cannot give you account of it.

While I paused a little, having written thus far, I hear that the two mentioned in the first line have alienated your house. If it be so, I am heartily sorry, that what we have so many years desired and hoped for, we shall be thus deprived of, viz. your neighborhood, which we do highly value, and therefore cannot but look upon our loss as exceeding great. My wife received Mrs. Winthrop's loving token, the sugar loaf she was pleased to send her, for which she returneth her many thanks, yet is sorry to have it from her, to whom she accounteth herself obliged otherwise rather to send unto her. With mine, my wife's and son's humble services to you both, and respectful and affectionate salutations to your daughters, commending you both, and yours, unto the everlasting arms, I rest, Sir,

Yours, exceedingly obliged,

JOHN DAVENPORT.

The 5th day of the 2d month, (April,) 1660.

We desire to receive some intelligence of your and Mrs. Winthrop's coming to us, whose house shall be as your own; and you will much cheer us if you say we shall enjoy you here shortly.

VII.

[*Superscription torn off.*]

HONORED SIR,

I received yours by Brother Benham, whom God preserved from being drowned in his journey homeward. The river by Mr. Yale's farm was swollen high; his wife was fearful of riding through it. God provided an help for her at the instant, by a passenger who traveled from Windsor to Brandford to Mr. Crane's, whose daughter he had married. He helped Sister Benham over a tree. But her husband adventuring to ride through, a foot of his horse slipped; so he fell into the water, and his horse, as he thinketh, fell upon him or struck him with his foot, for he had a blow on his head. But through the mercy of God he is now well. This day, Mr. Atwater, being at our lecture, speaks of a letter newly received from his wife, who writes her fears that she shall never see him again, doubting that he was cast away the last storm, whereby, she saith, sundry vessels about Boston have suffered much hurt, and some persons were cast away, and a ship also, if I mistake not, at Cape Cod. But God ordered things so, by his good providence, that Mr. Atwater was then at New London in a safe harbor. Even now, Major Hawthorne and Mr. Richards are come from the Dutch. They are gone into the town to despatch some business, but will return to sup and lodge at my house. I do not yet know whether they purpose to return to Boston by land or sea, yet prepare these lines, *in omnem eventum*, to send by them if they go by land, or by some other conveyance if I can hear of any.

Sir, I thank you for my sight of Mr. Knowles' letter to Mr. Joanes. That which he speaks of a parliament in Scotland, I cannot receive. For I suppose England will not suffer it. I still hope that things in England are in a hopeful way. The Lord Jesus dwell with you in peace! Mine, my wife's and son's humble services are affectionately presented to yourself and Mrs. Winthrop, with our salutations to your daughters. Having other letters to write, in answer to friends in the Bay, I am compelled to take off my pen, but shall always remain, Sir,

Your exceedingly obliged,

JOHN DAVENPORT.

NEW HAVEN, *the* 13*th of the* 2*d*, [*April*,] 1660.

Mr. Price, of Salem, and his wife, present their services to yourself and Mrs. Winthrop, in a letter brought to me by Major Hawthorne. They are importunately desirous to stay Mr. Higginson with them at Salem, for continuance, and in way of office.

VIII.

To the Right Worshipful John Winthrop, Esq., Governor of Connecticut colony, these present in [*Hartford.*]

HONORED SIR,—

I perceive you have received from others the sad intelligence of the decease of our honored governor, my very dear and precious friend.* We hoped that he was in a good way of recovery from his former sickness, and were comforted with his presence in the assembly two Lord's days, and at one meeting of the Church on a week day, without any sensible inconvenience. And on the morning of the day of public thanksgiving, he found himself encouraged to come to the public assembly. But after the morning sermon, he told me that he found himself exceedingly cold fr m head to toe, yet, having dined, he was refreshed, and came to the meeting again in the afternoon, the day continuing very cold. That night he was very ill;

* The governor here spoken of, is Governor Newman.

yet he did not complain of any relapse into his former disease, but of inward cold, which he and we hoped might be removed by his keeping warm and using other suitable means. I believe he did not think that the time of his departure was so near, or that he should die of this distemper, though he was always prepared for his great change. The last day of the week he desired my son to come to him the next morning to write a bill for him to be prayed for, according to his direction. My son went to him after the beating of the first drum; but finding himself not fit to speak much, he prayed him to write for him what he thought fit. When the second drum beat, I was sent for to him. But before I came, though I made haste, his precious immortal soul was departed from its house of clay unto the souls of just men made perfect. We were not worthy of him, a true Nathaniel, an Israelite indeed who served God in Christ, in sincerity and truth. He honored God in his personal conversation, and in his administration of chief magistracy in this colony; and God hath given him honor in the hearts of his people. My loss and my son's, who took great contentment in his company, as he also did in his, is very great, and our grief answerable. But the public loss is far greater; and answerably it is generally bewailed, God recompensing his faithfulness with his living desired, and dying lamented. It becomes us to lay our hands upon our mouths, yea, to put our mouths in the dust, remembering whose doing this is. Yet, in respect of means, I could wish two things; first, that in his former sickness, he had wholly and only followed your directions; secondly, that he had forborne coming forth that cold day. But God's counsels shall stand, whose will is the first and best cause of all things; and the very errors of men shall serve to accomplish his purposes, who is holy in all his ways and righteous in all his works.

Sir, what I wrote in my former letter concerning Mrs. Coglien, I had from Anthony Elcock, who received it in the Bay, viz. that she was discontented that she had no suitors, and that she had encouraged her farmer, a mean man, to make a motion to her for marriage, which accordingly he propounded, prosecuted, and proceeded in it so far that afterwards, when she reflected upon what she had done, and what a change of her outward condition she was bringing herself into, she was discontented, despaired, and took a great quantity of ratsbane, and so died. *Fides sit penes auctorem.* Sir, I humbly thank you for the intelligence you was pleased to give me of an opportunity of transmitting a letter for London, which is a thing that I earnestly desire, and do make bold to commit it to your own care, seeing you are pleased to give me that liberty, and hearing that the vessel is yet at Hartford. The letter is of great importance. The safe and speedy handing of it to Mr. Robert Newman will be a real advantage to me, and the miscarriage of it no small disadvantage. In which respect, if you conceive it will be more speedily and certainly conveyed to him by this way than by the ship at Boston, I desire it may be sent accordingly with the more engagement for committing it to a sure hand at Barbadoes, to be delivered to Mr. Newman in London, as the matter is of more consequence; that an answer may be returned from him, by the first ship from London to Boston in the spring. Having thus opened the case, I crave leave to commit it wholly to yourself to take that course with it which you shall judge most suitable. I shall not add, but mine, my wife's and son's humble service to yourself and

Mrs. Winthrop with our respectful and affectionate salutation to your son and daughters, praying the Lord to continue your life unto them, and theirs unto you, and to multiply his favors and blessings upon you and them through Jesus Christ; in whom I rest, Sir,

Yours, ever obliged,

JOHN DAVENPORT.

NEW HAVEN, *this 27th d. of the 9th m.* [*November*,] 1660.

The miscarriage of a letter which I formerly sent to London by way of Barbadoes, makes me so desirous that this may not miscarry.

IX.

Rev. John Davenport to Hon. John Leverett.

[The following letter from Rev. John Davenport to Major-General Leverett, is copied from "Miscellanies" published by the younger Hutchinson.]

HONORABLE SIR,

Let my first salutation be my congratulation for this addition of a further expression of God's people's affection and confidence in your courage, wisdom, and faithfulness for the interest of our Lord Jesus, and the good and welfare of church and commonwealth in that they have unanimously called you to be one of the assistants for governing the civil affairs in the court, as well as to be their Major General in the camp. The good Lord assist and govern you by his Spirit of wisdom and courage, and of the fear of the Lord in both.

Sir: I received yours, dated 27th 3d month, 1665, for which I return humble and hearty thanks, and for the inclosed narrative, whereby I perceive that the powers of darkness which have prevailed in other parts of the world are at work here also, to subvert the kingdom of Christ in these ends of the earth. But God hath not yet said that this is their hour in reference to New England, though our unthankfulness for the Gospel, unfaithfulness under it, disobedience to it, declensions from the simplicity that is in Christ, and sinful compliances, &c., have deserved that our hedge should be broken down. That admonition which Christ sent unto the church at Ephesus, should sound in our hearts continually: "Repent, and do thy first works." For even David had his first and his latter ways. Therefore it is noticed concerning Jehoshaphat, in 2 Chron. 17 : 3, that the Lord was with him, because he walked in the first ways of his father David. If New England would return to the first ways of reformation here begun, according to gospel rules and patterns (from which the compass of the last synod's conclusions seems to be varied by some degrees toward the antarctic, or is newly discovered to be other than I formerly apprehended to have been the way of these churches), I would hope that the same only wise God, who disappointed the counsel of that arch-prelate in the reign of the last king (whereby your patent was once and again demanded by the said king, and as often refused by your general court, to be returned to England), would also still appear, in this juncture, by frustrating the general design, and making it an abortion, or a mere trial of the country, whether they will stand to their church rights and privileges, or permit them to be invaded and violated by such attempts, which, when they are tried and found unsuccessful, will cease for the future. For the Lord is and will be with his people while they are with him; and if ye seek him he will be found of you. An experiment hereof you had in the quiet proceeding of your elections as a gracious answer to prayers. Their claiming power to sit authoritatively as a court of Appeals, and that to be managed in an arbitrary way, was a manifest laying of a ground-work to undermine your whole government established by your charter. If you had consented thereunto, you had plucked down with your own hands that house which wisdom had built for you and your posterity. For all your courts would then have signified nothing; the sentences of them being liable to be disannulled, upon complaints of commissioners, made by delinquents, as appeareth in the case of Mr. Thomas Deane, &c., and the execution of the justest censure might be hindered, and the course of Justice obstructed as you have already found in the case of John Potter. Nor can I see that your preserving that authority and jurisdiction, which the last king, by his royal charter, gave you, can rationally be accounted as opposing the sovereignty which this king hath over you, seeing *id possunt reges quod jure possunt.* There is indeed a verbal profession of preserving your liberties. But if the commission of these gentlemen be of such a latitude as they say, it is a real destruction of that which they promise to preserve. *Quid verba audiam, cum facta videam.* Therefore, to me the matter of your answer seems to be rational, just, and necessary. As for the solemnity of publishing it, in three places, by sounding a trumpet, I believe you did it upon good advice, and therefore, suspending my own thoughts, I shall wait to see how it is resented at the court in England. Yet upon serious second and third thoughts, I see not but it was your prudent way so to do, considering that,—1. It was the answer of the general court. 2. Published in the king's name. 3. For the cognizance of the whole country concerned in it. 4. For declaring the courage and resolution of the whole country to define their charter liabilities and privileges, and not to yield up their right voluntarily, so long as they can hold it, in dependence upon God in Christ, whose interest is in it, for his protection and blessing, who will be with you while you are with him. If my advice were worth anything, I would say, let a collection of your grievances occasioned by the coming over of these Commissioners, and by their actings, in one place and another, and of the three commissioners in prejudicing the Indians against the English, whereby the good work for their conversion is in danger to be hindered, and the safety and peace of the English to be hazarded for the future; let, I say, all instances of their illegal and injurious proceedings throughout the country be fully collected, and clearly proved, and speedily transmitted and represented to the King, the Lord Chancellor, &c., by your next address, and therein let them fully and plainly understand that the whole country (for the generality of them) are much aggrieved at these doings, and humbly desire to be resettled in their former state, according to their charter, and that they may be freed from those new encroachments; wherein the petition to the general court, presented in the names of so many non-freemen, declaring their full satisfaction in the settled government, as it is, with their earnest desire that it may be still continued without alteration, may be signified to the higher powers, to good purpose. Sir, you see whether my zeal for preserving Christ's interests in your parts (though in New

Haven Colony it is miserably lost) and my unfeigned love to your colony, and my fervent desire of the welfare of the churches and commonwealth (so far as they may be promoted and perpetuated by your circumspection) hath carried me, through my confidence in your wisdom and faithfulness, that you will make no other use of this my scribbling than such as shall be safe both to you and me. To the honorable Governor you may communicate it, if you please, presenting also to him my humble and affectionate service.

Sir: I return your copy of the articles which concern Commameene,* having received them formerly from yourself and lately from Mr. Bishop, with many thanks to you for the sight and loan of them from us both. But I am and shall be discouraged from reading such agreement made by a subject, though honorable, till I see your charter, sealed by the late King, and obliging his heirs and successors, really as well as verbally confirmed and performed, toward the purchasing whereof I paid £50, and Mr. Eaton £100, and sundry other merchants the same sums respectively, we being members for the London Corporation for N. E., which doth engage me to desire and endeavor, what I can and may, that the intended effects thereof may remain, for the service of Christ and for the good of all his people, both at present and for the future. I hear well of your last address to the King. I should take it for a favor if I might peruse it, and the King's answer. I shall now cease from giving you any further trouble, but not from praying for a good issue of your and our present

* Supposed to be a subordinate Indian Chief.

afflictive exercises, and not ours only, but of the distressed churches of Christ, in whom I rest.

Sir, your obliged and assured,
JOHN DAVENPORT.

New Haven, the 24th of the 4th Month, 1665.

X.

Rev. John Davenport to Rev. John Cotton.

To the Reverend, and his worthily much honoured friend and brother, Mr. John Cotton, Teacher to ye Church in Boston these present.

REVEREND AND WORTHY SIR,—

Yours dated ye 22th of ye 1st m. 1649, was not brought to my hand till this 2d day of the 3d month 1650—whereby I understand that Brother Pierce hath delivered unto you a copie of some sermons preached by me in our weekly lecture, wherein my intentt was to stablish the hearers in assurance that Jesus ye sonne of ye virgin Mary is the onely true Messiah. The forenamed brother diligently wrote as his manner was, but finding that his head and pen could not carry away some material expressions, he earnestly desired me to lett him have my notes, to perfect his owne by them, which I promised him in ye winter was twelve months. Having other hindrances, he called not for them, when he was here, but being in ye Bay, and unresolved about his stay there, or passage for England, or returne hither, he wrote for those notes, clayming my promise, wh accordingly I sent to him by brother Livermore with a double charge, 1. yt when he had transcribed them, he would return my copie again by a safe land-messenger, not by sea; remembering that I lost my autographs of all ye sermons I preached out of the Epistle of Christ to the Church of Philadelphia, (Rev. 3,) concerning ye hours of Temptation, and sundry others about Christ's shaking heaven and earth to establish his kingdom, in (Heb. 12) wh I gave Mr. Gregson, at his request, to carry with him when he went hence for England. My 2d charge was, that when he had transcribed them he would show them unto you, and make no other use of them than privately for himself, but by your advise. This I added, because I feared yt he had a purpose for ye presse, from some words that I observed now and then to fall from him. Now I am glad that you have them with you to peruse, where I pray keep them till you have sifted them thoroughly. I thank you for your faithfull advise about ye Interpretation of Phil. 2 : 6, 7, 8, which I did afterwards handle at large, unto 12, in sundry sermons, according to ye method I had propounded for handling the grounds of religion. In those sermons I did interpret that scripture in ye largest and most comprehensive sense; and particularly, as holding forth Christ's personal Godhead-humbling himself to assume our human nature. Nor can I tell what other or narrower interpretation I adhered unto, in the notes under your hand: but well knowing yt ye one way and ye other will suite the scope of that discourse, I leave it wholly to your wisdom to add or alter, as you find expedient, and analogous with other Scriptures, that allegation with its interpretation. I shall further pray you to cast your eye upon yt type, the rock in ye wilderness, to see whether I have safely expressed the rocks following ym, wh, I conceive, was that ye water flowing from ye rock followed ym all ye way in ye wilderness, meaning it of y[t] 2[d] rock in Rephidim, and kept by y[m] here and there in wells digged (Numb. 20 : 18), which also Tertullian (lib.depap.) seemeth to intend by his *petræ aquatilem sequetam.* Such have been my thoughts, but whether I did there so wright y[m] down, I doe not remember. Others have other apprehensions of it. If you meet with anything in y[t] or anything else, y[t] you doe not approve, deleatur. I thought it better to lett him have myne own notes to rectifye his by them, than to lett him print great mistakes for want of that helpe. I wish the wrong y[t] is done Reipub. literariæ by imp'fect copies may warne you to improve ye present season for ye perfecting of as many Tractates and commentarys as you have for ye publick good. One thing more give me leave to propound, and as earnestly as my modesty will p'mit, to importune, that you would take into your serious thoughts the question about single testimony of severall p'sons who speak fully to y[e] things and with concurrence therein, though not joyntly in y[e] circ'stances of time & place, and to answer that logicall quirk w'ch M[r] Prudden told you of, and what other Argum'ts you find in y[t] postscript of M[r] Cheivers, his answer to y[e] church, & which you have elsewhere mett with. You will much oblige me, if you will hasten a copie of y[or] labours upon that subject. If you list not to appear in this controversie, you shall be wholly concealed by me. For the managing of my speech or silence your letter of advice shall have the force of a law with me. Onely be intreated to dispatch it unto me by the 1st opportunity, whether by land or sea. *Bis dat qui cito dat.* The reason of this my earnestness for a speedy return, I will give at your demand by the next, which I believe you will judge to be weighty.

I had rather ease than add to your burdens, but that we are in a speciall manner, called to a serious consideration and determination concerning this point. The Lord Jesus dwell with you in peace, and preserve your life, & health & comforts, & crowne your holy labours with a plentifull blessing. In whom I rest,

Your obliged friend & brother,

JOHN DAVENPORTE.

NEW HAVEN, *ye 6th d. of ye* 3 *m.* 1650.

I am told that this vessell will speedily returne againe. I hope that you will return an answer by him if no other passenger leave sooner, with speed w'ch I earnestly desire.

XI.

Rev. John Davenport to John Winthrop, Jr.

To his Honoured freind John Winthrop, Esqre, these present, in Pequot.

HOND SIR—

We did earnestly expect your coming hither, with Mrs Winthrop and your familie, the last light moone, according to your purpose signified to us, having also intelligence that a vessel wayted upon you, at Pequot, for that end, and were thereby encouraged to provide your house, that it might be fitted, in some measure, for your comfortable dwelling in it, this winter.

My wife was not wanting in her endeavours to set all wheeles on going, all hands, that she could procure, on worke, that you might finde all things to your satisfaction. Though she could not accomplish her desires, to the full;

yet she proceeded as farr as she could ; whereby many things are done, viz. the house made warme, the well cleansed, the pumpe fitted for your use, some provision of wood is layed in, and 20 loades will be ready, whensoever you come: and sundry, who have received help from you have, by my wife's instigation, prepared 30 bush. of wheate for the present and sister Glover hath 12lb. of candles ready for you. My wife hath also procured a maid-servant for you, who is reported to be cleanly, and saving, her mother is of the Church, and she is kept from a place in Connectacut (where she was much desired) to serve you. At last Joseph Alsop arrived here, in safety, on the Lords day, and, in the Assembly, gave thancks for his comfortable passage. By him I received (instead of yourselfe and yours, whose presence was heartily desired by us all) a letter from you, dated on the day before his arrivall, whereby I understood that some providences intercurring hindred and disappointed your reall Intentions of coming, with your family, to us, both before, and by him. The hazzard and danger suspected, you now see, was more in ungrounded imaginacōns of those who laboured to hinder your proceeding, than in the reality and trueth of the cause prætended by them. Yet we have hope that, by another vessel (I heare, Mr Yongs, ni fallor) you will be accomodated, for transportation of your familye, and what you purpose to bring hither, and that you incline to improve that opportunity—whereof I am glad. Many hands are daily at worke for the iron-buisnes: onely your presence is wanting, to sett all things in a right course. If Mrs Winthrop knew how wellcome she will be to us, she would, I believe, neglect whatsoever others doe, or may be forward to suggest, for her discouragement. Salute her, with due respect, in my name and my wifes, most affectionately, together with Mrs Lake. The Lord Jesus pave your waye, and make your journey to us speedy and prosperous! In whom I rest, Sir, Yours exceedingly obliged,

JOHN DAVENPORTE.

NEWHAVEN *this* 22 *of the* 9*th* 55.

My wife had a man in pursuite that would be very fitt to manadge your Island, and the motion proceedes in an hopefull way, if a marriage, which he is about, doth not hinder. My sonne presents his humble service to yourselfe and Mrs Winthrope.

Sir William Constable, and Mr Tillinghast are taken away by death in England, boath buryed; the one, in London; the other, in Norfolke with great honour. Also Capt. Fen is dead at Barbadoes, and Mr Nowel, at Charles Towne. Mr Leverets wifes violent aversenes from his settling in the Colledge, he saith, causeth him to desist from that buiseness. So, that worke must waite for a better season.

My wife complaineth of a paine in the soles of her feete, especially in the evening, sometimes it burnes. Yet in the day, and after she hath bene a while in bed, it doth not trouble her.

Sir) I thanck you for the 2 bookes you sent me to peruse, which I am reading diligently.

[Labelled, "Mr Davenport."]

XII.

Rev. John Davenport to John Winthrop, Jr.

To the Right Worshipll and worthily much Honoured John Winthrope Esqr Governor of Connectacute these present in Hartford.

Honoured Sir)

Yours, datd ye 27th of this moneth, I received, by one of Farefield, whose name I know not, and in it an Almanack inclosed, for boath which I returne many thancks, and send inclosed a copie of a wrighting, which Mr Atwater brought from the Baye, which I read with joy and thancksgiving unto God, beleiving it to be a true Narration of the state of things in England, and the last that is come to our hands. So that the other reports of Naylers being Governour of Bristow, and of the fight betweene General Munck and Lambert etc. I looke at as misreports. I hope also that the fight reported to have bene in London will not be found true, in all particulars, at least. I am sorry for your loss of Mr Talcot, of whose decease I heard, but not how his diseases were found to be incurable, til I read your letter, whereby it is most cleare to me that no art of man could cure him. I hope now that you will either receive your son safely arrived, in the next ship, from London, at Boston, or good newes from him. By this time I am apt to thinck that a Parliament is assembled for the establishment of that great Commonw.(ealth) upon sure foundacōns of trueth and righteousnes, by the blessing of the most High, to whose grace, in Jesus Christ, with myne, my wifes, and sons humble services presented to you boath and affectionate salutations to your daughters, I heartily commend your selfe, and all yours, resting in him

yours ever obliged

JOHN DAVENPORTE.

NEWHAVEN *ye 29th of ye 1st m.* 1660.

[Labelled, "Mr. Davenport."]

XIII.

Rev. John Davenport to John Winthrop, Jr.

To the Right Worshipll John Winthrope Esqr Governor of Connectacute, these present at Hartford.

HONOURED SIR)

I received a former letter from you, by Mr Bishop, who, in his returne from your parts hitherward, tooke a wrong path twise and was so bewildred that he lost his way, from Wethersfield, and lay in the woods, in a very cold night, and came not to us, til the last day of the weeke towards noone. But, I hope, he hath no hurte, but is returned in safety and health, by the mercy of God to his family. I will not now trouble you with the reasons of my returning those papers unto you, but accept, thanckfully your freindly admonition, for the future, not to erre againe, on that hand. We boath pray you to accept our hearty thancks for your supplies of Rubila, both then, and now againe, by this bearer. The report is true which you have heard of much sicknes in this towne and the Farmes about it. The Lord be merciful to his people and rebuke our distempers, and sanctifie his afflicting hand to them and us all. It is true also that Mr Pierse is come. Brother Rutterford also and Brother Alsop are come to us, and have brought with them our Teacher whose deare wife, and our much beloved sister the most High hath taken to himselfe, both from him and us. She was buried the day before his arrival. They have also brought Mr Joanes, and his wife, Mrs Hannah Eaton, and her infant, with 2 sons of his, by a former wife, and 2 servants &c. They have declared themselves to be unsatisfyed with brother Yales selling away sundry things in the house, and with his agreement with Mr Hill about the division made of Mr Eatons estate. Some discouragement seemes to be upon theyre spirits concerning theyre settling here, yet they are buisyed about disposing the goods they have brought with them and accomodating theyre dwelling in the house. Time will shew what theyre future resolution will be. Edmond is come, who presenteth his humble service to your selfe and to Mrs Winthrope. He found out your son, who is Captaine of a Troope of horse in Colonel Reades regiment, whom he also saw, upon the Exchange. Your son is well recovered, by the mercy of God, from the small poxe. He was with him againe, the day before his coming away, by his bed side, and brought letters from him to your selfe &c which he gave to Mr Amos Richardson, at his desire, purposing, as he said, a journey to New London, where he was to meete with you. But, when Edmund saw that he went not, but stayed above a weeke, Edmond, being to come for N. Haven, desired him to lett him have the letters againe, that he might bring them unto you more speedily then, he suspected, they would be handed to you, by Mr A. R. But he utterly refused to let Edm. have them. So they remaine stil in his hands. Concerning Mr Peters I heare litle, onely from brother Hooke, that the lord Craven waytes hopefully for the restitucōn of his lands, wherein, he saith, M[r] Peters hath a share, he is of kinne to Monck, and sometimes dineth with him. Your son told Edmond that he purposeth to returne for N. E. the next yeare. My brother Hooke is valetudinarious, having bene afflicted with a very greate fluxe of Rheume, accompanied with an Erisipilus unto danger of death; he hath stil an ill stomach, and spleenish distempers. His wife also hath her bodily infirmities. He hath prevailed with a kinsman of yours to wright unto you the story of these late years in Engl. whom he commends for a great wit, parts, and copious language, and choise for Intelligence &c. His letter I send inclosed, with some others, and one from M[r] Hartlib, who thinckes you live in this plantacōn, and hath sent a large wrighting unsealed, that I might peruse it, which though I want time to read over, I choose rather to send it to you, then to detaine it. He hath sent also sundry wrightings, and bookes, some to your selfe, some to me. But I cannot heare of them, in the pinnases, which makes me doubt, they are stayed in the Bay, at M[r] Ushers, which I the rather suspect, because M[r] Hartlib, and brother Hooke certifie me that M[r] Drury also hath sent some papers and bookes to the 2 Teaching Elders at Boston, and to me. If it shall please you to employ Mr A. R. therein, he will inquire of Mr Usher, and procure them to be conveyed to your selfe, and myne, by your helpe, to me. Many things I might add, which it would be too tædious to wright, and would be more fittly communicated to you, if we might injoy your much desired presence here. The 2 gentlemen of greate qualitie arrived in the Baye, are Colonel Whaley, and his son in law, Lieutenant Goffe. I hope to see them here, after the Commissioners are gone, if not before. I might hope to see them before, upon my letter, but I defer that, on purpose, that your chamber may be free for your reception and Mrs Winthropes, when the Commissioners meete. I must now breake off, rather than conclude, with myne, my wifes, and sons humble services presented to yourselfe and Mrs Winthrope, and our prayers for all good to you boath and yours, remayning

Sir, yours exceeding obliged

JOHN DAVENPORTE.

NEWHAVEN *ye 11th d. of the 6th m.* 1660.

[On a little piece of paper wafered to the side of the letter, Mr. Davenport adds this note :—]

Sir, I mistooke, in my letter, when I said, Colonel Whalye was one of the gentlemen &c. It is Commissary Generall Whaley, sister Hookes brother, and his son in law who is with him, is Colonel Goffe; boath godly men, and escaped pursute in Eng. narrowly.

Etiam atque etiam vale.

[Endorsed by Governor Winthrop, "Mr Davenport. Aug. 11, 1660. Papers from Mr Hartlib &c. and the papers about Wethersfeild church."]

XIV.

Rev. John Davenport to John Winthrop, Jr.

To the Right Worship^ll John Winthrope Esqr Governour of Connectacute Colonie, these present at Hartford.

HONOURD SIR)

Though I am, at present, in preparacōn for the lecture, to morrow, yet having newly received a letter from Capt. Clarke, and hearing that one at the ordinary purposeth a journey towards the Baye, in the morning, who, I suppose, will goe by Hartford, I make bold to send you the Intelligence which I receive from England, by way of Newfoundland, to the middle of July, which informes, that those who were of the High Court of justice and condemned the former King, theyre estates are confiscate, 20 of them imprisoned, three of them like to die, viz. Jones, Harrison, and Say (if I doe not misreade) and that Dr Goodwin, Mr Nie, and Mr Peters, are in prison, and likely to lose theyre lives, and that there is a consultacōn to settle church discipline, in a way of joyning Episcopacy and Presbytery, by agreement that each Bishop in his Diocess shall have a select number of presbyters joyned with him, the common prayer to be established, but with some alteracōns: some ceremonies to be left indifferent; as bowing at the name of Jesus, the surpliss, cross in Baptisme &c. That good men are under some sufferings, many being turned out of theyre places: but greater things feared: Spaine like to make peace: France like to differ. The good Lord prepare his people, in Old England, and New, for what they and we may expect, and, in the meane time, give us hearts to sympathize with afflicted Joseph! We, at Newhaven, are stil under Gods afflicting hand. The good Lord sanctifie it, to us all! Our Governor stil continues very weake, eates litle, and ill digests what he eates, is ill after it, yet, til he takes something, findes a gnawing at his stomach, is commonly coldish. Once he tooke the Rubila, but finding himself sundrie times ready to faint away, hath not bene willing to take it againe, nor his wife that he should, though we perswaded and encouraged him thereunto. I feare what the issue may be, if some better course be not taken for his recovery then [Mr Augur *] prescribes. Also our

* "Erased by Governor Winthrop."

Teacher is very sick. The last lecture day, he purposed to preach, though he found an Aguish distemper, the day before, and continued in that purpose til the 2d drumme, but then was compelled to take his bed. So there was no sermon. Afterward he hoped that it would be a quotidian, and leave him at the 4th fitt, as it did here, in the spring, and, once, before, at Milford. . . . . . . The good Lord direct to the meanes, which he will bless for his recovery! Mr Jones tooke the Rubila 4 times and followed your other directions, and is, by the blessing of God, in an hopefull way. His fittes, he thincks, have left him, though some grudgings he findes hanging about him he doth not know of my wrighting, at this time. I believe Mr Jones himselfe will wright to you, when he findes himselfe able. And I am persuaded that your advise will prevaile with our Governour to take what course you may please to prescribe. He knoweth not of my wrighting at this time, because my letter is now to be sent away, the messenger being to be gone, betimes, in the morning. The Lord Jesus dwell with you, and yours in mercy and peace and loving kindnesses! With our humble service to yourselfe and Mrs Winthrope, and our loving salutations to all your branches, my wife, and son joyning with me therein, I rest

Yours exceedingly obliged

JOHN DAVENPORTE.

NEWHAVEN, *ye 17th d. of ye 8th m.* 1660.

We heare that Mr Paine and Mr Web are boath dead.

[Labelled, "Mr Davenport—October 17, 1660."]

XV.

Rev. John Davenport to Sir Thomas Temple.

[The following letter of Mr. Davenport was transcribed at her Majesty's State paper office, London, Sept. 9, 1842, by Hon. James Savage, LL.D., Boston, by permission of Lord Aberdeen, from Vol. 1st., of papers called "New England papers," 147, and was published in the Massachusetts Historical Collections, Vol. viii., 3d series, page 327.]

NOBLE SIR,

Whom though unknowne to me by Face, as allso I am to yourselfe, I Honnour for your noble disposition & for your neare Relation, to my, Ever Honoured, Lord, Viscount, Say And Sele, unto whom I have bene continually neare 40 years Past, Exceedingly obliged for Sundry Testimoneyes of his Speciall Favors towardes me when I lived in London, & when I was in Holland, & after my Returne thence to London, And since my abode in this Wildernesse, which hath bine above 24 yeares. If the most high hath taken him From us, by Death, as I am Informed he hath, The King hath lost the Best of his Peeres & Counsaleirs for Godley Wisdome & Faithfulnesse, The Church and People of god an Assured Pattron, The Commons and Parliament a most Emminent Patriott, the Nobility a Singular Pattiren and ornament, And my Poore Worthlesse Selfe a most Honorable & Faithfull frend, And that in a time when I have most need of his helpe, which I am assured Would not have Failed my Confident Expectation, if any Complaint against me had bene Presented to his Honor with the rest of his Maj'ties most Hono'ble Councell. Multis ille Bonis Flebilis occiditt, Nulli Flebilior quam mihi. Yet as long as his right honorable Son, my lord Fines liveth, he cannot Die, For in him & I hope in his Posterity that Noble Familey will be like that Golden tree the Boughes and Branches whereof Flourished in a Continuall Succession.

Uno Avulso non defficit alter
Aureus Et Simili Frondescens Virga Mettallo.

Sir, being Encouraged by some Expressions of your good affection toward mee, Brought to my Knowledge by one who came lateley, from Boston, heither, I take the Boldnesse to desier this Favor, that you would be pleased to cast your eyes uppon the Enclosed Appoligie, which I formerly transmitted to the Deputy Govenor of Massachusets to be by him Communicated to the General Courte. In it you will Find myne Innocyency in Referance to the 2 Collonells to be shuch as might secure me From all feare of Danger & Futher molestation from his Ma'tie in that Respecte, yet because I am sensible of Possible misrepresentations of mine actions, & Intentions, I humbly Crave leave to Intreate you to lay up in the Repositorie of your minde, your memorie, The true State of my Case that you may Speake a good an Seasonable word of truth in the Cause of the Dumbe & deafe, when God shall have Brought you in Safety to London, as occasion may be offired in the King's Courte, would my age which is past the great Climactericall yeare, & the weakness of my Boddy, which is under sensible decaies as well Shute with so long a Voyage as my minde is Propense to it, I should not Fear to answer anything that can be Suggested or objected against mee, in his Ma'tie presence, being Confident in the King's Justice and æqunimitie, that uppon a faire hearing I should be acquitted, & some in Boston who raile against mee, should have their Injurious mouthes Stopped, what Libbirty is denyed unto me, if God Inclyne

& Encourage your hearte theirunto, a word From your noble selfe Spoken in Season may be blessed of god to make up, with advantage, & to worke Favorable & Right apprehensions and perswations of mee in his Ma'tie & shuch of his most Hono'ble Councells as you maye have occasion of Discourse with aboute these matters.

This is my great Intendment in this lines, humbly to Crave your mindfulnesse of me & helpefulness Toward mee in this Exigent, And not for myselfe alone doe I make this humble Request, But also on the Behalfe of this Poore Colloney & of our Govenor & majestrates, who wanted neither will nor Industery to have served his Ma'tie in apprehending ye 2 Collonells, but were Prevented & Hindered by gods overruilling Providence, which withheld them that they Could not Exciqute their true Purpose therein; And the same Providence Could have done ye same, in the Same Curcumstances, if they had bine in London, or in the Tower, The Case was thus, The Collones hearing that some who had Entertained them, at their Houses, were in Extreme danger, uppon that Accompt to Prevent the same, Came from another Colloney where they were, & had bine somtime, to N. H: Professing, that their true Intentions, in their Coming at that time was to yeld themselves to be apprehended, for the afforesaid Purpose & accordingly they staied 2 dayes, This was knowne in the Towne, The D. G. waited for the Comming of the Govenor & other majestrats to this towne on the 2d. day, which they allso did according to Former Aggrement, Imediately uppon their Coming together, they fell into a Consultation, being out of any Feare of that which Followed, Before they had Issued their Consultation which was not long, the Collonels were gon away, no man knowing how nor whether, Thereuppon a Diligent Search was Renewed, & many were sent Forth on Foote & horsebacke, to recover them in to their hands, But all in vaine. I belive if his Ma'tie Rightly understood the Curcumstances of this Event he would not be displeased with our majestrates, but to accquiesce in the Providence of the most high well Knowing that the way of man is not in himselfe, but god worketh all things according to the Counsaile of his owne will, It is now high time that I begge pardon for putting so much trouble uppon you, & that I Conclude with my Prayers to him, whom windes & seas obey to Fill your sailes with Favorable windes & to Carrie your Person as uppon Eagles winges Far above the reach of all hurtfull Dangers, till he shall have landed you safe at your desiered Port, & then to make you a Blessed Instrument of some good unto this Poore Colloney & to myselfe, For which I shall Remaine

Noble Sir, your Humble Servt. & obliged
Faithfull Frend JOHN DAVENPORTE.

N. H y'e 19th day of ye 6 *mounth*
Called Augst. 1661.

Sir,

If my lord Saye be yet in vivis, be pleased to Communicate ye inclosed to him, with ye reason of my not writing to his honor at Present, & my Earnest desier of his Favorable helpe, that ye King may be rightly informed Concerning me in this matter; if you shall find he is not in ye land of ye living my humble request is the same to my lord Fines. But if his honor have not Sufficient Interest in those about his ma'tie for shuch a purpose, my Intreaty to yourselfe is ye same aforementioned. Allso if the Deputy Govenor Mr. Bellingham hath not Rec'd. yt. Letter & ye Appologie to ye General Courte wch I sent above 5 weekes since be pleased to let him peruse this & gett a Coppie of it (I meane ye appologie) transcribed & Retturne yours againe to your Noble Selfe, to be Improved as you find opertunity to ye best advantage on my behalfe, lastley lett it please you to accept a booke newly come forth wch I make bold to Present unto you for a vade mecum, in your voyage at sea, & for an helpe to Fix your Anchor aright when you come to land & for ever, ye lord Jesus be with you both at sea & land & to Etternity as a mighty Saviour

Amen Farewell, interim.

XVI.

Rev. John Davenport to John Winthrop, Jr.

To the Honble John Winthrope Governour of Connectecute Colonie, these present at Hartford.

HONOURBLE SIR—

Many hearty thancks being præmised, to God, and you; to God as to the principal efficient, who stirred up your heart, and guided your minde to pitch upon such meanes as his blessing made effectual; and to yourselfe, as to a blessed Instrument in God's hand, for our recovery, my sons especially, from that weakness, and those great paines, wherewith he was lately and long afflicted, unto this measure of strength, whereby he was enabled to come into the publick assembly, the last Lords day, to bless God the Author of all blessings upon your endeavours: which, I pray, may be stil continued, for the good of many!

Yet, in the midst of our familie-comforts, I feele at my heart no small sorrow for the publick divisions and distractions at Hartford. Were M[r] Hooker now in vivis; it would be as a sword in his bones, that the *Church*, which he had planted there, should be thus disturbed, by innovacōns, brought in and urged so Vehemently, by his young successour in office, not in his spirit: who was so far from these laxe waies that he opposed the baptizing of grand-children, by their grandfathers right: much more would he have decryed the baptising of Adopted children, by their Adoptants right: most of all, the baptising of servants, borne in the house, or bought with monie, quâ tales, unles they had a spiritual right, by being regularly joyned to the Church, according to Gospel-rules. But he is at rest: and the people there gro woefully divided, and the better sorte are exceedingly greived, while the looser and worser party insult, hoping that it will be as they would have it, viz., that the plantacōns shall be brought into a parish-way, against which Mr Hooker hath openly borne a strong Testimonie in print. The most of the churches, in this jurisdicōn, are professedly against this new way, both in judgment and practise, upon Gospel grounds, n, Newhaven, Milford, Stratford, Brandford, Gillford, Norwalke, Stamford, and those nearer to Hartford, n, Farmington, and the sounder parte of Windsor, together with their Reverend Pastor, Mr Warham, and, I thinck, Mr Fitch, and his church also. Nor may it be thought that we all are mere spectatours, or that we shall be allwaies silent, as persons not concerned. It is the cause of Christ, for which we must pleade: it is no slight matter, as dė lanâ caprinâ, that is now agitated, but that which concernes the preserving of Christian Churches in peace, and Gospel-ordinances in purity: it is the faith and order of the Churches of Christ, which we are called to contend for, that they may be preserved intyre and incorrupted. when the Bay-Synod published theire booke: I saw where their Temptation lay, and printed my answer to it: whereunto, when a seeming reply was made, I declared and proved the insufficiency of it, and sent my MSS. to the Baye, where it lyeth, in friends hands unprinted, til further occasion shall obstetricate it: Sed quorsum hæc? I shall breifly suggest unto you what I have heard. viz. that before the last lecture-day, when it was yong Mr Heynes his turne to preach, he sent 3 of his partie to tell Mr Whiting, that, the nexte Lecture-day, he would preach about his way of baptizing, and would begin the practising of it, on that day. Accordingly he preached, and water was prepared for Baptisme (which, I suppose, was never administered, in a weeke day, in that Church, before) But Mr Whiting, as his place and duty required, testifyed against it, and refused to consent to it. Much was spoken, to litle purpose, by some of Mr Heynes his partie. But, when Mr Warham began to speake, one of the Church rudely hindered him, saying, to this purpose, What hath Mr Warham to do to speake in our Church matters? This check stopped Mr Warhams proceeding, at that time. The objectour considered not that this matter was not res propria to that church alone, but res communis, it being of common concernment to all the churches in these parts, and to the Teaching Officers of them, and to Mr Warham more especially; For tum sua res agitur paries cum proximus ardet, which he might have answered. But we live in times and places, where the faces of the

Elders are not duely honoured; and therefore its justly to be feared that God will soone take away the most Godly and judicious Leaders from so unthanckful and unworthy people, and leave them to be mislead by superficial verbalists. Yourselfe prudently concluded that, that day was not a fit season to begin theire purposed practise, seeing it was not consented to. But opposed. And so it ceased, for that time. But Mr Heynes urged for a dispute about it with Mr Whiting, the next Lecture day, which will be the 20th day of this month, which also, they say, is agreed upon. But cui bono? No good issue can rationally be expected of a verbal dispute, at that time, and in that place, where so many are likely to disturbe the buisenes with interruptions and clamours, and to prepare a sufficient number to overvote the better party for establishment of the worser way. So Trueth shall be dethroned and errour set up in the throne. What then is to be done, in this Case? Let M[r] Heynes give in wrighting to M[r] Whiting, his position, and his Arguments to prove it: and let M[r] Whiting have a convenient time to returne his Answer in wrighting. This is the most suitable way for a peaceable issuing of the dispute, with solid judgment, and with due moderation and satisfaction: and let all practise of M[r] Heynes his opinion be forborne, til the trueth be cleared. But if M[r] Heynes refuseth this way; I shall suspect that he more confides in the clamours of his party, than in the goodnes of his cause or in the strength of his Arguments, or in his ability for disputacōn. These things I make bold to present to your serious consideracōn, that, by your wisdom and care of the publick good and common peace, according to the duety of your place, the fire alreadie kindled may be speedily quenched, and the banckes may be seasonably strengthened, to prevent the irruption of waters, that may cause an inundation, not to be stopped afterward.

Our service to yourselfe and Mrs Winthrope, with our affectionate salutacōns to all yours, being presented, I rest, in Jesus Christ

Yours obliged, assured

John Davenporte Senior.

N. H. *the* 14*th d. of the* 4*th m.* 1666.

Poster. My Revd brother, Mr Street, being with me, and hearing this letter read, earnestly desired me, once and againe, to declare unto you, his full consent to the contents thereof: so that you may take it as from us boath. He also thincks that a Synod of the Elders and Messengers of the churches, on this side of the countrey, i. e. of this jurisdiction, might be a suitable expedient motos componere fluctus. But that I leave to further consideracōn. In the meane time, it will be operæ præmium that you interpose your Authority and wisdom to stop all further proceedings and actings in this irregular and tumultuous way.

[Labelled, "Mr Davenport, Senior—received Junij 19. 1666."]

John Davenport, Jr., to John Winthrop, Jr.

Boston, 30. 2. 1675.

Honble Sir—

Yours I rec'd, and returne thankfull acknowledgments for the Rubela and the directions about my arme, which I have used, and hope it hath done good but yet remaines some paine in the shoulder and upper parte of the arme and a weaknes so as that I could not nor can lift up my hand to my hat, for which I request your further helpe and advice, there is no swelling but an itching especially (at times) on my shoulder. My bodily health and appetite (through the mercy of God) is better then before my sicknes.

The College busines (as I heare) is not yet settled. We heare the uncomfortable state of our Relations at Jersey.

Many are the afflictions of the righteous, but the Lord delivers out of all, it is good both to hope and quietly waite for the salvacōn of God: we live in a changable troublesome world, but there is an unchangable God who is the object of the hope of beleivers which is a strong ground of consolation.

The Lord preserve your life and health for the good of many in whome with our service presented, crave leave to subscribe

Honble Sir, your humble servant

J. Davenport.

["Labelled, 'Mr J. Davenport recd May 7.' The superscription is gone. This letter is written in the hand of old age,—neither the spelling nor punctuation is as good as was usual with the writer's father, who died March 15, 1670."]

INVENTORY OF THE REV. JOHN DAVENPORT.

"The inventory of the goods and chattels of Mr. John Davenport, deceased, late pastor of the First Church of Christ in Boston, taken by us, whose names are hereto subscribed, the 22d of the 5th Mo. 1670:—

In the Hall.

A feather bed and bolster, rugs, blanket, with damask curtains and valance, and bedstead,	£8	00	0
A drawing table,	2	00	0

Item	£	s.	d.
To 10 high chairs, 2 low chairs, a form, a joint stool, and a chest,	4	15	0
6 pair of sheets,	2	00	0
18 napkins, 3 short table cloths, and 5 towels	2	00	0
A pair of wampum, with trenchers, and several small things,	3	00	0

In the Study.

Item	£	s.	d.
Books prized by Mr. John Oxenbridge, our pastor, and by Mr. James Allen, our teacher, as appeared to us by a note under their hands, to the value of	233	17	0
A clock, with appurtenances,	5	00	0
7 high chairs, 3 stools, a low chair,	3	00	0
A skreen, 4 curtain rods, 4 boxes,	2	00	0
For wt. sugar, a little trunk, and a box,	1	05	0

In the Upper Chamber.

Item	£	s.	d.
3 rings, 4 blankets, a coverlet,	4	13	0
A feather bed, boulster, 3 pillows, a boulster and case, with feathers and bedstead,	7	10	0
3 chests, a court cupboard, and 4 trunks	8	00	0
5 chairs, 2 boxes, and a table,	3	00	0
6 cushions and darnic carpet, 2 striped carpets, a valure carpet, a cupboard, cloth and blanket, and 11 pair of sheets,	25	00	0
For several small things, as yarn thread,	1	00	0
7 pair of sheets,	4	00	0
17 napkins, cupboard cloth, 9 pillow biers, and 3 coarse towels,	3	00	0
1 pair of sheets, 11 pillowbiers, 4 short table cloths, 18 towels, and 4 napkins,	3	18	0
16 towels, 13 napkins, 3 pillowbiers, and 7 short table cloths,	2	00	0
80 yards of Holland, at 4s.	16	00	0
For some remnants of Holland lawn and dowlas,	3	10	0
6 pillows,	2	00	0
A basket, with Manchester binding,		5	0

In the Kitchen Chamber.

Item	£	s.	d.
A feather bed, a rug, two blankets, bedstead, a bolster, tick, and 2 pillow cases,	6	10	0

For his apparel, woolen and linen....................	30	00	0
In gold and English money, ...	13	08	7½
In Spanish money, ...	1	18	9
In New England money,..........................	95	10	0
A quilt, rug, 5 blankets, a pair of curtains and valance, with buckram and yarn,.........................	5	00	0
3 yards of br. clash, 11 yards of red kersey, 2 yards of Pennistone, a carpet, 1 yard of serge, ...	8	04	0
For several yards of tape,.........................		15	0
21 pair of sheets,.................................	17	00	0
For hangings and darnic curtains, ...	3	00	0
3 yards of Holland, 4½ yards dimity, 3 of thread, 11 quires of paper, 1½ dozen of pins, and 1 piece of brown tape and ribbon,..................................	2	17	0
3 pair of sheets, 6 diaper table cloths, 10 table cloths of diaper and towels, 4½ doz. of diaper napkins, and 3 diaper towels, ...	20	00	0
A dozen of plain napkins, 6 towels, 8 table cloths, 4 cupboard cloths, 17 pillowbiers, 6 diaper cloths, 6 doz. of plain cloths, ...	10	00	0
14 yards of Holland, ...	4	07	0
4½ yards of lawn and cambric, ...	2	00	0
5 yards of tufted Holland, ...		12	6
4 fine Holland beds for children,.....................		15	0
6 trunks, 3 chests, and some boxes, ...	5	00	0
In plate, ...	50	00	0
In china and earthen ware, ...	5	00	0

In the Garret.

In bedding, flax, sheep's wool, malt, Indian corn, with divers other things,..............................	20	00	0

In the Parlor.

A feather bed, bolster, pillow, a pair of sheets, pillowbiers, a pair of blankets, curtains, valance and bedstead,	12	00	0
A cupboard,......................................		10	0
A red chair, 5 small chairs and 1 joint stool, 1 little table and 6 cushions, ...	2	14	0
A feather bed, bolster, and 2 pillows, a pair of blankets, bedstead curtains and valance,......	6	00	0

Item	£	s.	d.
A flock bed, bolster, 1 pair of sheets, blanket, rug, trundle bed,..	3	00	0
For glass bottles, 1 jug, and some nutmegs,............		12	0
In the Kitchen.			
In pewter and tin ware,............................	20	00	0
A brass mortar, a marble mortar and pestles,..........	1	00	0
6 skillets, 6 brass candlesticks, with other brass things,..	3	00	0
3 brass kettles, 2 iron pots and still, 1 bed-pan, ...	4	00	0
5 pair of andirons, 3 pair of tongs, 1 iron fire-pan, 2 hooks, 1 iron peel, grid-iron, warming-pan, and frying-pan,..	4	00	0
3 sheets, with some other linen, a pair of brass scales, weights, chafing dish, and brass mortar, ...	3	00	0
In the Cellar.			
In cotton wool, 3 old kettles, a great copper kettle, a great pair of rackr, a still in salt, a great washing tub, with barrels, and other lumber, ...	20	00	0
The dwelling-house and land,.......................	400	00	0
	£1,147	15	10½

More presented to us :

Item	£	s.	d.
In English money, ...	£82	14	0
A bible, a gold ring, and sewing silk, ...	3	00	0
4 yards of bl. cr. cloth,............................	4	15	0
For silver clasp and silver hatband, ...	1	05	0
A saw, and 2 yards of flannel and fustian,.............	1	09	0
Total is............	£1,240	18	10½

JAMES PENN,
ANTHONY STODDART,
THOMAS CLARKE.

Item	£	s.	d.
One servant boy,................................	£10	00	0

Mr. John Davenport made oath before the Governor and Major Gen. John Leverett, appointed by the county court that last sat for that end, that this is a true Inventory of the estate he knows of his late father, and when he knows more he will discover it.

This done the first of the 7th Month, 1670.

As attest, FREEGRACE BENDALL, Clerk."

The above does not include the property the deceased left in New Haven, most of which, however, will be found included in the following Inventory of his son John Davenport, jr.

A part of his very valuable library, prized at more than one thousand dollars, seems to have been sold, or given away, before the death of his son; as the books then remaining were prized in the Boston inventory at less than £100. The largest portion passed to his grandson, the Rev. John Davenport, of Stamford, and others were divided among his other grandchildren.

A part appears to have passed, previous to the death of his son, to Dr. Increase Mather, and are now to be found, together with some of his manuscript works, in the library of the American Antiquarian Society, Worcester, Mass.

INVENTORY OF JOHN DAVENPORT, JR.

An Inventory of the effects of Mr. John Davenport, late of Boston, in New England, deceased, viz.: that part of it which is within the limits of New Haven, taken and apprised by us whose names are hereunto written, according to best information,—June 27, 1687.

Imprs.	The house and barnes, home-lot and orchard, at the town,	£200	00	0
	About sixteen acres of upland in that quarter, at the Sound side,	50	C0	0

Two acres of home-lot, joining to the aforesaid home-lot,...............................	20	00	0
About nineteen acres of wood-lot, near the mill,.	15	00	0
About eleven acres and half in the necks, ...	10	00	0
House and buildings, with the upland and meadow at the farm,.........................	450	00	0
One hundred and sixty acres of the third division	30	00	0
Right in the ox pasture and other commons of the town,—six cows and two small oxen and two 3-year old cattle at the farm, ...	35	00	0
One 2-year old mare,......................	2	00	0
Two cows and calves at the town, two ewes and two lambs, ...	9	10	0
Horses not known in the woods,			
Sum total,.............	£821	10	0

MOSES MANSFIELD,
ABRAM DICKEMAN.

The total of the Inventory of the said Mr. John Davenport's estate found at Boston is, according to a copy exhibited now in county court, held at New Haven, August 3d, 1687, ...	£836	12	6
Total of both is............	£1,658	02	6

May 27th, 1690.

Mrs. Abigail Davenport, widow, the relict and administratrix of Mr. John Davenport, of New Haven, deceased, at Boston, appeared in Court, in New Haven, and exhibited the above inventories, and requested the Court to make distribution of the estate according to law, to her the relict, and the four children of the said Mr. John Davenport, her dear husband deceased, viz., John, Elizabeth, Abigail, and Mary Davenport, for that the said deceased made no will whereby to dispose of his estate.

The Court therefore examined the above inventory, and

found that since it was made, one hundred and fifty-six pounds of the estate had been expended for the education and maintenance of the children, from their minority to this time, and for payment of debts and loss of fire, in Boston; and of the clear estate remaining, the Court grants and confirms to the relict and administratrix, a third part of the house at Boston, a third of the houses and lands at New Haven, during her natural life, and a third of the personal estate in her possession, amounting at present to £487 07*s.* 6*d.*, and also two-thirds of the plate, according to her deceased husband's mind, and the rest of the thirds to be used by her for the education and maintenance of the children, until they should be of lawful age, or the daughters married, when they shall receive their portion.

Besides the son's portion, he shall receive with the consent and good liking of the rest, £40 in books, Latin, Greek, and Hebrew, according to his father's mind; and the rest of the books, to the value of £50, to be distributed among the rest of the children, only the eldest daughter to have more than the younger, viz., £20 out of the £50.

For the children's portion, the Court grant unto John Davenport, the son, a double portion, viz. (including the £40 in books),	£409	18	10
To Elizabeth Davenport, the sum of (besides the £20 in books)	184	19	5
To Abigail Davenport, "	184	19	5
To Mary Davenport, "	184	19	5

The son to receive his portion at the age of 21, and the daughters at 18, or marriage, whichever may happen first.

The real estate of the widow's thirds, at her death, to go to the children, according to the aforementioned proportions.

COPY OF A DEED OF THE HEIRS OF JOHN DAVENPORT, Jr., TO THE FIRST CHURCH, BOSTON, 1693.

(*Drawn from Boston Town Records.*)

This Indenture made the tenth day of June, Anno Domini, one thousand six hundred and ninety-three, and in the fifth year of the reign of our sovereign Lord and Lady, William and Mary, King and Queen of England, BETWEEN Abigail Davenport, relict, widow and administratrix of the estate of her late husband John Davenport, late of Boston, in the county of Suffolk, within their Majesties' Province of Massachusetts Bay, in New England, merchant, deceased; John Davenport, of the town and county of New Haven, within their majesties colony of Connecticut, in New England, aforesaid, clerk [minister], son and heir of the said John Davenport, dec.; James Pierpont, of New Haven aforesaid, clerk, lately the husband of Abigail Davenport, deceased, one of the daughters of the said John Davenport, dec.; Elizabeth Davenport and Mary Davenport, of New Haven aforesaid, spinsters, two more daughters of the said John Davenport, dec., of the one part, and Robert Sanderson, sen., goldsmith, Henry Alline, carpenter, and Joseph Bridgham, tanner, all of Boston aforesaid, deacons of the First Church of Christ in Boston aforesaid, and as Trustees for and in behalf of the said First Church of Christ, on the other part, WITNESSETH, that the said Abigail Davenport, John Davenport, James Pierpont, Elizabeth Davenport and Mary Davenport, for and in consideration of the sum of one hundred and seventy pounds current money, in New England aforesaid, to them in hand, at or before the sealing and delivery of these presents, well and truly paid by the said Robert Sanderson, Sen., Henry Alline and Joseph Bridgham, in behalf of the aforesaid church, the receipt whereof to full amount and satisfaction they do hereby acknowledge, and thereof and of every part and parcel thereof they do acquit and exonerate and discharge the said Robert Sanderson, Sen., Henry Alline and Joseph Bridgham, and each and every of them, and each and every of their heirs, executors, administrators and assigns, as also this First Church now being, &c., their successors, forever, by these presents and for divers other good reasons and considerations them hereunto at this present especially moving, they the said Abigail Davenport, John Davenport, James Pierpont, Elizabeth Davenport and Mary Davenport, HAVE given, granted, bargained, sold, alienated, released, enfeoffed, conveyed and confirmed, And by these presents do fully, freely, and absolutely grant, bargain, sell, alien and release, enfeoffe, convey and confirm unto the said Robert Sanderson, Sen., Henry Alline and Joseph Bridgham, their heirs and assigns forever, to the use hereinto hereafter mentioned and expressed, ALL THAT CERTAIN MESSUAGE or Tenement, with the appurtenances and lands thereunto belonging, situate, lying and being in Boston aforesaid, being butted and bounded on the east with the street or highway leading from Prison Lane up to the Common or Training fields on the west, and with lands heretofore appertaining to Richard Bellingham, Esq., deceased (of which this land herein granted was once a part); on the south side with the garden and lands of the late Humphrey Davie, Esq., deceased, in the present tenure and occupation of Gabriel Barnon, merchant; and on the northerly side in part with the garden of Robert Howard, deceased, now appertaining to the said Gabriel Barnon, and in part by the land of the late John Hall, Esq., deceased, *Together* with all and singular houses, edifices, building and fences standing thereupon, yard, garden, wares, wells, waters, water courses, profits, privileges, advantages, commodities, hereditaments, emoluments and appurtenances whatsoever, to the said messuage or tenement belonging t or in anywise appertaining, or therewith now or heretof used or occupied, enjoyed, reputed, taken or known as pa parcel or member thereof, or of any part thereof, and th revision or revisions, remainder and remainders, rents and issues thereof, and all and each and every of their estated right, title, interest, inheritance, trust, property, possession, use, dower, claim and demand whatsoever of, into and out of the premises, and every part thereof, with all original deeds, writings and evidences whatsoever relating thereto, in their custody or power, TO HAVE AND TO HOLD the said messuage or tenement, with all the lands thereto belonging, butted and bounded as aforesaid, with all other the above granted premises, unto the said Robert Sanderson, Sen., Henry Alline and Joseph Bridgham, their heirs and assigns forever, to and for the sole proper use, benefit and behoof of the said First Church of Christ in Boston, aforesaid, now living, and their successors forever, and to no other use, intent or purpose whatsoever, absolutely without any manner of condition, redemption, or revocation in anywise: And the said Abigail Davenport, John Davenport, James Pierpont, Elizabeth Davenport and Mary Davenport, for themselves, their heirs and executors and administrators, and every of them do covenant, grant and agree to and with the said Robert Sanderson, Sen., Henry Alline, and Joseph Bridgham, their heirs and assigns, and to and with each and every of them, by these presents in manner and form following (that is to say) :—That at and immediately before the time of their sealing and delivery of these presents, they the said Abigail Davenport, John Davenport, James Pierpont, Elizabeth Davenport, and Mary Davenport, or some or one of them, are the true, sole and lawful owner or owners of all the aforebargained premises, And stand lawfully seized thereof in their or some of their own proper right of a good, perfect, and absolute estate of inheritance in fee simple, without any remainder of condition, revision, or limitation of use or uses whatsoever, so as to alter, change, defeat or make void the same, Leaving to themselves full power, good right and lawful authority to grant, sell, convey, alien, enfeoffe, release and confirm the same in manner and form as aforesaid, and according to the true intent and meaning of these presents, And that the said Robert Sanderson, Sen., Henry Alline and Joseph Bridgham, and their heirs and assigns shall and may by force and virtue of these presents from henceforth and at all times forever hereafter, lawfully, peaceably and quietly have, hold, use, occupy, possess and enjoy all the above granted premises, with their appurtenances, and receive and take the use and behoof aforesaid the rents and incomes thereof FREE AND CLEAR, and thereby acquitted, exonerated and discharged from all and all manner of former and other gifts, grants, bargains, sales, leases, mortgages, jointures, dowers, judgments, executions, entails, wills, forfeitures, seizures, amercements, and all and from all other titles, troubles, charges and incumbrances whatsoever; AND FURTHER, that the said Abigail Davenport, John Davenport, James Pierpont, Elizabeth Davenport and Mary Davenport do hereby covenant, promise, grant and agree and bind and oblige themselves, their heirs and executors and administrators, from henceforth and forever hereafter, to warrant and defend all the said above granted premises, with their appurtenances, and every part thereof, unto the said Robert Sanderson, Sen., Henry Alline and Joseph Bridgham, their heirs and assigns forever, to the uses aforesaid, against the lawful claims and demands of all and every person and persons whomsoever, and at any time or times hereafter, upon reasonable request or demand, and at the cost and charges of the above-named grantees, their heirs or assigns, to give and pass unto them such further and ample assurance and confirmation of these premises, as in law and equity can be reasonably desired, advised or required.

In witness whereof the said Abigail Davenport, John Davenport, James Pierpont, Elizabeth Davenport and Mary Davenport have hereunto set our hands and seals the day and year first above written.

ABIGAIL DAVENPORT, and a seal,
JOHN DAVENPORT, and a seal,
JAMES PIERPONT, and a seal,
ELIZABETH DAVENPORT, and a seal,
MARY DAVENPORT, and a seal.
} all on labels.

Signed, sealed and delivered in the presence of us,
SAMUEL BISHOP,
ISAAC JONES.

WILL OF MRS. ABIGAIL DAVENPORT, WIDOW OF JOHN DAVENPORT, JR.

"At a Court of Probate held at Newhaven Sept. 18th 1718, Present Warham Mather, Judge;
Joseph Whiting Clerk

Mr John Davenport nominated Exr. in the Last Will and Testament of Mrs Abigail Davenport late of Newhaven decd. exhibited the said Instrument in this Court which on the oath of two of the witnesses before John Bishop Esq. one of his Maj'ties Justices of the peace for the County of feirfeild as by him Certyfyed and the said Will was proved in Court and approved for Record and the said Execur accepted the trust therein Committed to him & Gave Bond for a faithful discharge thereof: And administration of the Intestate Estate or the Estate of which the Dec.d stood possessed as Tenant or Dower was Granted unto the aforesaid Mr. John Davenport on his own Bond."

Copy of the Will.

"In the Name of God, Amen, the 13th Day of August 1713 I Abigail Davenport of Newhaven, Widow, being weak of body but of sound mind and memory, blessed be God for it: Remembering the Mortality of my body Do make & ordain this my Last Will & Testament—that is to say principally & first of all I Give & Commend my Spirit into the hands of God that Gave it & my Lord Christ that Redeemed it & my body I Recommend to ye Earth Decently to be buried at the Direction of my Execur having a Good hope of the Resurection of the Just and as Touching Such worldly Estate as a Good God hath Lent me, my Last will & meaning is; that my Just Debts & funerall expences be first paid and perticularly as to the bill of mine To my worthy Son-in-Law Mather of six pounds Cash or thereabouts I do expect be allowed me as part payment for work I have done Thirty & Three shillings Cash which his wife knows very well besides much more I have Done and Do not account and my said Debts & expences being paid my will and meaning is that all my Remaining Estate be Committed into the hands of my

Executor hereafter named & be Dealt out perticulerly as is here under expressed & according to the Condition and order hereafter mentioned first I Give & Bequeath unto the Church of Newhaven my Silver Caudle Cup Desiring a Cup be made thereof for the service of that Church as Likely as y[t] will afford for the Vessel & its making out of my Love & affection to the house of God.*

Item. It is my will & meaning y[t] the biggest part by far of the Little I leave be in the hands of my Loving Son John Davenport to be improved for the education, encouragement & preparation of my Loving Grand Son Deodate Davenport.

Item. It is my will that my loving Grand Son John Davenport have a fashionable silver spoon made for him out of my plate.

Item. It is my will & meaning that the four daughters of my Son Davenport my Loving Grand Children to say Abigail, Martha, Sarah and Elizabeth Davenport have a pair of my Holland sheets each of them; and I give also to my Loving Grand-daughter Abigail Davenport the best of my Turkey work Chairs & a pair of holland pillowbers.

Item. It is my will & meaning that my cloathes be all of them Divided amongst my Three Children, my Loving son John Davenport & my Loving Daughter Elizabeth Mather, and my loving Daughter Mary Wade onely my said Daughter Mary Wade my will is that she hath a whole suit of woollen & Linen & my allamode whood & my allamode Scarfe also If it please the Lord y[t] I depart this Life by this sickness that my Loving sister Mary Bishop of Stamford have my Gray petty Coat which I wear every day.

* That cup is still used by the First Church of New Haven, at every monthly Communion.—*Communicated by Rev. Dr. Bacon*, 1850.

Item. Having Given a piece of Gold to my said Daughter Martha & two pieces of Gold remaining my will is that one of them be to my Son Davenport & the other to my Daughter Wade.

Item. My Will is y[t] my Loving Grand-daughter Abigail Pierpont have my Silver Spoon marked A: P: and ten shillings of money be Given among the other Dear Children of my worthy Son-in-Law the Rev[d] Mr James Pierpont of Newhaven as a token of my Love to them.

Item. Further my will & meaning is absolute in Reference to the Legacy of the Church of Newhaven but in all the other Declarations of this my will following after said Legacy is upon condition that my Estate will allow it, when my Just debts and funerall expences are paid & so far as my Estate will allow; the same order being observed in the performing my will as is expressed in this my will Desiring in no wise my Executor should be exposed to suffer damage by this my will. Moreover, I Disannul & Revoke all my former will or wills made by me & establish this onely to be my Last Will & Testament and I do nominate Constitute & appoint my well beloved Son John Davenport aforesaid to be my sole Executor.

And my desire mind & will is that my Dear Children Live in Love and the God of Love & peace will be with them.

I also do in these declare that in my Chamber are one Thousand & half of 8d nails and a thousand & about a quarter of sixes which belong to my Son Davenport & I bought with his of twenty shillings.

Signed with my hand & sealed with my seal in Stamford the day & year above written.

ABIGAIL DAVENPORT, [seal.]

Signed sealed published &
Declared by the said
Abigail Davenport as her
Last will & Testament in the
presence of us—

JONATH. BELL
ZACHARIAH ROBERTS
MARY (J. HOLLY
(her mark)

THE WILL OF REV. JOHN DAVENPORT, OF STAMFORD.

In the name of God amen. The 20th day of Jan'y anno Domini 1728–9. I John Davenport of the town of Stamford, alias Stemford, in Fairfield county, Connecticut colony, in New England, in America, clerk, sensible of the frailty of human life, but of sound mind and memory, for which Almighty God be thanked, whenever it shall please God to call me hence, do now declare my mind in this my last will and testament, as follows, viz.:

I give my soul into the hand of God my Creator, and the Lord Jesus Christ my all-sufficient Redeemer, and my body to the earth to be decently interred, according to the discretion of my executors hereafter named, having hope in the resurrection of the just; and as touching the worldly estate which the divine bounty hath been pleased to lend me, my last will and meaning is—

That first, my just debts and funeral expenses being

paid, and enough of my estate also reserved to answer for decent grave stones for my deceased mother's grave at New Haven, which my executors shall speedily and effectually care for, and also all the grain and meat, soap and fat, and candles, left at my decease, not to be inventoried, but to be for the use of those that are of my family, and residing therein, and that in common, under the management of my now wife; and farther—

Impr.—I give and bequeath to my dear and loving wife Elizabeth, one third both of my real and personal estate, the personal her own absolutely, and the real during her natural life.

Farther.—I will that my estate according to the apprising herein provided for; I say, my estate which I call dividable among my eight children be divided into twelve equal parts in value; eight of which equal parts to be to my four sons, to say, John, Deodate, Abraham, and James, but the remaining four equal parts to be to my four daughters, to say, Abigail, Martha, Sarah and Elizabeth.

Item.—I give and bequeath to my loving and eldest son John, two parts of said equal parts of my said dividable estate, and over and above that, I give said son the sum of thirty-one pounds and ten shillings. Now, if the legacy herein devised to my said son John will admit and fit according to apprising, my mind is, the said John have my land on Davenport Ridge, so called, as may appear by the note of laying out and seized to me, signed by Deacon Samuel Hait, Stephen Bishop, and John Holly, said note entered on the record of said Stamford, and also an addition of land northerly, and on the east side or east line of land laid out or belonging to Capt. Samuel Hait; I say northerly to my land contained in said note, I mean to the easterly part of my said land contained in said note. Now, the said addition of land may be thus known, viz.: from the south east corner of said land belonging to said Capt. Samuel Hait in said east line, let thirty five rods be exactly measured northerly, and a line from thence be drawn square till it come to the highway or path which hath been called Ponasses path, and the house and barn thereon: further, my meaning is that said house, to say mansion house and barn, be appraised according to their value at time of said appraising, and all said land be appraised according to their value at said time of said appraising, only I would have all the land improved by my said son John by the plough, or for pasture, and inclosed to be valued at no higher price than if they had lain wholly waste to said time of appraising, to be to my said son John, to him, his heirs and assigns forever, with the reservation, and also further conditions they may follow.

Item.—I give and bequeath to my loving son Deodate, two parts of said equal twelve parts of my said dividable estate, to be to him, my said son Deodate, to him, his heirs and assigns forever, and my meaning is, he said Deodate, may choose within one year after my decease, either to dwell on Noroten hill in Stamford aforesaid, or at my farm at said New Haven, long known by the name of Mr. Davenport's farm, or up in the wood of said Stamford, if on said Noroten; my mind is, said Deodate have all my land on Noroten hill, if on said farm he, said Deodate, may choose not to prejudice the remainder of said farm; if up in the wood, it shall be wholly the said Deodate's, where not interfering with the devise to said John: nevertheless, in case said Deodate have any trouble in the law on account of any said mother Davenport's last will and testament, my will is then, first, said Deodate will be cut out of the one half, the other half divided to my son Deodate.

Item.—I give and bequeath to my loving son Abraham, two parts of my said dividable estate, to be to him, my said son Abraham, to him, his heirs and assigns forever.

Item.—I give and bequeath to my loving son James, two parts of said equal parts of my said dividable estate, to be to him, my said son James, to him, his heirs and assigns forever.

Item.—I give and bequeath to my loving daughter Abigail, one part of the equal parts of my dividable estate, to be to my said daughter Abigail, to her, her heirs and assigns forever, of which said one part I account said Abigail hath already received of me one hundred and twenty-one pounds nine shillings and eleven pence.

Item.—I give and bequeath to my loving daughter Martha, one part of said equal parts of my dividable estate, to be to her, said Martha, to her, her heirs and assigns forever; also about one part, besides my special charge on a gift to said Martha, I do further give to her, said Martha, four score pounds, on compassion of said Martha having been lame from a child.

Item.—I give and bequeath to my loving daughter Sarah, one part of said equal parts of my said dividable estate, to be to her, said Sarah, to her, her heirs and assigns forever, of which said part said Sarah has already received one hundred and seven pounds four shillings and eleven pence.

Item.—I give and bequeath to my loving daughter Elizabeth, one part of said equal parts of my dividable estate, to be to her, said Elizabeth, to her, her heirs and assigns forever.

Also upon consideration of accounts between me and my

said son John, I find said son John hath already received of my estate seventy-one pounds and ten shillings.

Also about my books, my mind is, my loving wife choose two of them, and my children, to say, John, Deodate, Abigail, Martha, Sarah, Elizabeth, shall have each of them two of my English, if they have not had already, and all the rest of my books to belong to my said sons Abraham and James, in an equal proportion.

Further, my meaning is, that my said sons Abraham and James enter not on their respective portions till they have arrived at the full ages of twenty-one years also, and yet if only one of them, said Abraham and James, die in nonage, the other that surviveth shall have all the books of him that hath deceased, and as for the residue of the portion of him that hath deceased, my mind is, that said residue shall be equally divided into eight equal parts, and equally belong to my said wife, if surviving, and my seven children, or their lawful representatives, but if said sons Abraham and James die in nonage, my mind and meaning is that my present wife, if surviving, my said six children, to say, John, Deodate, Abigail, Martha, Sarah, Elizabeth, or their lawful representatives, shall have an equal share in the portions of the said Abraham and James, with this only difference, the said Martha have thirty pounds above an equal part, and to them, their heirs and assigns forever.

Also I give my said now wife Elizabeth, forty pounds of my estate in current bills of credit, or in bonds, and it is in affection to her, my said wife, and the improvement of whole or part to be, as I have told her, whereof she is not accountable.

And further together, my meaning about my estate which I call dividable among my eight children, and will have divided into twelve equal parts in value, I would have it understood thus, viz.: I consider these three articles on account; one article is the value of my said wife's thirds in my real estate, which are my said wife's during her natural life; a second article is the value of all the rest of my real estate; that is to say, of the other two thirds of my lands; a third article is the value of all my personal estate, besides my said wife's thirds, which are absolutely her own, nor in this third article must be accounted three hundred pounds four shillings and ten pence. Now I will that these three said articles be truly added into one sum: and further, I propose from said one sum be subtracted two hundred and ninety-one pounds ten shillings: now then, when said subtraction is made, the sum remaining, or residue, is the very thing I mean by my estate I call dividable among my eight children as aforesaid.

Further, I open the three hundred pounds four shillings and ten pence thus, viz.: said John hath had seventy-one pounds ten shillings; said Abigail hath had one hundred and twenty-one pounds nine shillings and eleven pence; said Sarah hath had one hundred and seven pounds four shillings and eleven pence, which brought into one sum, makes three hundred pounds four shillings and ten pence.

Further, I open the two hundred and ninety-one pounds and ten shillings thus, viz.: given my said son John, thirty-one pounds and ten shillings; given my said daughter Martha four score pounds; given my said wife Elizabeth forty pounds: now, if to these be added one hundred and forty pounds, the sum is two hundred and ninety-one pounds ten shillings, and of said one hundred and forty, I shall give account in what follows.

Further, however, I devise to my said children their parts in the third of my land belonging to my said wife during her natural life, my meaning is, my said wife enjoy the same, the term aforesaid, and that all my said children do wait for their respective parts in the same, until the term be fully completed.

Further, my mind is, that whatever of my real estate shall at any time or times fall to any of my said daughters, to say, Abigail, Martha, Sarah, Elizabeth, the whole, or any part or parts thereof, it shall be in the power of said John, or said Deodate, or my said wife, to have payment being made according to said appraising for the whole, or any part or parts, as aforesaid.

Also, my will is, that my said loving wife, while my widow, at her pleasure improve all the lands I have improved up my ridge for plough and pasture, and at her pleasure take in twenty acres more not within fence, at my decease, which is the reservation I mean, mentioned in my bequest to my said son John.

Also, I open the conditions, or further conditions mentioned in my bequest to said wife Martha, deceased, said land being at Fairfield, or Major Gold's farm, so called, in all which land my desire is my six children aforesaid named, viz.: John, Deodate, Abigail, Martha, Sarah, Elizabeth, have equal shares for them, their heirs and assigns forever, which, if they have not through said John's refusal or fault, then my will is, my said son John be cut out of the one half aforesaid, devised to him, said John; the other condition relates to my estate of my sister Martha, at said New Haven, or any other way which may fall to me or any child of mine by right of inheritance, wherein my desire is that all my said eight children, viz.: John, Deodate, Abraham, James, Abigail, Martha, Sarah, Elizabeth, shall have equal shares in fee, which, if they have not [illegible] them through said John's refusal or fault, then my last mind and meaning is, that my said son John be cut out of all before bequeathed to him, said John, but only the seventy and one pounds ten shillings which I account the said John hath already received of me, so much being the due to balance from said John to me, as must appear by the accounts drawn out by me, and signed with my name.

Further, in case of forfeiture made by said John, or said Deodate, whatsoever shall be forfeited, I give and bequeath to my other children, to each one alike, to be to them, their heirs and assigns forever.

Also, I commit it to my executors to get my land at said Stamford* and New Haven, &c., measured and appraised by persons under the solemnity of an oath.

Further, Whereas I have in the seventh and eighth lines of this very page or folio mentioned one hundred and forty pounds, my meaning and will is, that my executors reserve out of my estate to the value of one hundred and forty pounds, and if said executors think it needful, I commit it unto their power to make sale of lands of mine : now, said one hundred and forty pounds I intend on account of charges for measuring and appraising aforesaid, and also for undertaking in the law as my executor's council may apprehend convenient for asserting my right in land, or any other head ; my meaning also is, that besides the neat answering of the trouble and charges of my executors, that each said executors have twelve pounds gratuity ; and further, in case after all of said one hundred and forty pounds, there be any thing remaining, my mind and meaning is, about such remainder, or any other thing or things proper for me yet to order, I say my meaning is, that a division

* The Inventory of Mr. Davenport's estate shows him to have been possessed of about 4,000 acres of land within the township of Stamford.

thereof in equal proportion be among all my said children, or their lawful representatives.

Finally, I nominate, constitute and ordain my said loving wife Elizabeth, and my said loving son Deódate, executors of this my last will and testament, hereby revoking and disannulling all and every former wills and testaments executed, and confirming and ratifying this and no other to be my last will and testament, and seal, the day and year first written.

JOHN DAVENPORT, [a seal.]

Signed, sealed, published, pronounced, and declared by said John Davenport, the Testator, to be his last will and testament, in the presence of us, the subscribers.

JNO. BELL,
SAML. BLACHLEY,
ABIGAIL BLACHLEY.

THE REV. JAMES DAVENPORT'S CONFESSION AND RETRACTIONS.

(See pages 215–224.)

"ALTHOUGH I do not question at all, but there is great reason to bless God for a glorious and wonderful work of his power and grace in the edification of his children, and the conviction and conversion of numbers in New England, in the neighbouring governments and several other parts, within a few years past; and believe that the Lord hath favored me, though most unworthy, with several others of his servants, in granting special assistance and success; the glory of all which be given to Jehovah, to whom alone it belongs:

"Yet, after frequent meditation and desires that I might be enabled to apprehend things justly, and, I hope I may say, mature consideration, I am now fully convinced and persuaded that several things, which in the time of the work I was very industrious and instrumental in promoting, by a misguided zeal, were no parts of it, but of a different and contrary nature and tendency, and that I was much influenced in the affair by the false spirit; which, unobserved by me, did (as I have been brought to see since) prompt me to unjust apprehensions and misconduct in several articles; which have been great blemishes to the work of God; very grievous to some of God's children, no less ensnaring and corrupting to others of them, a sad means of many persons' questioning the work of God, concluding and appearing against it, and of the hardening of multitudes in their sins, and an awful occasion of the enemies blaspheming the right ways of the Lord; and withal very offensive to that God, before whom I would lie in the dust, prostrate in deep humility and repentance on this account, imploring pardon for the mediator's sake, and thankfully accepting the tokens thereof.

"The articles which I especially refer to, and would in the most public manner retract, and warn others against, are these which follow, viz.:

"I. The method I used, for a considerable time, with respect to some, yea, many ministers in several parts, in openly exposing such as I feared or thought unconverted, in public prayer or otherwise; herein making my private judgment, (in which also I much suspect I was mistaken in several instances, and I believe also that my judgment concerning several was formed rashly and upon very slender grounds,) I say, making my private judgment the ground of public actions or conduct; offending, as I apprehend (although in the time of it, ignorantly) against the ninth commandment, and such other passages of Scripture as are similar; yea, I may say, offending against the laws both of justice and charity; which laws were further broken,

"II. By my advising and urging to such separations from those ministers whom I treated as above, as I believe may be justly called rash, unwarrantable, and of sad and awful tendency and consequences. And here I would ask the forgiveness of those ministers, whom I have injured in both these articles.

"III. I confess I have been much led astray by following impulses or impressions as a rule of conduct, whether they came with or without a text of Scripture; and by neglecting, also duly to observe the analogy of Scripture. I am persuaded this was a great means of corrupting my experiences and carrying me off from the word of God, and a great handle, which the false spirit has made use of with respect to a number, and me especially.

"IV. I believe, further, that I have done much hurt to religion, by encouraging private persons to a ministerial and authoritative kind or method of exhorting; which is particularly observable in many, such being much puffed up and falling into the snare of the devil, whilst many others are thus directly prejudiced against the work.

"I have reason to be deeply humbled that I have not been duly careful to endeavour to remove or prevent prejudice, (where I now believe I might then have done it consistently with duty,) which appeared remarkable in the method I practised, of singing with others in the streets, in societies frequently.

"I would also penitently confess and bewail my great stiffness in retaining these aforesaid errors a great while, and unwillingness to examine into them with any jealousy of their being errors, notwithstanding the friendly counsels and cautions of real friends, especially in the ministry.

"Here may properly be added a paragraph or two, taken out of a letter from me to Mr. Barber of Georgia; a true copy of which I gave consent, should be published lately at Philadelphia: 'I would add to what brother T——— hath written on the awful affair of books and clothes at New London, which affords grounds of deep and lasting humiliation; I was, to my shame be it spoken, a ringleader in that horrid action; I was, my dear brother, under the powerful influence of the false spirit, almost one whole day together, and part of several days. The Lord showed me afterwards, that the spirit I was then acted by, was in its operations void of true inward peace, laying the greatest stress on externals, neglecting the heart, full of impatience, pride and arrogance; although I thought, in the time of it, that it was the Spirit of God in a high degree; awful, indeed! my body, especially my leg, much disordered at the same time,* which satan and my evil heart might make some handle of.'

"And now may the holy, wise and good God be pleased to guard and secure me against such errors for the future, and stop the progress of those, whether ministers or people, who have been corrupted by my words or example in any of the above mentioned particulars; and if it be his holy will, bless this public recantation to this purpose. And O! may he grant, withal, that such, as by reason of the aforesaid errors and misconduct, have entertained unhappy prejudices against Christianity in general, or the late glorious work of God in particular, may, by this account, learn to

* I had the long fever and the cankry humour, raging at once.

distinguish what is no part of the work, from the work itself, that which is vile and odious, from that which is precious, glorious and divine, and thus be entirely and happily freed from all those prejudices referred to, and this, in infinite mercy through Jesus Christ: and to these requests, may all God's children, whether ministers or others, say Amen.

JAMES DAVENPORT."

"July 28th, 1744.

"P. S.—Inasmuch as a number, who have fallen in with and promoted the aforesaid errors and misconduct, and are not altered in their minds, may be prejudiced against this Recantation, by a supposition or belief, that I came into it by reason of desertion or dulness and deadness in religion, it seems needful, therefore, to signify, what I hope I may say without boasting, and what I am able, through pure, rich grace, to speak with truth and freedom, that for some months in the time of my coming to the abovesaid conclusions and retractions, and since I have come through grace to them, I have been favored, a great part of the time, with a sweet calm, and serenity of soul, and rest in God, and sometimes with special and remarkable refreshments of soul, and these more free from corrupt mixtures than formerly. Glory to God alone. J. D."

SOME ADDITIONAL NOTICES OF REV. JOHN DAVENPORT, OF NEW HAVEN.

Rev. Dr. Bacon mentions the following incident, as an additional illustration of his public spirit:—"On the 11th of August, 1662, Mr. Davenport informed the town 'that he having occasion, by the Providence of God, to go into the Bay, and understanding that there are two merchants that are lately come from England, who, have a desire to come to these parts, wished to be authorized by the town to make them some such proposals as might induce them to come to this place. They are very godly men,' he said, 'and belong to a church in England, and so have a desire to have a place to sit down together (as brother Alsop reported, and Mr. Rutherford); they only desire home lots, and it may be some out lots.' After some discussion it was suggested that 'the Neck' might be the fittest place for them. Mr. Davenport then proposed the question whether the town would give up that tract of land to these strangers, on condition of their settling here. 'For his part, he had some land there himself, and he would willingly resign up his.' He argued that these merchants 'would bring shipping yearly from England, hither, and so cause manufacture, which is necessary, if we long subsist together.' The proposal being favorably received, he further propounded whether we should not consider them as coming from London and not knowing the state of a wilderness condition, and therefore extend our thoughts further than their desires, so as to accommodate them with land, and meadow for cows, and also liberty for cutting fire wood, and timber for building, equal with others of the planters, which may be a great encouragement to them when they should hear our thoughts extend beyond their desires. All which he purposed to acquaint them withal, when he understood the town's mind therein.' The result was a formal offer of 'the Neck,' a tract of about six hundred acres, and of the other accommodations and privileges proposed."

Rev. Mr. Dodd, in his East Haven Register, gives the following record:—"In 1649, 'It was ordered that Mr. Davenport, pastor of the church, shall have his meadow, and the upland for his second division, both together, on the east side of the East River, where himself shall choose, with all the conveniences the place can afford for a farm, together with the natural bounds of the place, whether by creeks or otherwise.' He accordingly laid out a tract of land of about a mile square, and containing about 600 acres above Dragon.

"In 1650 Alling Ball became his farmer, and was exempted from militia service while he continued in Mr. Davenport's employment." A portion of that farm has continued in the family till within the present century, when it became alienated.

In the Colony Records an expression of Mr. Davenport's is found, which is quite characteristic. In the trial of a case of defamation, "Thomas Staplies, of Fairfield, plaintiff, Mr. Roger Ludlow, late of Fairfield, defendant," 29th of May, 1654, Mr. and Mrs. Davenport were called by the plaintiff to testify to a conversation at their house, between them and the defendant. In regard to that conversation Mr. Ludlow asserted "that he required, and they promised secrecy;" to which Mr. Davenport replied, that "he is careful not to make unlawful promises; and when he hath made a lawful promise, he is, through the help of Christ, careful to keep it."

[I have never been able to ascertain either the maiden or Christian name of the wife of Mr. Davenport, or the date of their marriage. The earliest allusion to her is in a letter of his to Lady Vere, in 1628. In the records of New Haven she is frequently mentioned, but in all cases is called simply *Mrs.* Davenport. I have sought to obtain some information on this point, from the records of St. Stephens' Church, London, but as yet have been unsuccessful.

The Crest upon the Davenport Coat-of-Arms, as used by Mr. Davenport, is changed, to what, says Rev. Mr. Bromley, "on comparison of several seals, resembles a *wolf's head*, which might have been derived from the forest rights which our ancestors had in Macclesfield forest."]

The following Catalogue of the published works of Rev. John Davenport, to which, after careful research, but little in addition could be found, is mostly taken from the list given by Dr. Bacon, in his Historical Discourses, Appendix, page 389 :—

A Royal Edict for Military Exercises, published in a Sermon preached to the captains and gentlemen that exercise arms in the Artillery Garden, at their general meeting in Saint Andrew's Undershaft in London. (2 Sam. 1 : 18.) London, 1629. A copy of this is in the Atheneum Library, Boston.

Letter to the Dutch Classis, containing a just complaint against an unjust doer, &c., 1634, quarto. This is a complaint against Mr. Paget's proceedings in the English Church at Amsterdam.

Certain Instructions delivered to the Elders of the English Church deputed, which are to be propounded to the pastors of the Dutch Church in Amsterdam, 1634. Wood calls it a quarto paper.

1. *A Report of some Passages or Proceedings about his calling to the English Church in Amsterdam, against John Paget.* Quarto. 2. *Allegations of Scripture against the baptizing of some kind of infants.* Quarto. 3. *Protestation about the publishing of his writings.* Quarto. These three "little scripts," as Wood calls them, were all printed at Amsterdam in 1634. Mr. Paget replied in a book of 150 pages, quarto, entitled "*An Answer to the Unjust Complaints, &c.*" To this book Mr. Davenport made a rejoinder, in the following article:

An Apologetical Reply to a book called 'an answer to the unjust complaint of W[illiam] B[est].' &c., quarto. Rotterdam, 1636. A copy of this is among the books deposited by the Old South Church in the Library of the Massachusetts Historical Society.

An Answer of the Elders of the several Churches in New England, unto nine positions, sent over to them by divers reverend and godly ministers in England, written in 1639, and published in London in 1641.

Profession of Faith made publicly before the Congregation at his admission into one of the Churches of New England; containing twenty several heads. 1. Concerning the Scriptures, &c. London, 1642. One sheet, quarto.

The Messiah is already Come. A sermon on Acts ii. 36. London, 1653. This is supposed to be the same with the work next named.

The Knowledge of Christ, &c., wherein the types, prophecies, genealogies, miracles, humiliation, &c. of Christ are opened and applied. Quarto, printed in 1658, or before.

Catechism containing the chief Heads of the Christian Religion. London, 1659. Octavo. Published at the desire and for the use of the Church of Christ in New Haven. Wood says that Mr. Hooke had a hand in this work.

The Saints' Anchor-hold, in all storms and tempests, preached in sundry sermons, and published for the support and comfort of God's people in all times of trial. London, 1661. Duodecimo.

Another Essay for investigation of the truth, in answer to two questions, &c. Cambridge, 1663. Quarto. There is a copy in the possession of Rev. Thomas Robbins, D.D., of Hartford, Ct.

Election Sermon, at Boston, 1669.

God's Call to his People to turn unto Him, &c., in two sermons on two public fasting days in New England. London, 1670. Quarto.

The Power of Congregational Churches asserted and vindicated; in answer to a treatise of Mr. J. Paget's, entitled, 'The Defense of Church Government exercised in Classes and Synods.' London, 1672. Duodecimo. A copy of this is found in the Library of Harvard University.

A Discourse about Civil Government in a new plantation whose design is religion. Cambridge, 1673. Quarto.

He was also the author of a Latin Epistle to John Dury on the Union of Protestant Churches.

He also wrote several commendatory prefaces to other men's works, among which, Mather mentions an epistle before Scudder's Daily Walk, as worthy to be reckoned itself a book.

He also left ready for publication an Exposition of the Canticles, which was just going into the press at London, when the death of the undertaker of the publication stopped it. This is to be lamented, because it was prefaced by a life of the author, drawn up by Dr. Increase Mather, which is now lost.

Mr. Davenport also wrote an unprinted life of John Cotton, which was once in Governor Hutchinson's hands, but is now lost.

A volume of his earliest sermons in manuscript is preserved in the Library of Yale College, and several other small works and essays in manuscript are in the Library of the American Antiquarian Society at Worcester, Mass.

Some letters to Lady Digby also exist in the British Museum, supposed to be of an earlier date than those to Lady Vere.

THE END.

CPSIA information can be obtained
at www.ICGtesting.com
Printed in the USA
LVHW031913300323
743031LV00002B/264

9 789354 023378